THE VEGETARIAN *Gourmet*

THE VEGETARIAN *Gourmet*

Sebastian Kelly

This edition published in 1997 by
Sebastian Kelly
2 Rectory Road
Oxford OX4 1BW

Produced by
Anness Publishing Limited

ISBN 1 901688 10 0

A CIP catalogue record for this book is available from the British Library

Previously published as part of a larger compendium,
The Ultimate Vegetarian Cookbook

Publisher: Joanna Lorenz
Project Editor: Samantha Gray
Designer: Adrian Morris
Photographer: Michael Michaels
Home Economist: Wendy Lee

Printed in Singapore by Star Standard Industries Pte. Ltd.

1 3 5 7 9 10 8 6 4 2

THE LEAF SYMBOL NEXT TO A RECIPE INDICATES THAT IT IS SUITABLE FOR VEGANS.

MEASUREMENTS

Three sets of equivalent measurements have been provided in the recipes here, in the following order: Metric, Imperial and American.
It is essential that units of measurement are not mixed within each recipe.
Where conversions result in awkward numbers, these have been rounded for convenience, but are accurate enough to produce successful results.

CONTENTS

SOUPS & STARTERS

Tantalising appetizers range from traditional favourites – including soups that could be served either before a main course or on their own as a light and wholesome meal – to more exotic dishes for elegant dinners.

Egg Flower Soup

For the very best flavour, you do need to use a homemade stock for this soup. The egg sets into pretty strands giving the soup a flowery look, hence the name.

SERVES 6
1 litre/1¾ pints/4 cups stock
45 ml/3 tbsp light soy sauce
30 ml/2 tbsp dry sherry or vermouth
3 spring onions, diagonally sliced
small piece fresh root ginger, shredded
4 large lettuce leaves, shredded
5 ml/1 tsp sesame seed oil
2 eggs, beaten
salt and ground black pepper
sesame seeds, to garnish

1 Pour the stock into a large saucepan. Add all the ingredients except the eggs and seeds. Bring to the boil and then cook for about 2 minutes.

2 Very carefully, pour the eggs in a thin, steady stream into the centre of the boiling liquid.

3 Count to three then quickly stir the soup. The egg will begin to cook and form long threads. Season to taste, ladle the soup into warm bowls and serve immediately sprinkled with sesame seeds.

Broccoli and Blue Brie Soup

A popular vegetable, broccoli makes a delicious soup with an appetizing deep green colour. For a tasty tang, stir in some cubes of blue Brie cheese just before serving.

SERVES 6
1 onion, chopped
450 g/1 lb broccoli spears, chopped
1 large courgette, chopped
1 large carrot, chopped
1 medium potato, chopped
25 g/1 oz/2 tbsp butter
30 ml/2 tbsp sunflower oil
2 litres/3½ pints/8 cups stock or water
about 75 g/3 oz blue Brie (or Dolcellate) cheese, cubed
salt and ground black pepper
almond flakes, to garnish (optional)

VARIATION

Try using cauliflower instead of broccoli in this recipe. Stilton is a tasty alternative to Brie.

1 Put all the vegetables into a large saucepan, together with the butter and oil plus about 45 ml/3 tbsp stock or water.

2 Heat the ingredients until sizzling and stir well. Cover and cook gently for 15 minutes, shaking the pan occasionally, until all the vegetables soften.

3 Add the rest of the stock or water, season and bring to a boil, then cover and simmer gently for about 25–30 minutes.

4 Strain the vegetables and reserve the liquid. Purée the vegetables in a food processor or blender then return them to the pan with the reserved liquid.

5 Bring the soup back to a gentle boil and stir in the cheese until it melts. (Don't let the soup boil too hard or the cheese will become stringy.) Season to taste and garnish with a scattering of almond flakes.

Borscht

A simply stunning colour, this classic Russian soup is ideal to serve when you want to make something a little different. The flavour matures and improves too if it is made the day before it is needed.

SERVES 6
1 onion, chopped
450 g/1 lb raw beetroot, peeled and chopped
1 large cooking apple, chopped
2 celery sticks, chopped
½ red pepper, chopped
115 g/4 oz mushrooms, chopped
25 g/1 oz/2 tbsp butter
30 ml/2 tbsp sunflower oil
2 litres/3½ pints/8 cups stock or water
5 ml/1 tsp cumin seeds
pinch dried thyme
1 large bay leaf
fresh lemon juice
salt and ground black pepper
150 ml/¼ pint/⅔ cup soured cream
few sprigs fresh dill, to garnish

1 Place all the chopped vegetables into a large saucepan with the butter, oil and 45 ml/3 tbsp of the stock or water. Cover and cook gently for about 15 minutes, shaking the pan occasionally.

2 Stir in the cumin seeds and cook for a minute, then add the remaining stock or water, dried thyme, bay leaf, lemon juice and seasoning.

3 Bring to the boil, then cover and turn down to a gentle simmer. Cook for about 30 minutes.

4 Strain the vegetables and reserve the liquid. Pass the vegetables through a food processor or blender until they are smooth and creamy.

5 Return the vegetables to the pan, stir in the reserved stock and reheat. Check the seasoning.

6 Serve the borscht with swirls of soured cream and topped with a few sprigs of fresh dill.

VARIATION

This soup can be served fairly thick, as long as the vegetables are finely chopped first.

Beetroot is something of an under-valued vegetable, although popular in many European countries. For example, it is delicious served as a hot vegetable accompaniment with a creamy bechamel sauce and topped with crisp breadcrumbs. Alternatively, try it raw and coarsely grated, then tossed in dressing for a side salad.

Garlicky Mushrooms

Serve these on toast for a quick, tasty starter or pop them into small ramekins and serve with slices of warm crusty bread. Use some shitake mushrooms, if you can find them, for a richer flavour.

SERVES 4
450 g/1 lb button mushrooms, sliced if large
45 ml/3 tbsp olive oil
45 ml/3 tbsp stock or water
30 ml/2 tbsp dry sherry (optional)
3 garlic cloves, crushed
115 g/4 oz low fat soft cheese
30 ml/2 tbsp fresh parsley, chopped
15 ml/1 tbsp fresh chives, chopped
salt and ground black pepper

1 Put the mushrooms into a large saucepan with the olive oil, stock or water and sherry, if using. Heat until bubbling then cover and simmer for 5 minutes.

2 Add the garlic and stir well. Cook for a further 2 minutes. Remove the mushrooms with a slotted spoon and set them aside. Cook the liquor until it reduces down to 30 ml/2 tbsp. Remove from the heat and stir in the cheese and herbs.

3 Stir the mixture well until the cheese melts then return the mushrooms to the pan so that they become coated with the cheesy mixture. Season to taste.

4 Pile the mushrooms onto thick slabs of hot toast. Alternatively, spoon them into four ramekins and serve accompanied by slices of crusty bread.

Ricotta and Borlotti Bean Pâté

A lovely light yet full-flavoured pâté. For an attractive presentation, spoon the pâté into small, oiled ring moulds, turn out and fill with some whole borlotti beans, simply dressed with lemon juice, olive oil and fresh herbs.

SERVES 4
1 × 400 g/14 oz can borlotti beans, drained
1 garlic clove, crushed
175 g/6 oz ricotta cheese (or other cream cheese)
50 g/2 oz/4 tbsp butter, melted
juice of ½ lemon
salt and ground black pepper
30 ml/2 tbsp fresh parsley, chopped
15 ml/1 tbsp fresh thyme or dill, chopped
TO SERVE
extra canned beans (optional)
fresh lemon juice, olive oil and chopped herbs (optional)
salad leaves, radish slices and few sprigs fresh dill, to garnish

1 Blend the beans, garlic, cheese, butter, lemon juice and seasoning in a food processor until smooth.

2 Add the chopped herbs and continue to blend. Spoon into one serving dish or four lightly oiled ramekins, the bases lined with discs of non-stick baking paper. Chill the pâté so that it sets firm.

3 If serving with extra beans, dress them with lemon juice, olive oil and herbs, season well and spoon on top. Garnish with salad leaves and serve with warm crusty bread or toast.

4 If serving individually, turn each pâté out of its ramekin onto a small plate and remove the disc of paper. Top with radish slices and sprigs of dill.

VARIATION

You could try other canned pulses for this recipe, although the softer lentils would not be suitable. Butter (lima) beans are surprisingly good. For an attractive presentation fill the centre with dark red kidney beans and chopped fresh green beans.

Twice-baked Goats' Cheese Soufflés

A good chef's trick is to reheat small baked soufflés out of their ramekins to serve with a salad. They puff up again and the outsides become nice and crispy. If you prefer, you can substitute another full-flavoured cheese such as Cheddar or Parmesan.

SERVES 6
25 g/1 oz/2 tbsp butter
25 g/1 oz/3 tbsp plain flour
300 ml/½ pint/1¼ cups hot milk
pinch cayenne pepper
squeeze of lemon juice
salt and ground black pepper
100 g/3½ oz semi-hard goats' cheese, crumbled
2 eggs, separated
melted butter, for brushing
25 g/1 oz/3 tbsp dried breadcrumbs
25 g/1 oz/3 tbsp ground hazelnuts or walnuts
2 egg whites
salad garnish (optional)

1 Melt the butter and stir in the flour. Cook to a roux for a minute then gradually whisk in the hot milk to make a thick white sauce.

2 Simmer for a minute then season with cayenne, lemon juice, salt and pepper. Remove the pan from the heat and stir in the cheese until it melts. Cool slightly then beat in the egg yolks.

3 Brush the insides of six ramekins with the melted butter and coat them with the breadcrumbs and nuts mixed together. Shake out any excess.

4 Preheat the oven to 190°C/375°F/Gas 5 and prepare a bain marie – a roasting pan with boiling water.

5 Whisk the four egg whites to the soft peak stage and carefully fold them into the main mixture using a figure of eight motion. Spoon into the ramekins.

6 Place the soufflés in the bain marie and bake for about 12–15 minutes until risen and golden brown. You can of course serve them at this stage; otherwise allow to cool then chill.

7 To serve twice-baked, reheat the oven to the same temperature. Run a knife round the inside of each ramekin and turn out each soufflé onto a baking tray.

8 Bake the soufflés for about 12 minutes. Serve on prepared plates with a dressed salad garnish.

VARIATION

There is another good chef's trick – making soufflés in advance and chilling them unbaked. It helps to add an extra egg white or two when whisking, depending on the mixture. It is also possible to freeze unbaked soufflés in small ramekins and then to bake them from frozen, allowing an extra 5 or 10 minutes' baking time.

Stuffed Artichokes

Globe artichokes are a little fiddly to prepare but their delicious taste makes it all worthwhile, especially when stuffed with nuts, mushrooms and sun-dried tomatoes. This dish can be prepared in advance and reheated before serving.

SERVES 4
4 medium globe artichokes
salt
lemon slices
STUFFING
1 medium onion, chopped
1 garlic clove, crushed
45 ml/3 tbsp olive oil
115 g/4 oz mushrooms, chopped
1 medium carrot, grated
40 g/1½ oz sun-dried tomatoes in oil, drained and sliced
leaves from a sprig of thyme
about 45–60 ml/3–4 tbsp water
ground black pepper
115 g/4 oz/2 cups fresh breadcrumbs
extra olive oil, to cook
fresh parsley, chopped, to garnish

1 Boil the artichokes in plenty of salted water with a few slices of lemon for about 30 minutes, or until a leaf pulls easily from the base. Strain through a colander and cool the artichokes, laying them upside down.

2 To make the stuffing for the artichokes, gently fry the onion and garlic in the oil for 5 minutes, then add the mushrooms, carrot, sun-dried tomatoes and thyme.

3 Stir in the water, season well and cook for a further 5 minutes, then mix in the breadcrumbs.

VARIATION

For a lighter meal, rather than stuff the artichokes, you could simply fill the centres with home-made mayonnaise or serve with a dish of vinaigrette or melted butter for dipping the leaves.

4 Pull the artichoke leaves apart and pull out the purple-tipped central leaves. Using a small teaspoon, scrape out the hairy choke, making sure that you remove it all. Discard it.

5 Spoon the stuffing into the centre of the artichoke, and push the leaves back into shape. Put the artichokes into an ovenproof dish and pour a little oil into the centre of each one.

6 Half an hour before serving, heat the oven to 190°C/375°F/Gas 5 and bake the artichokes for about 20–25 minutes until heated through. Serve garnished with a little chopped fresh parsley on top.

Bruschetta with Goats' Cheese and Tapenade

Simple to prepare in advance, this appetizing dish can be served as a starter or at finger buffets. Make sure that you finely chop the ingredients for the tapenade.

SERVES 4–6

TAPENADE

1 × 400 g/14 oz can black olives, stoned and finely chopped
50 g/2 oz sun-dried tomatoes in oil, chopped
30 ml/2 tbsp capers, chopped
15 ml/1 tbsp green peppercorns, in brine, crushed
45–60 ml/3–4 tbsp olive oil
2 garlic cloves, crushed
45 ml/3 tbsp fresh basil, chopped, or 5 ml/1 tsp dried basil
salt and ground black pepper

BASES

12 slices Ciabatta or other crusty bread
olive oil, for brushing
2 garlic cloves, halved
115 g/4 oz soft goats' cheese (or plain cream cheese)
fresh herb sprigs, to garnish

1 Mix the tapenade ingredients all together and check the seasoning. It should not need too much. Allow to marinate overnight, if possible.

2 To make the bruschetta, grill both sides of the bread lightly until golden. Brush one side with oil and then rub with a cut clove of garlic. Set aside until ready to serve.

3 Spread the bruschetta with the cheese, roughing it up with a fork, and spoon the tapenade on top. Garnish with sprigs of herbs.

COOK'S TIP

The bruschetta is nicest grilled over a open barbecue flame, if possible. Failing that a grill will do, but avoid using a toaster – it gives too even a colour and the bruschetta is supposed to look quite rustic.

Warm Avocadoes with Tangy Topping

Lightly grilled with a tasty topping of red onions and cheese, this dish makes a delightful alternative to the rather humdrum avocado vinaigrette.

SERVES 4

1 small red onion, sliced
1 garlic clove, crushed
15 ml/1 tbsp sunflower oil
Worcestershire sauce
2 ripe avocadoes, halved and stoned
2 small tomatoes, sliced
15 ml/1 tbsp fresh chopped basil, marjoram or parsley
50 g/2 oz Lancashire or Mozzarella cheese, sliced
salt and ground black pepper

1 Gently fry the onion and garlic in the oil for about 5 minutes until just softened. Shake in a little Worcestershire sauce.

2 Preheat a grill. Place the avocado halves on the grill pan and spoon the onions into the centre.

3 Divide the tomato slices and fresh herbs between the four halves and top each one with the cheese.

4 Season well and grill until the cheese melts and starts to brown.

VARIATION

Avocadoes are wonderful served in other hot dishes too. Try them chopped and tossed into hot pasta or sliced and layered in a lasagne.

LIGHT LUNCHES & SUPPERS

For tempting lunches that are not too filling and tasty television suppers, experiment with these glorious recipes, from those that include protein-rich ingredients such as tofu to irresistible cheese and pasta dishes.

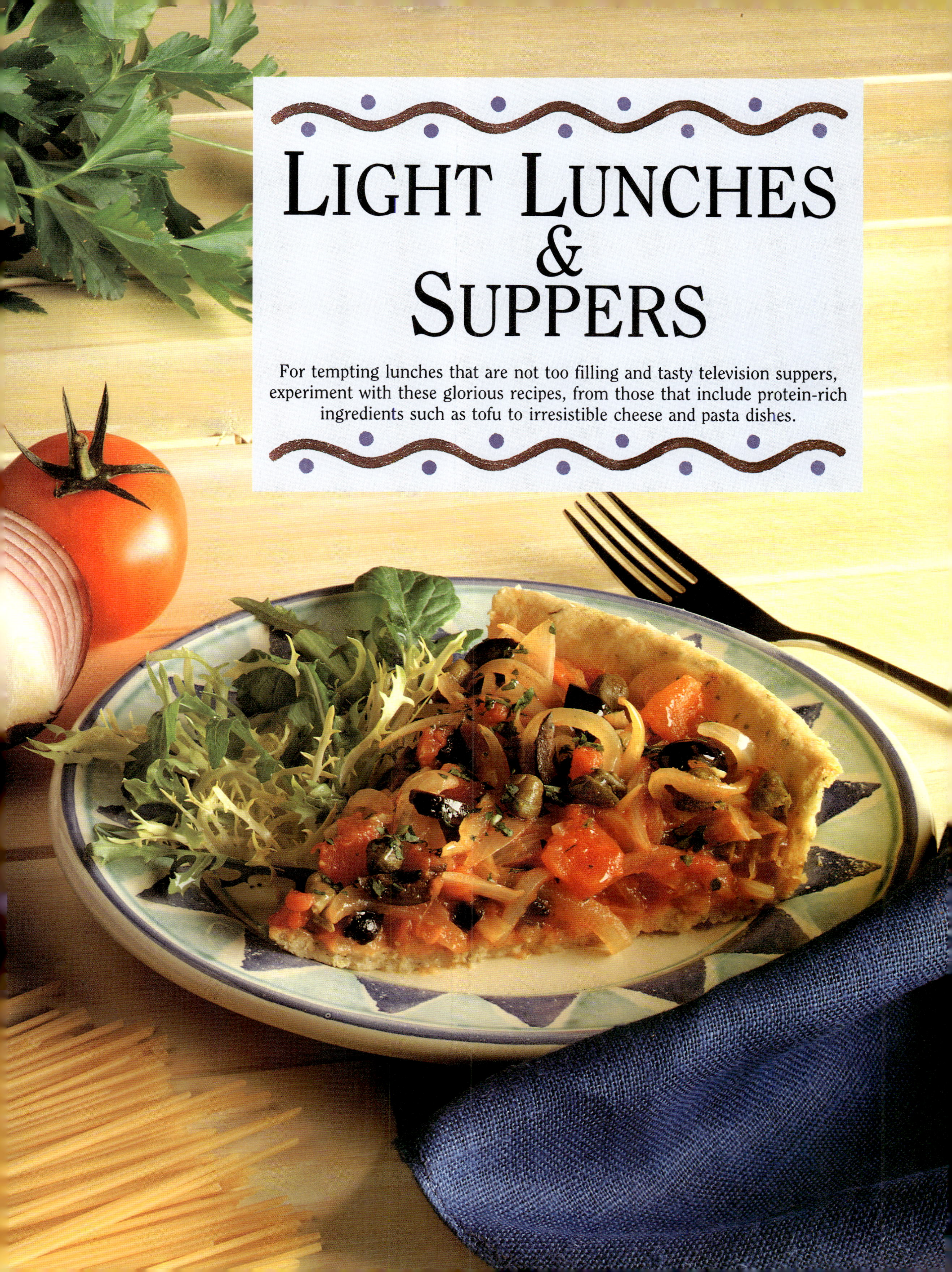

Mexican Brunch Eggs

Instead of eggs on toast, why not try them on fried corn tortillas with chillies and creamy avocado? Canned tortillas are readily available from larger supermarkets or delicatessens.

SERVES 4
oil, for frying
8 tortilla corn pancakes
1 avocado
1 large tomato
50 g/2 oz/4 tbsp butter
8 eggs
4 jalepeno chillies, sliced
salt and ground black pepper
15 ml/1 tbsp fresh coriander, chopped, to garnish

1 Heat the oil and fry the tortillas for a few seconds each side. Remove and drain. Keep the tortillas warm.

2 Halve, stone and peel the avocado, then cut into slices. Dip the tomato into boiling water, then skin and chop roughly.

3 Melt the butter in a frying pan and fry the eggs, in batches, sunny side up.

4 Place two tortillas on four plates, slip an egg on each and top with sliced chillies, avocado and tomato. Season and serve garnished with fresh coriander.

Fried Tomatoes with Polenta Crust

If you saw the film 'Fried Green Tomatoes' then you should enjoy this dish! No need to search for home-grown green tomatoes – any slightly under-ripe ones will do.

SERVES 4
4 large firm under-ripe tomatoes
115 g/4 oz/1 cup polenta or coarse cornmeal
5 ml//1 tsp dried oregano
2.5 ml/½ tsp garlic powder
plain flour, for dredging
1 egg, beaten with seasoning
oil, for deep fat frying

1 Cut the tomatoes into thick slices. Mix the polenta or cornmeal with the oregano and garlic powder.

2 Put the flour, egg and polenta into different bowls. Dip the tomato slices into the flour, then into the egg and finally into the polenta.

3 Fill a shallow frying pan a third full of oil and heat steadily until quite hot.

4 Slip the tomato slices into the oil carefully, a few at a time, and fry on each side until crisp. Remove and drain. Repeat with the remaining tomatoes, reheating the oil in between. Serve with salad.

Pissaladière

A French Mediterranean classic, this is a delicious and colourful tart full of punchy flavour. Ideally, put the base and fillings together just when serving so the base remains crisp.

SERVES 6

PASTRY

225 g/8 oz/2 cups plain flour
115 g/4 oz/8 tbsp butter or sunflower margarine
5 ml/1 tsp dried mixed herbs
pinch salt

FILLING

2 large onions, thinly sliced
2 garlic cloves, crushed
45 ml/3 tbsp olive oil
fresh nutmeg, grated, to taste
1 × 400 g/14 oz can chopped tomatoes
5 ml/1 tsp sugar
leaves from small sprig of thyme
salt and ground black pepper
75 g/3 oz/⅔ cup stoned black olives, sliced
30 ml/2 tbsp capers
fresh parsley, chopped, to garnish

1 Rub the flour and butter or margarine together until it forms fine crumbs, then mix in the herbs and salt. Mix to a firm dough with cold water. Preheat the oven to 190°C/375°F/Gas 5.

2 Roll out and line a 21 cm/9 in flan dish and bake blind, removing the baking beans and paper for the last 5 minutes for the pastry to crisp up. Cool.

3 Gently fry the onions and garlic in the oil for about 10 minutes until quite soft and mix in the nutmeg.

4 Stir in the tomatoes, sugar, thyme and seasoning and simmer gently for about 10 minutes until the mixture is reduced and slightly syrupy.

5 Remove from the heat and allow to cool. Mix in the olives and capers.

6 When ready to serve, spoon into the flan case, sprinkle with some fresh chopped parsley and serve at room temperature.

VARIATION

To serve Pissaladière hot, top with grated cheese and grill until the cheese is golden and bubbling. The crisp-baked pastry case can be used as a base for a number of other vegetable mixtures. Try filling it with a Russian Salad – chopped, cooked root vegetables, including potato and carrot, mixed with peas, beans and onions, blended with mayonnaise and soured cream. Top with slices of hard-boiled egg and garnish with chopped fresh herbs.

Multi Mushroom Stroganoff

A pan fry of sliced mushrooms swirled with soured cream is made especially interesting if two or three varieties of mushroom are used. It is even more delicious if you can incorporate woodland or wild mushrooms.

SERVES 3–4
45 ml/3 tbsp olive oil
450 g/1 lb edible mushrooms (including ceps, shiitakes or oysters), sliced
3 spring onions, sliced
2 garlic cloves, crushed
30 ml/2 tbsp dry sherry or vermouth
salt and ground black pepper
300 ml/½ pint/1¼ cups soured cream or crème fraîche
15 ml/1 tbsp fresh marjoram or thyme leaves, chopped
fresh parsley, chopped

1 Heat the oil in a large frying pan and fry the mushrooms gently, stirring them occasionally until they are softened and just cooked.

2 Add the spring onions, garlic and sherry or vermouth and cook for a minute more. Season well.

3 Stir in the soured cream or crème fraîche and heat to just below boiling. Stir in the marjoram or thyme then scatter over the parsley. Serve with rice, pasta or boiled new potatoes.

Butter Bean and Pesto Pasta

Buy good quality, ready-made pesto, rather than making your own. Pesto forms the basis of several very tasty sauces, and it is especially good with butter beans.

SERVES 4
225 g/8 oz pasta shapes
salt and ground black pepper
fresh nutmeg, grated
30 ml/2 tbsp extra virgin olive oil
1 × 400 g/14 oz can butter beans, drained
45 ml/3 tbsp pesto sauce
150 ml/¼ pint/⅔ cup single cream
TO SERVE
45 ml/3 tbsp pine nuts
cheese, grated (optional)
sprigs of fresh basil, to garnish (optional)

1 Boil the pasta until *al dente*, then drain, leaving it a little wet. Return the pasta to the pan, season, and stir in the nutmeg and oil.

2 Heat the beans in a saucepan with the pesto and cream, stirring it until it begins to simmer. Toss the beans and pesto into the pasta and mix well.

3 Serve in bowls topped with pine nuts, and add a little grated cheese and basil sprigs if you wish.

Eggs Benedict with Quick Hollandaise

Traditional Hollandaise sauce is tricky to make without it curdling. To make it quickly, yet still achieve a thick and creamy sauce, use a blender or food processor. Hollandaise sauce is simply delicious served over poached eggs on hot toasted muffins.

SERVES 4
2 egg yolks
5 ml/1 tsp dry mustard
good pinch each salt and ground black pepper
15 ml/1 tbsp wine vinegar or lemon juice
175 g/6 oz/¾ cup butter
4 muffins, split
butter or low fat spread
4 large eggs
30 ml/2 tbsp capers
a little fresh parsley, chopped, to garnish

1 Blend the egg yolks with the mustard and seasoning in a blender or food processor for a few seconds until well mixed. Mix in the vinegar or lemon juice.

2 Heat the butter until it is on the point of bubbling then, with the machine still running, slowly pour the butter onto the egg yolks.

3 The mixture should emulsify instantly and become thick and creamy. Switch off the blender and set the sauce aside.

4 Toast the split muffins. Cut four of the halves in two and lightly butter. Place the four uncut halves on warmed plates and leave unbuttered.

5 Poach the eggs either in gently simmering water or in an egg poacher. Drain well and slip carefully onto the muffin halves.

6 Spoon the sauce over the muffins and then sprinkle with capers and parsley. Serve immediately with the buttered muffin quarters.

VARIATION

This classic American brunch dish is said to have originated in New York, and is ideal to serve on a special occasion such as a birthday treat or New Year's day.

Instead of the toasted muffin, you could make more of a main meal by serving the dish on a bed of lightly steamed or blanched spinach mixed with quick fried sliced mushrooms and onions. The quick Hollandaise sauce is of course ideal as an all-purpose serving sauce for vegetables, baked potatoes, cauliflower and broccoli.

Quick Basmati and Nut Pilaff

Light and fragrant basmati rice from the foothills of the Himalayas cooks perfectly using this simple pilaff method. Use whatever nuts are your favourite – even unsalted peanuts are good, although almonds, cashews or pistachios are more exotic.

SERVES 4–6
225 g/8 oz/1¼ cups basmati rice
1 onion, chopped
1 garlic clove, crushed
1 large carrot, coarsely grated
15–30 ml/1–2 tbsp sunflower oil
5 ml/1 tsp cumin seeds
10 ml/2 tsp ground coriander
10 ml/2 tsp black mustard seeds (optional)
4 cardamom pods
450 ml/¾ pint/2 cups stock or water
1 bay leaf
salt and ground black pepper
75 g/3 oz/½ cup unsalted nuts
fresh chopped parsley or coriander, to garnish

RINSING BASMATI

For light, fluffy grains basmati rice is best rinsed before cooking to remove any surface starch. The traditional method is to put the rice into a large bowl of cold water. Swill the grains around with your hands then tip out the cloudy water. (The rice will quickly sink to the bottom.) Repeat this action about five times. Ideally, leave the rice to soak for 30 minutes in the last rinsing water. This ensures a lighter, fluffier grain.

1 Wash the rice either by the traditional Indian method (see note) or in a sieve under a running tap. If there is time, soak the rice for 30 minutes, then drain well in a sieve.

2 In a large shallow pan, gently fry the onion, garlic and carrot in the oil for a few minutes.

3 Stir in the rice and spices and cook for a further minute or two so that the grains are coated in oil.

4 Pour in the stock or water, add the bay leaf and season well. Bring to a boil, cover and simmer very gently for about 10 minutes.

5 Remove from the heat without lifting the lid – this helps the rice to firm up and cook further. Leave for about 5 minutes.

6 If the rice is cooked, there will be small steam holes in the centre. Discard the bay leaf and cardamom pods.

7 Stir in the nuts and check the seasoning. Scatter the mixture with the chopped parsley or coriander. This whole dish can be made ahead and reheated.

Spaghetti with Feta

We think of pasta as being essentially Italian but, in fact, the Greeks have a great appetite for it too and it complements beautifully the tangy, full-flavoured feta cheese.

SERVES 2–3
115 g/4 oz spaghetti
1 garlic clove
30 ml/2 tbsp extra virgin olive oil
8 cherry tomatoes, halved
a little freshly grated nutmeg
salt and ground black pepper
75 g/3 oz feta cheese, crumbled
15 ml/1 tbsp chopped fresh basil
a few black olives (optional), to serve

1 Boil the spaghetti in plenty of lightly salted water according to the instructions on the pack, then drain.

2 In the same pan gently heat the garlic clove in the oil for a minute or two then add the cherry tomatoes.

3 Increase the heat to fry the tomatoes lightly for a minute, then remove the garlic and discard.

4 Toss in the spaghetti, season with the nutmeg and seasoning to taste then stir in the crumbled feta and basil.

5 Check the seasoning, remembering that feta can be quite salty, and serve hot topped with olives if liked.

Potatoes with Blue Cheese and Walnuts

We are so used to eating potatoes as a side dish, we forget they can be a good main meal too. This dish is so versatile it can be served as either. Use Stilton, Danish blue, Blue Brie or any other blue veined cheese.

SERVES 4
450 g/1 lb small new potatoes
small head of celery, sliced
small red onion, sliced
115 g/4 oz blue cheese, mashed
150 ml/¼ pint/⅔ cup single cream
salt and ground black pepper
100 g/3½ oz/½ cup walnut pieces
30 ml/2 tbsp fresh parsley, chopped

1 Cover the potatoes with water and boil for about 15 minutes, adding the sliced celery and onion to the pan for the last 5 minutes or so.

2 Drain the vegetables and put them into a shallow serving dish.

3 In a small saucepan melt the cheese in the cream, slowly, stirring occasionally. Do not allow the mixture to boil but heat it until it scalds.

4 Season the sauce to taste. Pour it over the vegetables and scatter over the walnuts and parsley. Serve hot.

MAIN COURSES

Create healthy and satisfying meals that make the most of the wonderful variety of herbs and spices, as well as nutritious ingredients such as lentils, rice and vegetables.

Sprouting Beans and Pak Choi

Supermarkets are fast becoming cosmopolitan and many stock ethnic fresh vegetables.

SERVES 4
45 ml/3 tbsp groundnut oil
3 spring onions, sliced
2 garlic cloves, cut in slivers
2.5 cm/1 in cube fresh root ginger, cut in slivers
1 carrot, cut in thin sticks
150 g/5 oz sprouting beans (e.g. lentils, mung beans, chick peas)
1 × 200 g/7 oz pak choi cabbage, shredded
50 g/2 oz/½ cup unsalted cashew nuts or halved almonds
SAUCE
45 ml/3 tbsp light soy sauce
30 ml/2 tbsp dry sherry
15 ml/1 tbsp sesame oil
150 ml/¼ pint/⅔ cup cold water
5 ml/1 tsp cornflour
5 ml/1 tsp clear honey
ground black pepper

1 Heat the oil in a large wok and stir-fry the onions, garlic, ginger and carrot for 2 minutes. Add the sprouting beans and fry for another 2 minutes, stirring and tossing them together.

2 Add the pak choi and nuts or almonds and stir-fry until the cabbage leaves are just wilting. Quickly mix all the sauce ingredients together in a jug and pour them into the wok, stirring immediately.

3 The vegetables will be coated in a thin, glossy sauce. Season and serve as soon as possible.

Thai Tofu Curry

Thai food is a marvellous mixture of Chinese and Indian styles, plus other exotic ingredients.

SERVES 4
2 × 200 g/7 oz packs tofu curd, cubed
30 ml/2 tbsp light soy sauce
30 ml/2 tbsp groundnut oil
PASTE
1 small onion, chopped
2 fresh green chillies, seeded and chopped
2 garlic cloves, chopped
15 ml/1 tbsp grated gresh gallingale or 5 ml/1 tsp grated fresh ginger
2 Thai kaffir leaves or 5 ml/1 tsp lime rind, grated
10 ml/2 tsp coriander berries, crushed
10 ml/2 tsp cumin seeds, crushed
45 ml/3 tbsp fresh coriander, chopped
15 ml/1 tbsp Thai fish sauce (Nam pla) or soy sauce
juice of 1 lime or small lemon
5 ml/1 tsp sugar
25 g/1 oz creamed coconut dissolved in 150 ml/¼ pint/⅔ cup boiling water
GARNISH
thin slices fresh red chilli or red pepper
fresh coriander leaves

1 Toss the tofu cubes in soy sauce and leave to marinate for 15 minutes or so while you prepare the paste.

2 Put all the paste ingredients into a food processor and grind until smooth.

3 To cook, heat the oil in a wok until quite hot. Drain the tofu cubes and stir fry at a high temperature until well browned on all sides and just firm. Drain on kitchen paper towel.

4 Wipe out the wok. Pour in the paste and stir well. Return the tofu to the wok and mix it into the paste, reheating the ingredients as you stir.

5 Serve this dish on a flat platter garnished with red chilli or pepper and chopped coriander. Bowls of Thai fragrant or jasmine rice are the perfect accompaniment to the curry.

Festive Jalousie

An excellent puff pastry pie to serve either on Christmas Day or at anytime during the holiday period. Chinese dried chestnuts make an excellent substitute for fresh ones when soaked and cooked. Or you could drain a can of chestnuts.

SERVES 6
450 g/1 lb puff pastry, thawed if frozen
450 g/1 lb Brussels sprouts, trimmed
about 16 whole chestnuts, peeled if fresh
1 large red pepper, sliced
1 large onion, sliced
45 ml/3 tbsp sunflower oil
1 egg yolk, beaten with 15 ml/1 tbsp water

SAUCE
40 g/1½ oz/scant ½ cup plain flour
40 g/1½ oz/3 tbsp butter
300 ml/½ pint/1¼ cups milk
75 g/3 oz Cheddar cheese, grated
30 ml/2 tbsp dry sherry
good pinch dried sage
salt and ground black pepper
45 ml/3 tbsp fresh parsley, chopped

1 Roll out the pastry to make two large rectangles, roughly the size of your dish. The pastry should be about 6 mm/¼ in thick and one rectangle should be slightly larger than the other. Set the pastry aside in the refrigerator.

2 Blanch the Brussels sprouts for 4 minutes in 300 ml/½ pint/1¼ cups boiling water then drain, reserving the water. Refresh the sprouts under cold running water.

3 Cut each chestnut in half. Lightly fry the red pepper and onion in the oil for 5 minutes. Set aside till later.

4 Make up the sauce by beating the flour, butter and milk together over a medium heat. Beat the sauce continuously, bringing it to the boil, stirring until it is thickened and smooth.

5 Stir in the reserved sprout water, and the cheese, sherry, sage and seasoning. Simmer for 3 minutes to reduce and mix in the parsley.

6 Fit the larger piece of pastry into your pie dish and layer the sprouts, chestnuts, peppers and onions on top. Trickle over the sauce, making sure it seeps through to wet the vegetables.

7 Brush the pastry edges with beaten egg yolk and fit the second pastry sheet on top, pressing the edges well to seal them.

8 Crimp, knock up the edges then mark the centre. Glaze well all over with egg yolk. Set aside to rest somewhere cool while you preheat the oven to 200°C/400°F/Gas 6. Bake for 30–40 minutes until golden brown and crisp.

Greek Spinach Pies

These little horns of filo pastry are stuffed with a simple spinach and feta cheese filling to make a quick and easy main course.

SERVES 8
225 g/8 oz fresh leaf spinach
2 spring onions, chopped
175 g/6 oz feta cheese, crumbled
1 egg, beaten
15 ml/1 tbsp fresh dill, chopped
ground black pepper
4 large sheets or 8 small sheets of filo pastry
olive oil, for brushing

COOK'S TIP

The pies can be prepared ahead and chilled for a day or two, before baking and serving warm. Alternatively, open freeze on a wire rack, then wrap well in foil or cling film and freeze for up to one month. Uncover and thaw well before baking as the recipe above.

1 Preheat the oven to 190°C/375°F/Gas 5. Blanch the spinach in the tiniest amount of water until just wilted, then drain very well, pressing it through a sieve with the back of a wooden spoon.

2 Chop the spinach finely and mix with the onions, feta, egg, dill and ground black pepper.

3 Lay out a sheet of filo pastry and brush with olive oil. If large, cut the pieces in two and sandwich them together. If small, fit another sheet on top and brush with olive oil.

4 Spread a quarter of the filling on one edge of the filo at the bottom, then roll it up firmly, but not too tightly. Shape into a crescent and place on a baking sheet.

5 Brush the pastry well with oil and bake for about 20–25 minutes in the preheated oven until golden and crisp. Cool slightly then remove to a wire rack to cool further.

Chunky Vegetable Paella

This Spanish rice dish has become a firm family favourite the world over. There are very many versions: here is one with aubergine and chick peas.

SERVES 6
good pinch saffron strands
1 aubergine, cut in thick chunks
salt
90 ml/6 tbsp olive oil
1 large onion, sliced
3 garlic cloves, crushed
1 yellow pepper, sliced
1 red pepper, sliced
10 ml/2 tsp paprika
225 g/8 oz/1¼ cups risotto rice
600 ml/1 pint/2½ cups stock
450 g/1 lb fresh tomatoes, skinned and chopped
ground black pepper
115 g/4 oz sliced mushrooms
115 g/4 oz cut green beans
1 × 400 g/14 oz can chick peas

1 Steep the saffron in 45 ml/3 tbsp hot water. Sprinkle the aubergine with salt, leave to drain in a colander for 30 minutes, then rinse and dry.

2 In a large paella or frying pan, heat the oil and fry the onion, garlic, peppers and aubergine for about 5 minutes, stirring occasionally. Sprinkle in the paprika and stir again.

3 Mix in the rice, then pour in the stock, tomatoes, saffron and seasoning. Bring to a boil then simmer for 15 minutes, uncovered, shaking the pan frequently and stirring occasionally.

4 Stir in the mushrooms, green beans and chick peas (with the liquor). Continue cooking for a further 10 minutes, then serve hot from the pan.

Green Lentil Kulbyaka

This traditional Russian dish, usually made with fish and dough, can be adapted to make a light, crisp vegetarian centrepiece using filo pastry and green lentils.

SERVES 6

175 g/6 oz/1 cup green lentils, soaked for 30 minutes
2 bay leaves
2 onions, sliced
1.2 litres/2 pints/5 cups stock
175 g/6 oz/¾ cup butter, melted
225 g/8 oz/1¼ cups long grain rice, ideally basmati
salt and ground black pepper
60 ml/4 tbsp fresh parsley, chopped
30 ml/2 tbsp fresh dill, chopped
1 egg, beaten
225 g/8 oz mushrooms, sliced
about 8 sheets filo pastry
3 eggs, hard-boiled and sliced

1 Drain the lentils then simmer with the bay leaves, one onion and half the stock for 25 minutes until cooked and thick. Season well, cool and set aside.

VARIATION

You could use a vegetarian puff pastry. In this case, use two blocks of pastry, placing one on top of the other and rolling to a large rectangle. Alternatively, you could make two separate kulbyakas. Divide the filling between the pastry and seal the edges well, glazing the tops with beaten egg.

2 Gently fry the remaining onion in another saucepan with 30 ml/2 tbsp of the butter for 5 minutes. Stir in the rice then the rest of the stock.

3 Season, bring to the boil, then cover and cook gently for 12 minutes for basmati, 15 minutes for long grain. Leave to stand, uncovered for 5 minutes then stir in the fresh herbs. Cool, then beat in the raw egg.

4 Fry the mushrooms in 45 ml/3 tbsp of the butter for 5 minutes until they are just soft. Cool and set aside.

5 Brush the inside of a large, shallow ovenproof dish with more butter. Lay the sheets of filo in it, covering the base and making sure most of the pastry overhangs the sides. Brush well with butter in between and overlapping the pastry as required. Ensure there is a lot of pastry to fold over the mounded filling.

6 Into the pastry lining, layer rice, lentils and mushrooms, repeating the layers at least once and tucking the sliced egg in between. Season as you layer and form an even mound of filling.

7 Bring up the sheets of pastry over the filling, scrunching the top into attractive folds. Brush all over with the rest of the butter and set aside to chill and firm up.

8 Preheat the oven to 190°C/375°F/Gas 5. When ready, bake the kulbyaka for about 45 minutes until golden and crisp. Allow to stand for 10 minutes before you cut it and serve.

Chilli con Queso

Known as a 'bowl of red', this classic Mexican dish is just as tasty when made with all-red beans. For an extra good flavour, use small cubes of smoked cheese, and serve with rice. Epazote is a traditional Mexican herb found in specialist stores.

SERVES 4
225 g/8 oz/2 cups red kidney beans, soaked and drained
45 ml/3 tbsp sunflower oil
1 onion, chopped
1 red pepper, chopped
2 garlic cloves, crushed
1 fresh red chilli, chopped (optional)
15 ml/1 tbsp chilli powder (mild or hot)
5 ml/1 tsp ground cumin
1 litre/1¾ pints/4 cups stock or water
5 ml/1 tsp crushed dried epazote leaves (optional)
ground black pepper
salt
15 g/½ oz granulated sugar
115 g/4 oz cheese, cubed, to serve

1 Rinse the beans. In a large saucepan heat the oil and gently fry the onion, pepper, garlic and fresh chilli for about 5 minutes.

2 Stir in the spices and cook for another minute, then add the beans, stock or water, epazote (if using) and a grinding of pepper. Don't add salt at this stage.

3 Boil for 10 minutes, cover and turn down to a gentle simmer. Cook for about 50 minutes checking the water level and adding extra if necessary.

4 When the beans are tender, season them well with salt. Remove about a quarter of the mixture and mash to a pulp or pass through a food processor.

5 Return the purée to the pan and stir well. Add sugar and serve hot with the cheese sprinkled on top. Great with plain boiled long grain rice.

Big Barley Bowl

Barley seems to have slipped from fashion in recent years – a pity as it is a delicious grain with a marvellous nutty texture. Serve this with crisp cheesy croûtes.

SERVES 6
1 red onion, sliced
½ fennel bulb, sliced
2 carrots, cut in sticks
1 parsnip, sliced
45 ml/3 tbsp sunflower oil
115 g/4 oz/1 cup pearl barley
1 litre/1¼ pints/4 cups stock
5 ml/1 tsp dried thyme
fresh parsley, chopped, to garnish
salt and ground black pepper
115 g/4 oz/⅔ cup green beans, sliced
1 × 425 g/15 oz can pinto beans, drained
CROÛTES
1 medium sized baguette, sliced
olive oil, for brushing
1 garlic clove, cut in half
60 ml/4 tbsp grated Parmesan cheese

1 In a large, heatproof casserole, sauté the onion, fennel, carrots and parsnip gently in the oil for 10 minutes.

2 Stir in the barley and stock. Bring to a boil, add the herbs and seasoning, then cover and simmer gently for 40 minutes.

3 Stir in the green beans and pinto beans and continue cooking – covered – for a further 20 minutes.

4 Meanwhile, preheat the oven to 190°C/375°F/Gas 5. Brush the baguette slices with olive oil and place them on a baking sheet.

5 Bake for about 15 minutes until light golden and crisp. Remove from the oven and quickly rub each croûte with the garlic halves. Sprinkle over the cheese and return to the oven to melt.

6 Ladle the barley into warm bowls and serve sprinkled with parsley, accompanied by the cheesy croûtes. This dish is nicest eaten with a spoon.

Vegetables Julienne with a Red Pepper Coulis

Just the right course for those watching their weight. Choose a selection of as many vegetables as you feel you can eat. Cut them into equal size finger lengths and steam them over aromatic, bubbling water.

SERVES 2

A selection of vegetables. Choose from: carrots, turnips, asparagus, parsnips, courgettes, green beans, broccoli, salsify, cauliflower, mangetouts

RED PEPPER COULIS

1 small onion, chopped
1 garlic clove, crushed
15 ml/1 tbsp sunflower oil
15 ml/1 tbsp water
3 red peppers, roasted, skinned and chopped
120 ml/8 tbsp fromage frais
squeeze of fresh lemon juice
salt and ground black pepper
sprigs of fresh thyme
2 bay leaves
fresh green herbs, to garnish

1 Prepare the vegetables by cutting them into thin fingers or small, bite size pieces.

2 Make the coulis: lightly sauté the onion and garlic in the oil and water for 3 minutes then add the peppers and cook for a further 2 minutes.

3 Pass the coulis through a food processor, then work in the fromage frais, lemon juice and seasoning.

4 Boil some salted water with the fresh thyme and bay leaves, and fit a steamer over the top.

5 Arrange the prepared vegetables on the steamer, placing the harder root vegetables at the bottom and steaming these for about 3 minutes.

6 Add the other vegetables according to their natural tenderness and cook for a further 2–4 minutes.

7 Serve the vegetables on plates with the sauce to one side. Garnish with fresh green herbs, if you wish.

VARIATION

The red pepper coulis makes a wonderful sauce for many other dishes. Try it spooned over fresh pasta with lightly steamed or fried courgettes, or use it as a pouring sauce for savoury filled crêpes.

Curried Parsnip Pie

Sweet, creamy parsnips are beautifully complemented by the addition of curry spices and cheese. This unusual but delicious combination of flavours makes for a very tasty pie.

SERVES 4

PASTRY
115 g/4 oz/8 tbsp butter or margarine
225 g/8 oz/1 cup plain flour
salt and ground black pepper
5 ml/1 tsp dried thyme or oregano
cold water, to mix

FILLING
8 baby onions, or shallots, peeled
2 large parsnips, thinly sliced
2 carrots, thinly sliced
25 g/1 oz/2 tbsp butter or margarine
30 ml/2 tbsp wholemeal flour
15 ml/1 tbsp mild curry or tikka paste
300 ml/½ pint/1¼ cups milk
115 g/4 oz mature cheese, grated
salt and ground black pepper
45 ml/3 tbsp fresh coriander or parsley, chopped
1 egg yolk, beaten with 10 ml/2 tsp water

1 Make the pastry by rubbing the butter or margarine into the flour until it resembles fine breadcrumbs. Season and stir in the thyme or oregano, then mix to a firm dough with cold water.

2 Blanch the baby onions or shallots with the parsnips and carrots in just enough water to cover, for about 5 minutes. Drain, reserving about 300 ml/½ pint/1¼ cups of the liquid.

3 In a clean pan, melt the butter or margarine, and stir in the flour and spice paste to make a roux. Gradually whisk in the reserved stock and milk until smooth. Simmer for a minute or two.

4 Take the pan off the heat, stir in the cheese and seasoning, then mix into the vegetables with the coriander or parsley.

COOK'S TIP

This pie freezes well and makes a good stand-by for a mid-week meal. For best results, make up to the final stage and freeze unbaked. Open freeze until solid, then wrap well in freezer cling film, seal and label. Use within one month.

Cauliflower, broccoli or any other favourite vegetable can be added to the filling to give a variety of flavours and textures.

5 Pour into a pie dish, fix a pie funnel in the centre and allow to cool.

6 Roll out the pastry, large enough to fit the top of the pie dish. Re-roll the trimmings into long strips.

7 Brush the pastry edges with egg yolk wash and fit on the pastry strips. Brush again with egg yolk wash.

8 Using a rolling pin, lift the rolled out pastry over the pie top and fit over the funnel, pressing it down well onto the strips underneath.

9 Cut off the overhanging pastry and crimp the edges. Cut a hole for the funnel, brush all over well with the remaining egg yolk wash and make decorations with the trimmings, glazing them too.

10 Place the pie dish on a baking sheet and chill for 30 minutes while you preheat the oven to 200°C/400°F/Gas 6. Bake the pie for about 25–30 minutes until golden brown and crisp on top.

Vegetables under a Light Creamy Crust

This light main course dish is ideal for a summer supper. The subtle flavours of leeks, courgettes and mushrooms are topped by a tasty crust of fromage frais, cheese and breadcrumbs.

SERVES 4
2 leeks, thinly sliced
3 courgettes, thickly sliced
350 g/12 oz sliced mushrooms, including oyster and shitake mushrooms
2 garlic cloves, crushed
30 ml/2 tbsp olive oil
25 g/1 oz/2 tbsp butter
15 ml/1 tbsp plain flour
300 ml/½ pint/1¼ cups stock
5 ml/1 tsp dried thyme
salt and ground black pepper
30 ml/2 tbsp fromage frais

TOPPING
450 g/1 lb fromage frais
25 g/1 oz/2 tbsp butter, melted
3 eggs, beaten
salt and ground black pepper
fresh nutmeg, grated
freshly grated cheese and dried breadcrumbs, to sprinkle

1 Preheat the oven to 190°C/375°F/ Gas 5. In a saucepan, gently fry the leeks, courgettes, mushrooms and garlic in the oil and butter for about 7 minutes, stirring occasionally, until the vegetables are just soft.

2 Stir in the flour then gradually mix in the stock. Bring to a boil, stirring until thickened. Add the thyme and seasoning. Take the pan off the heat and stir in the fromage frais. Pour the vegetable mixture into a shallow ovenproof dish.

3 Beat the topping ingredients together, seasoning them well and adding the nutmeg to taste. Spoon on top of the vegetables and sprinkle with cheese and breadcrumbs.

4 Bake for about 30 minutes until a light golden, firm crust forms. Serve hot with pasta or crusty bread.

Potato and Parsnip Amandine

Shells of baked potatoes are filled with a spicy parsnip and crunchy almond mix. They make an unusual alternative to plain jacket potatoes.

SERVES 4
4 large baking potatoes
olive oil, for greasing
225 g/8 oz parsnips, diced
25 g/1 oz/2 tbsp butter
5 ml/1 tsp cumin seeds
5 ml/1 tsp ground coriander
30 ml/2 tbsp single cream or natural yogurt
salt and ground black pepper
115 g/4 oz Gruyère or Cheddar cheese, grated
1 egg, beaten
50 g/2 oz/¼ cup flaked almonds

1 Rub the potatoes all over with oil, score in half, then bake at 200°C/400°F/ Gas 6 for about 1 hour until cooked.

2 Meanwhile, boil the parsnips until tender, then drain well, mash and mix with the butter, spices and cream or natural yogurt.

3 When the potatoes are cooked, halve, scoop out and mash the flesh then mix with the parsnip, seasoning well.

4 Stir in the cheese, egg and three quarters of the almonds. Fill the potato shells with the mixture and sprinkle over the remaining almonds.

5 Return to the oven and bake for about 15–20 minutes until golden brown and the filling has set lightly. Serve hot with a side salad.

Autumn Glory

Glorious pumpkin shells summon up the delights of autumn and seem too good simply to throw away. Use one instead as a serving pot. Pumpkin and pasta make marvellous partners, especially as a main course served from the baked shell.

SERVES 4

1 × 2 kg/4 lb pumpkin
1 onion, sliced
2.5 cm/1 in cube fresh root ginger
45 ml/3 tbsp extra virgin olive oil
1 courgette, sliced
115 g/4 oz sliced mushrooms
1 × 400 g/14 oz can chopped tomatoes
75 g/3 oz/1 cup pasta shells
450 ml/¾ pint/2 cups stock
salt and ground black pepper
60 ml/4 tbsp fromage frais
30 ml/2 tbsp fresh basil, chopped

1 Preheat the oven to 180°C/350°F/ Gas 4. Cut the top off the pumpkin with a large, sharp knife and scoop out and discard the seeds.

2 Using a small sharp knife and a sturdy tablespoon extract as much of the pumpkin flesh as possible, then chop it into chunks.

3 Bake the pumpkin with its lid on for 45 minutes to one hour until the inside begins to soften.

4 Meanwhile, make the filling. Gently fry the onion, ginger and pumpkin flesh in the olive oil for about 10 minutes, stirring occasionally.

5 Add the courgette and mushrooms and cook for a further 3 minutes, then stir in the tomatoes, pasta shells and stock. Season well, bring to a boil, then cover and simmer gently for 10 minutes.

6 Stir the fromage frais and basil into the pasta and spoon the mixture into the pumpkin. (It may not be possible to fit all the filling into the pumpkin shell, so serve the rest separately if this is the case.)

Festive Lentil and Nut Roast

An excellent celebration mould which can be served with all the trimmings, including vegetarian gravy. Garnish it with fresh cranberries and French parsley for a really festive effect.

SERVES 6–8
115 g/4 oz/⅔ cup red lentils
115 g/4 oz/1 cup hazelnuts
115 g/4 oz/1 cup walnuts
1 large carrot
2 celery sticks
1 large onion
115 g/4 oz mushrooms
50 g/2 oz/4 tbsp butter
10 ml/2 tsp mild curry powder
30 ml/2 tbsp tomato ketchup
30 ml/2 tbsp Worcestershire sauce
1 egg, beaten
10 ml/2 tsp salt
60 ml/4 tbsp fresh parsley, chopped
150 ml/¼ pint/⅔ cup water

1 Soak the lentils for 1 hour in cold water then drain well. Grind the nuts in a food processor until quite fine but not too smooth. Set the nuts aside.

2 Chop the carrot, celery, onion and mushrooms into small chunks, then pass them through a food processor or blender until they are quite finely chopped.

3 Fry the vegetables gently in the butter for 5 minutes then stir in the curry powder and cook for a minute. Cool.

4 Meanwhile, mix the soaked lentils with the nuts, vegetables, ketchup, Worcestershire sauce, egg, salt, parsley and water.

5 Grease and line the base and sides of a long 1 kg/2 lb loaf tin with greaseproof paper or a sheet of foil. Press the mixture into the tin. Preheat the oven to 190°C/375°F/Gas 5.

6 Bake for about 1–1¼ hours until just firm, covering the top with a butter paper or piece of foil if it starts to burn.

7 Allow the mixture to stand for about 15 minutes before you turn it out and peel off the paper. It will be fairly soft when cut as it is a moist loaf.

Vegetarian Gravy

Make up a large batch of this and freeze it in small containers ready to reheat and serve. A delicious alternative to the meaty version.

MAKES ABOUT 1 LITRE/1¾ PINTS
1 large red onion, sliced
3 turnips, sliced
3 celery sticks, sliced
115 g/4 oz mushrooms, halved
2 whole garlic cloves
90 ml/6 tbsp sunflower oil
1.5 litres/2½ pints/6 cups vegetable stock or water
45 ml/3 tbsp soy sauce
good pinch of granulated sugar
salt and ground black pepper

1 Cook the vegetables and garlic on a moderately high heat with the oil in a large saucepan, stirring occasionally until nicely browned but not singed. This should take about 15–20 minutes.

2 Add the stock or water and soy sauce, bring to the boil then cover and simmer for another 20 minutes.

3 Purée the vegetables, adding a little of the stock, and return them to the pan by rubbing the pulp through a sieve with the back of a ladle or wooden spoon.

4 Taste for seasoning and add the sugar. Freeze at least half of the gravy to use later and reheat the rest to serve with the lentil and nut roast.

Homemade Ravioli

It is a pleasure to make your own fresh pasta and you might be surprised at just how easy it is to fill and shape ravioli. Allow a little extra time than you would for ready-made or dried pasta. A food processor will save you time and effort in making and kneading the dough. A pasta rolling machine helps with the rolling out, but both these jobs can be done by hand if necessary.

SERVES 6
200 g/7 oz/1½ cups strong plain flour
5 ml/½ tsp salt
15 ml/1 tbsp olive oil
2 eggs, beaten
FILLING
1 small red onion, finely chopped
1 small green pepper, finely chopped
1 carrot, coarsely grated
15 ml/1 tbsp olive oil
50 g/2 oz/½ cup walnuts, chopped
115 g/4 oz ricotta cheese
30 ml/2 tbsp fresh Parmesan or Pecorino cheese, grated
15 ml/1 tbsp fresh marjoram or basil, chopped
salt and ground black pepper
extra oil or melted butter, to serve

1 Sift the flour and salt into a food processor. With the machine running, trickle in the oil and eggs and blend to a stiff but smooth dough.

2 Allow the machine to run for at least a minute if possible, otherwise remove the dough and knead it by hand for 5 minutes.

3 If you are using a pasta machine, break off small balls of dough and then feed them through the rollers, several times, according to the machine manufacturer's instructions.

4 If rolling the pasta by hand, divide the dough into two and roll out on a lightly floured surface to a thickness of about 6 mm/¼ in.

5 Fold the pasta into three and re-roll. Repeat this up to six times until the dough is smooth and no longer sticky. Roll the pasta slightly more thinly each time.

6 Keep the rolled dough under clean, dry tea towels while you complete the rest and make the filling. You should aim to have an even number of pasta sheets, all the same size if rolling by machine.

7 Fry the onion, pepper and carrot in the oil for 5 minutes, then allow to cool. Mix with the walnuts, cheeses, herbs and seasoning.

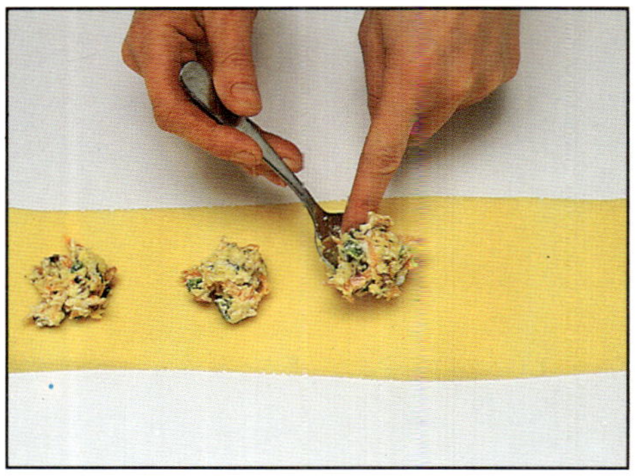

8 Lay out a pasta sheet and place small scoops of the filling in neat rows about 5 cm/2 in apart. Brush in between with a little water and then place another pasta sheet on the top.

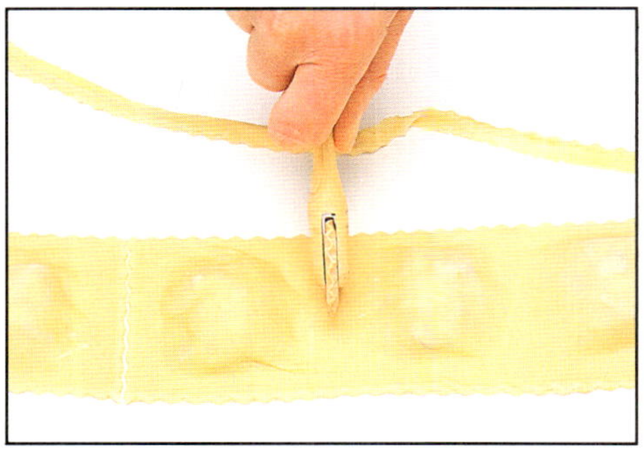

9 Press down well in between the rows then, using a ravioli or pastry cutter, cut into squares. If the edges pop open occasionally, press them back gently with your fingers.

10 Leave the ravioli to dry in the refrigerator, then boil in plenty of lightly salted water for just 5 minutes.

11 Toss the cooked ravioli in a little oil or melted butter before serving with homemade tomato sauce or extra cheese.

Artichoke and Leek Crêpes

Fill thin pancakes with a mouth-watering soufflé mixture of Jerusalem artichokes and leek to serve for a special main course.

SERVES 4
115 g/4 oz/1 cup plain flour
pinch of salt
1 egg
300 ml/½ pint/1¼ cups milk
oil, for brushing
SOUFFLÉ FILLING
450 g/1 lb Jerusalem artichokes, peeled and diced
1 large leek, sliced thinly
50 g/2 oz/4 tbsp butter
30 ml/2 tbsp self-raising flour
30 ml/2 tbsp single cream
75 g/3 oz mature Cheddar cheese, grated
30 ml/2 tbsp fresh parsley, chopped
fresh nutmeg, grated
2 eggs, separated
salt and ground black pepper

1 Make the crêpe batter by blending the flour, salt, egg and milk to a smooth batter in a food processor or blender.

2 Using a crêpe or omelette pan with a diameter of about 20 cm/8 in, make a batch of thin pancakes. You will need about 30 ml/2 tbsp of batter for each one.

3 Stack the pancakes under a clean tea towel as you make them. Reserve eight for this dish and freeze the rest.

4 Cook the artichokes and leek with the butter in a covered saucepan on a gentle heat for about 12 minutes until very soft. Mash with the back of a wooden spoon. Season well.

5 Stir the flour into the vegetables and cook for 1 minute. Take the pan off the heat and beat in the cream, cheese, parsley and nutmeg to taste. Cool, then add the egg yolks.

6 Whisk the egg whites until they form soft peaks and carefully fold them into the leek/artichoke mixture.

7 Lightly grease a small ovenproof dish and preheat the oven to 190°C/375°F/Gas 5. Fold each pancake in four, hold the top open and spoon the mixture into the centre.

8 Arrange the crêpes in the prepared dish with the filling uppermost if possible. Bake for about 15 minutes until risen and golden. Eat immediately!

COOK'S TIP

Make sure the pan is at a good steady heat and is well oiled before you pour in the batter. It should sizzle as it hits the pan. Swirl the batter round to coat the pan, and then cook quickly.

Mushroom Gougère

A savoury choux pastry ring makes a marvellous main course dish that can be made ahead then baked when required. Why not try it for a dinner party? It looks so very special.

SERVES 4
115 g/4 oz/½ cup strong plain flour
2.5 ml/½ tsp salt
75 g/3 oz/6 tbsp butter
200 ml/7 fl oz/¾ cup cold water
3 eggs, beaten
75 g/3 oz/¾ cup diced Gruyère or mature Gouda cheese

FILLING
1 small onion, sliced
1 carrot, coarsely grated
225 g/8 oz button mushrooms, sliced
40 g/1½ oz/3 tbsp butter or margarine
5 ml/1 tsp tikka or mild curry paste
25 g/1 oz/2 tbsp plain flour
300 ml/½ pint/1¼ cups milk
30 ml/2 tbsp fresh parsley, chopped
salt and ground black pepper
30 ml/2 tbsp flaked almonds

1 Preheat the oven to 200°C/400°F/Gas 6. Grease a shallow ovenproof dish about 23 cm/9 in long.

2 To make the choux pastry, first sift the flour and salt onto a sheet of greaseproof paper.

3 In a large saucepan, heat the butter and water until the butter just melts. Do not let the water boil. Fold the paper and shoot the flour into the pan all at once.

4 With a wooden spoon, beat the mixture rapidly until the lumps become smooth and the mixture comes away from the sides of the pan. Cool for 10 minutes.

5 Beat the eggs gradually into the mixture until you have a soft, but still quite stiff, dropping consistency. You may not need all the egg.

6 Stir in the cheese, then spoon the mixture round the sides of the greased ovenproof dish.

7 To make the filling, sauté the onion, carrot and mushrooms in the butter or margarine for 5 minutes. Stir in the curry paste then the flour.

8 Gradually stir in the milk and heat until thickened. Mix in the parsley, season well, then pour into the centre of the choux pastry.

9 Bake for 35–40 minutes until risen and golden brown, sprinkling on the almonds for the last 5 minutes or so. Serve at once.

COOK'S TIP

Choux pastry is remarkably easy to make, as no rolling out is required. The secret of success is to let the flour and butter mixture cool before beating in the eggs, to prevent them from setting.

Cabbage Roulades with Lemon Sauce

Cabbage or chard leaves filled with a rice and lentil stuffing and served with a light eggy lemon sauce makes a light and tasty main course.

SERVES 4–6
12 large cabbage or chard leaves, stalks removed
salt
30 ml/2 tbsp sunflower oil
1 onion, chopped
1 large carrot, grated
115 g/4 oz sliced mushrooms
600 ml/1 pint/2½ cups stock
115 g/4 oz/½ cup long grain rice
60 ml/4 tbsp red lentils
5 ml/1 tsp dried oregano or marjoram
ground black pepper
100 g/3½ oz soft cheese with garlic
SAUCE
30 g/1 oz/3 tbsp plain flour
juice of 1 lemon
3 eggs, beaten

1 Blanch the leaves in boiling, salted water until they begin to wilt. Drain, reserve the water and pat the leaves dry with kitchen paper.

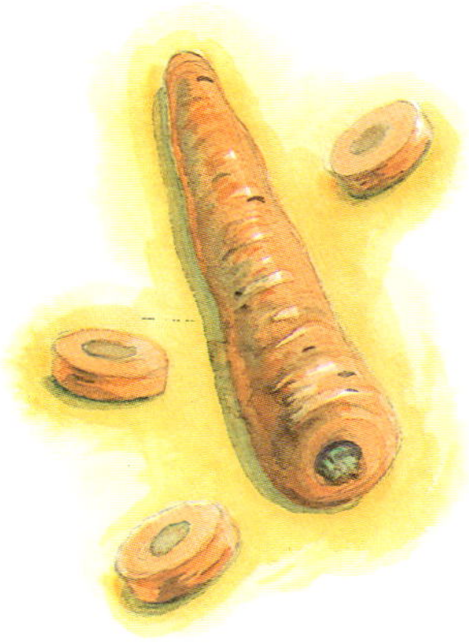

2 Heat the oil and lightly fry the onion, carrot and mushrooms for 5 minutes, and then pour in the stock.

3 Add the rice, lentils, herbs and seasoning. Bring to a boil, cover and simmer gently for 15 minutes. Remove, then stir in the cheese. Preheat the oven to 190°C/375°F/Gas 5.

4 Lay out the chard or cabbage leaves rib side down, and spoon on the filling at the stalk end. Fold the sides in and roll up.

5 Place the join side down in a small roasting pan and pour in the reserved cabbage water. Cover with lightly greased foil and bake for 30–45 minutes until the leaves are tender.

6 Remove the cabbage rolls from the oven, drain and place on a serving dish. Strain 600 ml/1 pint/2½ cups of the cooking water into a saucepan and bring to a boil.

7 Blend the flour to a runny paste with a little cold water and whisk into the boiling stock, together with the lemon juice.

8 Beat the eggs in a heatproof jug and slowly pour on the hot stock, whisking well as you go.

9 Return to the stove and on the lowest heat, stir until smooth and thick. Do not allow the sauce to boil or it will curdle. Serve the rolls with some of the sauce poured over and the rest handed separately.

Irish Colcannon

This lovely warming winter's dish bears a slight resemblance to Eggs Florentine. Here, baked eggs nestle among creamy potatoes with curly kale or cabbage and a topping of grated cheese.

SERVES 4
1 kg/2 lb potatoes, cut in even pieces
225 g/8 oz curly kale or crisp green cabbage, shredded
2 spring onions, chopped
butter or margarine, to taste
fresh nutmeg, grated
salt and ground black pepper
4 large eggs
75 g/3 oz mature cheese, grated

1 Boil the potatoes until just tender, then drain and mash well.

2 Lightly cook the kale or cabbage until just tender but still crisp. Preheat the oven to 190°C/375°F/Gas 5.

3 Drain the greens and mix them into the potato with the onions, butter or margarine and nutmeg. Season to taste.

4 Spoon the mixture into a shallow ovenproof dish and make four hollows in the mixture. Crack an egg into each and season well.

5 Bake for about 12 minutes or until the eggs are just set, then serve sprinkled with the cheese.

Pasta with Caponata

The Sicilians have an excellent sweet and sour vegetable dish called *caponata*, which naturally enough goes wonderfully well with pasta.

SERVES 4
1 medium aubergine, cut into sticks
2 medium courgettes, cut into sticks
8 baby onions, peeled or 1 large onion, sliced
2 garlic cloves, crushed
1 large red pepper, sliced
60 ml/4 tbsp olive oil, preferably extra virgin
450 ml/¾ pint/scant 2 cups tomato juice or 1 × 500 ml/17 fl oz carton creamed tomatoes
150 ml/¼ pint/⅔ cup water
30 ml/2 tbsp balsamic vinegar
juice of 1 lemon
15 ml/1 tbsp sugar
30 ml/2 tbsp sliced black olives
30 ml/2 tbsp capers
salt and ground black pepper
400 g/14 oz tagliatelle or other pasta ribbons

1 Lightly salt the aubergine and courgettes and leave them to drain in a colander for 30 minutes. Rinse and pat dry with kitchen paper towel.

2 In a large saucepan, lightly fry the onions, garlic and pepper in the oil for 5 minutes, then stir in the aubergine and courgettes and fry for a further 5 minutes.

3 Stir in the tomato juice or creamed tomatoes plus the water. Stir well, bringing the mixture to the boil, then add all the rest of the ingredients except the pasta. Season to taste and then simmer for 10 minutes.

4 Meanwhile, boil the pasta according to the instructions on the pack, then drain. Serve the caponata with the pasta.

Spinach Gnocchi

This wholesome Italian dish is ideal for making in advance then baking when required. Serve it with a fresh tomato sauce.

SERVES 4–6
400 g/14 oz fresh leaf spinach or 150 g/6 oz frozen leaf spinach, thawed
750 ml/1¼ pints/good 3 cups milk
200 g/7 oz/1¼ cups semolina
50 g/2 oz/4 tbsp butter, melted
50 g/2 oz Parmesan cheese, freshly grated, plus extra to serve
fresh nutmeg, grated
salt and ground black pepper
2 eggs, beaten

1 Blanch the spinach in the tiniest amount of water then drain and squeeze dry through a sieve with the back of a ladle. Chop the spinach roughly.

2 In a large saucepan, heat the milk and when just on the point of boiling, sprinkle in the semolina in a steady stream, stirring it briskly with a wooden spoon.

3 Simmer the semolina for 2 minutes then remove from the heat and stir in half the butter, most of the cheese, nutmeg and seasoning to taste and the spinach. Allow to cool for 5 minutes.

4 Stir in the eggs then tip the mixture out onto a shallow baking sheet, spreading it to a 1 cm/½ in thickness. Allow to cool completely then chill until solid.

5 Stamp out shapes using a plain round cutter with a diameter of 4 cm/1½ in. Reserve the trimmings.

6 Grease a shallow ovenproof dish. Place the trimmings on the base and arrange the gnocchi rounds on top with each one overlapping.

7 Brush the tops with the remaining butter and sprinkle over the last of the cheese.

8 Preheat the oven when ready to bake to 190°C/375°F/Gas 5 and cook for about 35 minutes until golden and crisp on top. Serve hot with fresh tomato sauce and extra cheese.

VARIATION

For a special occasion, make half plain and half spinach gnocchi and arrange in an attractive pattern to serve. Use the same recipe as above but halve the amount of spinach and add to half the mixture in a separate bowl to make two batches. Stamp out and cook the gnocchi as normal. For a more substantial, healthy meal, make a tasty vegetable base of lightly sautéed peppers, courgettes and mushrooms and place the gnocchi on the top.

Red Rice Rissoles

Risotto rice chills to a firm texture yet remains light and creamy when reheated as crisp crumbed rissoles. These contain small nuggets of cheese for extra creaminess.

SERVES ABOUT 8
1 large red onion, chopped
1 red pepper, chopped
2 garlic cloves, crushed
1 red chilli, finely chopped
30 ml/2 tbsp olive oil
25 g/1 oz/2 tbsp butter
225 g/8 oz/1¼ cups risotto rice
1 litre/1¾ pints/4½ cups stock
4 sun-dried tomatoes, chopped
30 ml/2 tbsp tomato purée
10 ml/2 tsp dried oregano
salt and ground black pepper
45 ml/3 tbsp fresh parsley, chopped
150 g/6 oz cheese, e.g. Red Leicester or smoked Cheddar
1 egg, beaten
115 g/4 oz/1 cup dried breadcrumbs
oil, for deep frying

1 Fry the onion, pepper, garlic and chilli in the oil and butter for 5 minutes. Stir in the rice and fry for a further 2 minutes.

2 Pour in the stock and add the tomatoes, purée, oregano and seasoning. Bring to the boil, stirring occasionally, then cover and simmer for 20 minutes.

3 Stir in the parsley then turn into a shallow dish, cool and chill until firm. When cold, divide into 12 and shape into balls.

4 Cut the cheese into 12 pieces and press a nugget into the centre of each of the rissoles.

5 Put the beaten egg in one bowl and the breadcrumbs into another. Dip the rissoles first into the egg then into the breadcrumbs, coating each one evenly.

6 Lay the coated rissoles on a plate and chill again for 30 minutes. Fill a deep fat frying pan one-third full of oil and heat until a cube of day-old bread browns in under a minute.

7 Fry the rissoles in batches, reheating the oil in between, for about 3–4 minutes. Drain on kitchen paper and keep warm, uncovered, before serving.

Broad Bean and Cauliflower Curry

A tasty mid-week curry to serve with rice (especially a brown basmati), small popadums and maybe a cucumber raita.

SERVES 4
2 garlic cloves, chopped
2.5 cm/1 in cube fresh root ginger
1 fresh green chilli, seeded and chopped
15 ml/1 tbsp oil
1 onion, sliced
1 large potato, chopped
30 ml/2 tbsp ghee or softened butter
15 ml/1 tbsp curry powder, mild or hot
1 medium size cauliflower, cut into small florets
600 ml/1 pint/2½ cups stock
25 g/1 oz/2 tbsp creamed coconut
salt and ground black pepper
1 × 285 g/10 oz can broad beans, with liquor
juice of half a lemon (optional)
fresh coriander or parsley, chopped, to serve

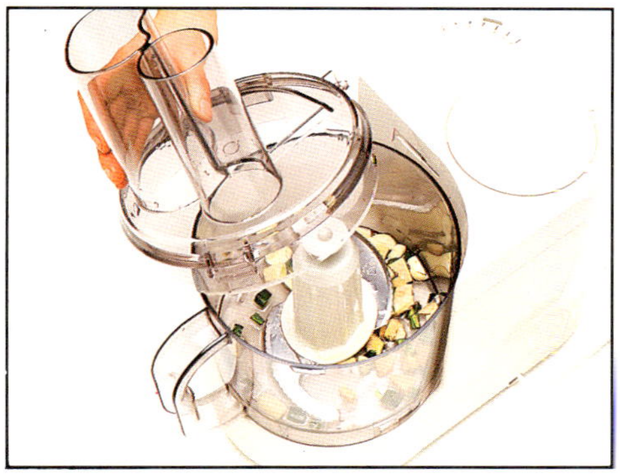

1 Blend the garlic, ginger, chilli and oil in a food processor until they form a smooth paste.

2 In a large saucepan, fry the onion and potato in the ghee or butter for 5 minutes then stir in the spice paste and curry powder. Cook for 1 minute.

3 Add the cauliflower florets and stir well into the spicy mixture, then pour in the stock. Bring to a boil and mix in the coconut, stirring until it melts.

4 Season well then cover and simmer for 10 minutes. Add the beans and their liquor and cook uncovered for a further 10 minutes.

5 Check the seasoning and add a good squeeze of lemon juice if liked. Serve hot garnished with coriander or parsley.

SALADS & VEGETABLE DISHES

Here is a delightful range of colourful salads and scrumptious vegetable dishes and accompaniments. Varied but easy to obtain ingredients ensure the perfect recipe for every style of meal.

Bean Sprout Stir-fry

Homegrown bean sprouts taste so good, tossed into a tasty stir-fry. They have more flavour and texture than shop bought varieties and are very nutritious, being rich in vitamins and high in fibre. (Old dried beans will not sprout, so use beans that are well within their 'Use by' date.)

SERVES 3–4
30 ml/2 tbsp sunflower or groundnut oil
225 g/8 oz mixed sprouted beans
2 spring onions, chopped
1 garlic clove, crushed
30 ml/2 tbsp soy sauce
10 ml/2 tsp sesame oil
15 ml/1 tbsp sesame seeds
30 ml/2 tbsp fresh coriander or parsley, chopped
salt and ground black pepper

1 Heat the sunflower or groundnut oil in a large wok and stir-fry the sprouting beans, onion and garlic for 3–5 minutes.

2 Add the remaining ingredients, cook for 1–2 minutes more and serve hot.

HOME SPROUTING BEANS

Use any of the following pulses to grow your own sprouts: green or brown lentils, aduki beans, mung beans, chick peas, flageolet and haricot beans, soya beans or Indian massor dal.

Cover 45 ml/3 tbsp of your chosen pulses with lukewarm water. Leave to soak overnight, then drain and rinse.

Place in a large clean jam jar or special sprouting tray. Cover with muslin and secure with a rubber band. If using a jam jar, lay the jar on its side and shake it so the beans spread along the length. Leave somewhere warm.

Rinse the beans night and morning with plenty of cold water, running this through the muslin, and drain. Carefully place the jar back on its side.

Repeat this twice a day until roots and shoots appear. (If nothing happens after 48 hours, the beans are probably too old.) When the shoots are at least twice the length of the bean, rinse finally and store in the fridge for up to two days.

Panzanella Salad

If sliced juicy tomatoes layered with day old bread sounds strange for a salad, don't be deceived – it's quite delicious. A popular Italian salad, this dish is ideal as a starter or an accompaniment. Use full-flavoured tomatoes for the best result.

SERVES 4–6
4 thick slices day-old bread, either white, brown or rye
1 small red onion, thinly sliced
450 g/1 lb ripe tomatoes, thinly sliced
115 g/4 oz Mozzarella cheese, thinly sliced
5 ml/1 tbsp fresh basil, shredded, or marjoram
salt and ground black pepper
120 ml/4 fl oz/½ cup extra virgin olive oil
45 ml/3 tbsp balsamic vinegar
juice of 1 small lemon
stoned and sliced black olives or salted capers, to garnish

1 Dip the bread briefly in cold water, then carefully squeeze out the excess water. Arrange on the bottom of a shallow salad bowl.

2 Soak the onion slices in cold water for about 10 minutes while you prepare the other ingredients. Drain and reserve.

3 Layer the tomatoes, cheese, onion, basil or marjoram, seasoning well in between each layer. Sprinkle with oil, vinegar and lemon juice.

4 Top with the olives or capers, cover with cling film and chill in the refrigerator overnight, if possible.

Caesar's Salad

On Independence Day 1924, in Tijuana, Mexico, a restauranteur – Caesar Cardini – created this masterpiece of new American cuisine. It has all the elements of a good salad – being light, flavoursome, attractive and nutritious with a good crunch.

SERVES 4
- 2 thick slices crustless bread
- 2 garlic cloves
- sunflower oil, for frying
- 1 Cos lettuce, torn in pieces
- 50 g/2 oz/½ cup fresh Parmesan cheese, coarsely grated
- 2 eggs

DRESSING
- 30 ml/2 tbsp extra virgin olive oil
- 10 ml/2 tsp French mustard
- 10 ml/2 tsp Worcestershire sauce
- 30 ml/2 tbsp fresh lemon juice

1 Cut the bread into cubes. Heat one of the garlic cloves slowly in about 45 ml/ 3 tbsp of the sunflower oil in a saucepan then toss in the bread cubes. Remove the garlic clove.

2 Heat an oven to 190°C/375°F/Gas 5. Spread the garlicky cubes on a baking sheet and bake the bread for about 10–12 minutes until golden and crisp. Remove and allow to cool.

3 Rub the inside of a large salad bowl with the remaining garlic clove and then discard it.

4 Toss in the torn lettuce, sprinkling between the leaves with the cheese. Cover and set the salad aside.

5 Boil a small saucepan of water and cook the eggs for 1 minute only. Remove the eggs, and crack them open into a jug or bowl. The whites should be milky and the yolks raw.

6 Whisk the dressing ingredients into the eggs. When ready to serve pour the dressing over the leaves, toss well together and serve topped with the croûtons.

VARIATION

Why not try a refreshing Italian version of this salad? Use cubed ciabatta bread for the croûtons. Rub the inside of a salad bowl with garlic and spoon in 30–45 ml/ 2–3 tbsp of good olive oil. Add a selection of torn salad leaves, including rocket, together with some shaved Parmesan cheese. Do not mix yet. Just before serving, add the croûtons, season well, then toss the leaves with the oil, coating well. Finally squeeze over the juice of a fresh lemon.

Chef's Salad

This is basically whatever you make of it – a lovely large salad containing all your favourite ingredients. It is also a good opportunity to use up leftover vegetables and small pieces of cheese from the refrigerator. For these reasons, quantities are approximate.

SERVES 6
450 g/1 lb new potatoes, halved if large
2 carrots, grated coarsely
½ small fennel bulb or 2 sticks celery, sliced thinly
50 g/2 oz sliced button mushrooms
¼ cucumber, sliced or chopped
small green or red pepper, sliced
60 ml/4 tbsp garden peas
200 g/7 oz/1 cup cooked pulses, e.g. red kidney beans or green lentils
1 Ice Gem or baby lettuce or 1 head chicory (endive)
2–3 hard boiled eggs, quartered and/or grated cheese, to serve
½ carton salad cress, snipped

1 Put all the vegetables and pulses (except the lettuce or chicory) into a large mixing bowl.

DRESSING
60 ml/4 tbsp mayonnaise
45 ml/3 tbsp natural yogurt
30 ml/2 tbsp milk
30 ml/2 tbsp chopped fresh chives or spring onion tops
salt and ground black pepper

2 Line a large platter with the lettuce or chicory leaves – creating a nest for the other salad ingredients. Mix the dressing ingredients together and pour over the salad in the mixing bowl.

3 Toss the salad thoroughly in the dressing, season well then pile into the centre of the lettuce nest.

4 Top the salad with the eggs, cheese or both and sprinkle with the snipped cress. Serve lightly chilled.

Potato and Radish Salad

So many potato salads are dressed in thick sauce. This one is quite light and colourful with a flavoursome yet delicate dressing.

SERVES 4–6
450 g/1 lb new potatoes, scrubbed
45 ml/3 tbsp olive oil
15 ml/1 tbsp walnut or hazelnut oil (optional)
30 ml/2 tbsp wine vinegar
10 ml/2 tsp coarse grain mustard
5 ml/1 tsp clear honey
salt and ground black pepper
about 6–8 radishes, thinly sliced
30 ml/2 tbsp fresh chives, chopped

1 Boil the potatoes until just tender. Drain, return to the pan and cut any large potatoes in half.

2 Make a dressing with the oils, vinegar, mustard, honey and seasoning. Mix them together thoroughly in a bowl.

3 Toss the dressing into the potatoes while they are still cooling and allow them to stand for an hour or so.

4 Mix in the radishes and chives, chill lightly, toss again and serve.

COOK'S TIP

The secret of a good potato salad is to dress the potatoes while still warm in a vinaigrette-style dressing in order to let them soak up the flavour as they cool. You can then mix in an additional creamy dressing of mayonnaise and natural yogurt if liked. Sliced celery, red onion and chopped walnuts would make a good alternative to the radishes and, for best effect, serve on a platter lined with frilly lettuce leaves.

Thai Rice and Sprouting Beans

Thai rice has a delicate fragrance and texture that is delicious whether served hot or cold. This salad is a colourful collection of popular Thai flavours and textures.

SERVES 6
30 ml/2 tbsp sesame oil
30 ml/2 tbsp fresh lime juice
1 small fresh red chilli, seeded and chopped
1 garlic clove, crushed
10 ml/2 tsp grated fresh root ginger
30 ml/2 tbsp light soy sauce
5 ml/1 tsp clear honey
45 ml/3 tbsp pineapple juice
15 ml/1 tbsp wine vinegar
225 g/8 oz/1¼ cups Thai fragrant rice, boiled
2 spring onions, sliced
2 rings canned pineapple in natural juice, chopped
150 g/5 oz/1¼ cups sprouted lentils or bean sprouts
1 small red pepper, sliced
1 stick celery, sliced
50 g/2 oz/½ cup unsalted cashew nuts, roughly chopped
30 ml/2 tbsp toasted sesame seeds
salt and ground black pepper

1 Whisk together the sesame oil, lime juice, chilli, garlic, ginger, soy sauce, honey, pineapple juice and vinegar in a large bowl. Stir in the lightly boiled rice.

2 Toss in all the remaining ingredients and mix well. This dish can be served warm or lightly chilled. If the rice grains stick together on cooling, simply stir them with a metal spoon.

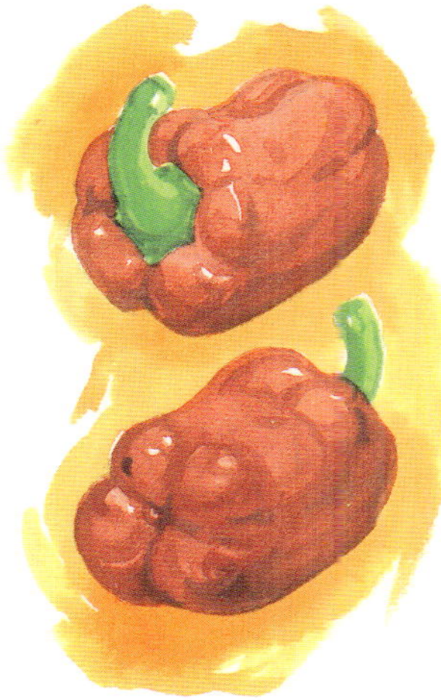

Chicory, Carrot and Rocket Salad

A bright and colourful salad which is ideal for a buffet or barbecue party. Use watercress if you are unable to obtain any rocket.

SERVES 4–6
3 carrots, coarsely grated
about 50 g/2 oz fresh rocket or watercress, roughly chopped
1 large head chicory
DRESSING:
45 ml/3 tbsp sunflower oil
15 ml/1 tbsp hazelnut or walnut oil (optional)
30 ml/2 tbsp cider or wine vinegar
10 ml/2 tsp clear honey
5 ml/1 tsp grated lemon rind
15 ml/1 tbsp poppy seeds
salt and ground black pepper

1 Mix the carrot and rocket or watercress together in a large bowl and season well.

2 Shake the dressing ingredients together in a screw-topped jar then pour onto the carrot and greenery. Toss the salad thoroughly.

3 Line a shallow salad bowl with the chicory leaves and spoon the salad into the centre. Serve lightly chilled.

Bountiful Bean and Nut Salad

This is a good multi-purpose dish. It can be a cold main course, a buffet party dish, or a salad on the side. It also keeps well for up to three days in the refrigerator.

SERVES 6
75 g/3 oz/½ cup red kidney, pinto or borlotti beans
75 g/3 oz/½ cup white cannellini or butter beans
30 ml/2 tbsp olive oil
175 g/6 oz cut fresh green beans
3 spring onions, sliced
1 small yellow or red pepper, sliced
1 carrot, coarsely grated
30 ml/2 tbsp dried topping onions or sun-dried tomatoes, chopped
50 g/2 oz/½ cup unsalted cashew nuts or almonds, split

DRESSING
45 ml/3 tbsp sunflower oil
30 ml/2 tbsp red wine vinegar
15 ml/1 tbsp coarse grain mustard
5 ml/1 tsp caster sugar
5 ml/1 tsp dried mixed herbs
salt and ground black pepper

1 Soak the beans, overnight if possible, then drain and rinse well, cover with a lot of cold water and cook according to the instructions on the pack.

2 When cooked, drain and season the beans and toss them in the olive oil. Leave to cool for 30 minutes.

3 In a large bowl, mix in the other vegetables, including the sun-dried tomatoes but not the crisp topping onions, if using, or the nuts.

4 Make up the dressing by shaking all the ingredients together in a screw topped jar. Toss the dressing into the salad and check the seasoning again. Serve sprinkled with the topping onions, if using, and the split nuts.

Garden Salad and Garlic Crostini

Dress a colourful mixture of salad leaves with good olive oil and freshly squeezed lemon juice, then top it with crispy bread crostini.

SERVES 4–6
3 thick slices day old bread, e.g. ciabatta
120 ml/4 fl oz/½ cup extra virgin olive oil
garlic clove, cut
½ small Cos or Romaine lettuce
½ small oak leaf lettuce
25 g/1 oz rocket leaves or cress
25 g/1 oz fresh flat leaf parsley
a few leaves and flowers of nasturtium
flowers of pansy and pot marigold
a small handful of young dandelion leaves
sea salt flakes and ground black pepper
juice of 1 fresh lemon

1 Cut the bread into medium size pieces about 1 cm/½ in square.

2 Heat half the oil gently in a frying pan and fry the bread cubes in it, tossing them until they are well coated and lightly browned. Remove and cool.

3 Rub the inside of a large salad bowl with the garlic and discard. Pour the rest of the oil into the bottom of the bowl.

4 Wash, dry and tear the leaves into bite size pieces and pile them into the bowl. Season with salt and pepper. Cover and keep chilled until ready to serve.

5 To serve, toss the leaves in the oil at the bottom of the bowl, then sprinkle with the lemon juice and toss again. Scatter over the crostini and serve immediately.

Californian Vim and Vit Salad

Full of vitality and vitamins, this is a lovely light healthy salad for sunny days when you feel full of energy, or need an extra boost.

SERVES 4
1 small crisp lettuce, torn in pieces
225 g/8 oz young spinach leaves
2 carrots, coarsely grated
115 g/4 oz cherry tomatoes, halved
2 celery sticks, thinly sliced
75 g/3 oz/½ cup raisins
50 g/2 oz/½ cup blanched almonds or unsalted cashew nuts, halved
30 ml/2 tbsp sunflower seeds
30 ml/2 tbsp sesame seeds, lightly toasted
DRESSING:
45 ml/3 tbsp extra virgin olive oil
30 ml/2 tbsp cider vinegar
10 ml/2 tsp clear honey
juice of 1 small orange
salt and ground black pepper

1 Put the salad vegetables, raisins, almonds or cashew nuts and seeds into a large bowl.

2 Put all the dressing ingredients into a screw top jar, shake them up well and pour over the salad.

3 Toss the salad thoroughly and divide it between four small salad bowls. Season and serve lightly chilled.

Scandinavian Cucumber and Dill

It's amazing what a touch of salt can do to simple cucumber slices. They take on a contradictory soft yet crisp texture and develop a good, full flavour. However, juices continue to form after salting, so this salad is best dressed just before serving. It is particularly complementary to hot and spicy food.

SERVES 4
2 cucumbers
salt
30 ml/2 tbsp fresh chives, chopped
30 ml/2 tbsp fresh dill, chopped
150 ml/¼ pint/⅔ cup soured cream or fromage frais
ground black pepper

1 Slice the cucumbers as thinly as possible, preferably in a food processor or a slicer.

2 Place the slices in layers in a colander set over a plate to catch the juices. Sprinkling each layer well, but not too heavily, with salt.

3 Leave the cucumber to drain for up to 2 hours, then lay out the slices on a clean tea towel and pat them dry.

4 Mix the cucumber with the herbs, cream or fromage frais and plenty of pepper. Serve as soon as possible.

COOK'S TIP

Lightly salted (or degorged) cucumbers are also delicious as sandwich fillings in wafer thin buttered brown bread. These sandwiches were always served at the traditional British tea-time.

Spinach Roulade

A simple purée of spinach baked with eggs rolled around a creamy red pepper filling makes an exotic and colourful side dish. Even better, this can be prepared in advance and then reheated when required.

SERVES 4
450 g/1 lb leaf spinach, well washed and drained
fresh nutmeg, grated
good knob of butter
45 ml/3 tbsp Parmesan cheese, grated
45 ml/3 tbsp double cream
salt and ground black pepper
2 eggs, separated
1 small red pepper, chopped
1 × 200 g/7 oz pack soft cheese with garlic and herbs

1 Line and then grease a medium-sized Swiss roll tin. Preheat the oven to 190°C/375°F/Gas 5.

2 Cook the spinach with a tiny amount of water then drain well, pressing it through a sieve with the back of a ladle. Chop the spinach finely.

3 Mix the spinach with the nutmeg, butter, Parmesan cheese, cream and seasoning. Cool for 5 minutes then beat in the egg yolks.

4 Whisk the egg whites until they form soft peaks and carefully fold in to the spinach mixture. Spread in to the prepared tin, level and bake for 12–15 minutes until firm.

5 Turn the spinach out upside down on to a clean tea towel and allow it to cool in the tin for half an hour.

6 Meanwhile, simmer the pepper in about 30 ml/2 tbsp of water in a covered pan until just soft, then either purée it in a blender or chop it finely. Mix with the soft cheese and season well.

7 When the spinach has cooled, peel off the paper. Trim any hard edges and spread it with the red pepper cream.

8 Carefully roll up the spinach and pepper in the tea towel, leave for 10 minutes to firm up, then serve on a long platter, cut in thick slices.

VARIATION

A thick vegetable purée of any root vegetable also works well as a roulade. Try cooked beetroot or parsnip, flavouring lightly with a mild curry-style spice such as cumin or coriander. The fillings can be varied too, such as finely chopped and sautéed mushroom and onion or grated carrot mixed with fromage frais and chives. Roulades are delicious served warm as well. Sprinkle with cheese and bake in a moderately hot oven for 15 minutes or so.

Indian Spiced Okra with Almonds

Long and elegantly shaped, it's not surprising these vegetables have the popular name of 'lady's fingers'. Although commonly used in many international dishes, okra are particularly well suited to all the Indian spices.

SERVES 2–4
225 g/8 oz okra
50 g/2 oz/½ cup blanched almonds, chopped
25 g/1 oz/2 tbsp butter
15 ml/1 tbsp sunflower oil
2 garlic cloves, crushed
2.5 cm/1 in cube fresh root ginger, grated
5 ml/1 tsp cumin seeds
5 ml/1 tsp ground coriander
5 ml/1 tsp paprika

1 Trim just the tops of the okra stems and around the edges of the stalks. They have a sticky liquid which oozes out if prepared too far ahead, so trim them immediately before cooking.

2 In a shallow fireproof dish, fry the almonds in the butter until they are lightly golden, then remove.

3 Add the oil to the pan and fry the okra, stirring constantly, for 2 minutes.

4 Add the garlic and ginger and fry gently for a minute, then add the spices and cook for another minute or so, stirring all the time.

5 Pour in about 300 ml/½ pint/1¼ cups water. Season well, cover and simmer for about 5 minutes or so until the okra feel just tender.

6 Finally, mix in the fried almonds and serve piping hot.

VARIATION

Okra are also popular in Louisiana cooking and are an essential ingredient for gumbo, a thick, spicy stew served over hot, steaming rice. Indeed, 'gumbo' was the old African word for okra used by the American slaves. You can make a ratatouille-style vegetable stew using okra instead of aubergines, and adding onions, peppers, garlic and tomatoes. Or try them sliced, fried in garlic and spices, then stirred into a pilaff of basmati rice with cauliflower florets and carrots. This makes a colourful and delicious dish – especially when topped with crushed grilled popadums.

Roasted Peppers in Oil

Peppers take on a delicious, smoky flavour if roasted in a very hot oven. The skins can easily be peeled off and the flesh stored in olive oil. This oil can then be used to add extra flavour to salad dressings.

6 large peppers of differing colours
450 ml/¾ pint/scant 2 cups olive oil

1 Preheat the oven to the highest temperature, about 230°C/450°F/Gas 8. Lightly grease a large baking sheet.

2 Quarter the peppers, remove the cores and seeds then squash them flat with the back of your hands. Lay the peppers skin side up on the baking tray.

3 Roast the peppers at the top of the oven until the skins blacken and blister. This will take about 12–15 minutes.

4 Remove the peppers from the oven, cover with a clean tea towel until they are cool, then peel off the skins.

5 Slice the peppers and pack them into a clean preserving jar.

COOK'S TIP

These pepper slices make very attractive presents, especially around Christmas time. You can either buy special preserving jars from kitchen equipment shops, or wash out large jam jars, soaking off the labels at the same time. The jars should then be sterilized by placing upside down in a low oven for about half an hour. Fill the jars while still hot with the sliced peppers, and fill with a good olive oil. Cover immediately with the lid and fix on an attractive label.

6 Add the oil to the jar to completely cover the peppers, then seal the lid tightly.

7 Store the peppers in the refrigerator and use them within 2 weeks. Use the oil in dressing or for cooking once the peppers have been eaten.

Potato Latkes

These little potato pancakes make a pleasant and unusual alternative to chips or roast potatoes.

MAKES ABOUT 24
1 kg/2 lb potatoes, peeled and coarsely grated
40 g/1½ oz/scant ½ cup self-raising flour
2 eggs
15 ml/1 tbsp onion, grated
fresh nutmeg, grated
salt and ground black pepper
oil, for shallow frying

1 Soak the grated potato in plenty of cold water for about an hour, then drain well and pat dry with a clean tea towel.

2 Beat together the flour, eggs, onion and nutmeg, then mix in the potato. Season well.

3 Heat a thin layer of oil in a heavy based frying pan and drop about a tablespoon of potato batter into the pan, squashing it flat, if necessary.

4 Cook the potato until golden brown, then flip over and cook the other side. Drain on kitchen paper towel and keep warm, uncovered in the oven. Repeat with the rest of the mixture.

Stir-fry Aubergine

A speedy side dish with an Oriental touch. The aubergine is stir-fried with red pepper and black beans which gives it an exotic and colourful appearance. Salted black beans are sold either dried or canned. Dried ones will need soaking.

SERVES 4
30 ml/2 tbsp groundnut oil
1 aubergine, sliced
2 spring onions, sliced diagonally
1 garlic clove, crushed
1 small red pepper, sliced
30 ml/2 tbsp oyster sauce
25 g/1 oz/1 tbsp Chinese salted black beans, soaked if dried
ground black pepper
15 ml/1 tbsp fresh coriander or parsley, chopped, to garnish

1 Heat the oil in a wok and stir-fry the aubergine for 2 minutes. Add the onions, garlic and pepper and cook for a further 2 minutes.

2 Add the oyster sauce, black beans and pepper. Cook for a further 1 minute, season with pepper only and serve with fresh coriander or parsley.

Potato and Parsnip Dauphinoise

Layers of potatoes and parsnips are baked slowly in creamy milk with grated cheese. This is an ideal special side dish or light supper dish.

SERVES 4–6
1 kg/2 lb potatoes, thinly sliced
1 onion, thinly sliced
450 g/1 lb parsnips, thinly sliced
2 garlic cloves, crushed
50 g/2 oz/4 tbsp butter
125 g/4 oz Gruyère or Cheddar cheese, grated
fresh nutmeg, grated
salt and ground black pepper
300 ml/½ pint/1¼ cups single cream
300 ml/½ pint/1¼ cups milk

1 Lightly grease a large shallow ovenproof dish. Preheat the oven to 180°C/350°F/Gas 4.

2 Layer the potatoes with the onion and parsnips. In between each layer, dot the vegetables with garlic and butter, sprinkle over most of the cheese, add the nutmeg and season well.

3 Heat the cream and milk together in a saucepan until it is hot but not boiling. Slowly pour the creamy milk over the vegetables, making sure it seeps underneath them.

4 Scatter the remaining cheese over the vegetables and grate a little more nutmeg on top. Bake for about an hour or so until the potatoes are tender and the cheesey top is bubbling and golden.

Asparagus Mimosa

Pretty spears of fresh, tender asparagus are tossed in a buttery sauce and served with a chopped egg and chervil dressing. This also makes an excellent starter.

SERVES 2
225 g/8 oz fresh asparagus
salt
ground black pepper
50 g/2 oz/4 tbsp butter, melted
squeeze of fresh lemon juice
2 eggs, hard-boiled and chopped
15 ml/1 tbsp fresh chervil, chopped

1 Trim the asparagus stalks and peel off the tough outer layers at the base with a vegetable peeler.

2 Poach the asparagus spears in lightly salted water, until just tender. This will take between 3–6 minutes. (Use a clean, deep frying pan if you don't have an asparagus steamer.)

3 Drain the asparagus well and arrange it on two small plates or one large one. Season well.

4 Mix the melted butter with the lemon juice. Trickle over the spears, sprinkle with the eggs and garnish with the chervil. Serve warm.

Braised Fennel and Tomato

Fennel is a very undervalued vegetable but it is excellent cooked in a light tomato sauce. This dish can be gently simmered on the cooker or baked inside a moderate oven.

SERVES 4–6
2 fennel bulbs
1 small onion or 3 shallots, sliced
1 garlic clove, crushed
30 ml/2 tbsp olive oil
4 medium sized tomatoes, skinned and chopped
45 ml/3 tbsp dry white wine
15 ml/1 tbsp fresh marjoram, chopped
150 ml/¼ pint/⅔ cup stock or water
salt and ground black pepper

1 Trim the fennel then cut it into wedges. Reserve any fronds for a garnish.

2 Lightly sauté the fennel with the onion or shallots and garlic in the oil in a fireproof dish for 5 minutes.

3 Add the tomatoes, wine, marjoram and stock or water. Season.

4 Cover and either simmer very gently for 20 minutes, or bake in a preheated oven for 30 minutes at 190°C/375°F/Gas 5. Garnish with any reserved fronds and serve immediately.

Creamed Winter Vegetables

A mixture of chunky mashed root vegetables, such as carrots, parsnips and turnips or swedes, makes a wonderfully warming winter side dish.

SERVES 4–6
225 g/8 oz carrots, chopped
225 g/8 oz parsnips, chopped
1 small swede, chopped
25 g/1 oz/2 tbsp butter
10 ml/2 tsp mild curry paste
salt and ground black pepper
115 g/4 oz/½ cup fromage frais
15 ml/1 tbsp fresh chives, chopped

1 Boil the carrots, parsnips and swede in plenty of lightly salted water until tender. Drain the vegetables then return them to the pan with the butter, curry paste and seasoning.

2 Mash the vegetables lightly with a fork so that you end up with a chunky purée; you want to retain a good texture.

3 Stir in the fromage frais and chives. Check the seasoning and serve hot. This is a good dish to prepare in advance and reheat when required.

COOK'S TIP

Vegetable purées are a popular accompaniment with any dish which could be a little on the dry side, providing a good contrast of textures and colours. Suitable vegetables are Brussels sprouts, carrots, peas, broccoli and leeks.

PARTIES & PICNICS

From informal meals, ideal for outdoor entertaining, to elegant and delicious dishes that will add style to special occasions, here are recipes to suit every festivity.

Spicy Potato Strudel

Wrap up a tasty mixture of vegetables in a spicy, creamy sauce with crisp filo pastry. It makes a perfect dish for a special family supper.

SERVES 4
1 onion, chopped
2 carrots, coarsely grated
1 courgette, chopped
350 g/12 oz potatoes, chopped
65 g/2½ oz/5 tbsp butter
10 ml/2 tsp mild curry paste
2.5 ml/½ tsp dried thyme
150 ml/¼ pint/⅔ cup water
salt and ground black pepper
1 egg, beaten
30 ml/2 tbsp single cream
50 g/2 oz Cheddar cheese, grated
8 sheets filo pastry
sesame seeds, to sprinkle

1 Fry the onion, carrots, courgette and potatoes in half the butter for 5 minutes until they are soft then add the curry paste and cook for a further minute.

2 Add the thyme, water and seasoning. Continue to cook gently, uncovered for another 10 minutes.

3 Allow the mixture to cool and mix in the egg, cream and cheese. Chill until ready to fill and roll.

4 Melt the remaining butter and lay out four sheets of filo pastry, slightly overlapping them to form a large rectangle. Brush with butter and fit the other sheets on top. Brush again.

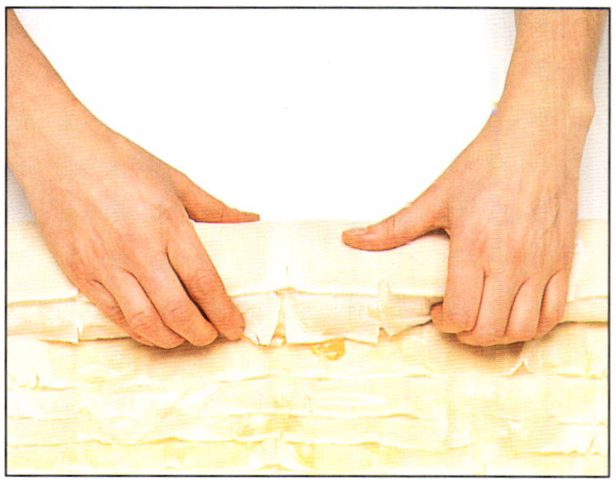

5 Spoon the filling along one long edge, then roll up the pastry. Form it into a circle and brush again with the last of the butter. Sprinkle over the sesame seeds and set on a baking sheet.

6 Heat the oven to 190°C/375°F/Gas 5 then bake the strudel for about 25 minutes until golden and crisp. Allow to stand for 5 minutes or so before cutting.

Coronation Salad

This famous salad dressing was created especially for the coronation dinner of Queen Elizabeth II. It is a wonderful accompaniment to eggs and vegetables.

SERVES 6
450 g/1 lb new potatoes
salt
45 ml/3 tbsp vinaigrette dressing
3 spring onions, chopped
ground black pepper
6 eggs, hard-boiled and halved
frilly lettuce leaves, to serve
¼ cucumber, sliced then cut in shreds
6 large radishes, sliced
carton of salad cress

DRESSING
30 ml/2 tbsp olive oil
1 small onion, chopped
15 ml/1 tbsp mild curry
powder or korma spice mix
10 ml/2 tsp tomato purée
30 ml/2 tbsp lemon juice
30 ml/2 tbsp sherry
300 ml/½ pint/1¼ cups mayonnaise
150 ml/¼ pint/¾ cup natural yogurt

1 Boil the potatoes in salted water until tender. Drain them and toss in the vinaigrette dressing.

2 Allow the potatoes to cool, stirring in the spring onions and seasoning. Cool the mixture thoroughly.

3 Meanwhile, make the coronation dressing. Heat the oil and fry the onion for 3 minutes until it is soft. Stir in the spice powder and fry for a further minute. Mix in all the other dressing ingredients.

4 Stir the dressing into the potatoes; add the eggs then chill. Line a serving platter with lettuce leaves and pile the salad in the centre. Scatter over the cucumber, radishes and cress.

Pasta and Wild Mushroom Mould

Bake pasta shapes in a golden crumb coating layered with a rich bechamel sauce and mushrooms. Scrumptious!

SERVES 4–6
200 g/7 oz pasta shapes
600 ml/1 pint/2½ cups milk
1 bay leaf
small onion stuck with 6 cloves
50 g/2 oz/4 tbsp butter
45 ml/3 tbsp breadcrumbs
10 ml/2 tsp dried mixed herbs
40 g/1½ oz/⅓ cup plain flour
60 ml/4 tbsp Parmesan cheese, freshly grated
fresh nutmeg, grated
salt and ground black pepper
2 eggs, beaten
1 × 15 g/½ oz pack porcini dried mushrooms
350 g/12 oz button mushrooms, sliced
2 garlic cloves, crushed
30 ml/2 tbsp olive oil
30 ml/ 2 tbsp fresh parsley, chopped

1 Boil the pasta according to the instructions on the pack. Drain and set aside. Heat the milk with the bay leaf and clove-studded onion and stand for 15 minutes. Remove bay leaf and onion.

2 Melt the butter in a saucepan and use a little to brush the inside of a large oval pie dish. Mix the crumbs and mixed herbs together and use them to coat the inside of the dish.

3 Stir the flour into the butter, cook for a minute then slowly add the hot milk to make a smooth sauce. Add the cheese, nutmeg, seasoning and cooked pasta. Cool for 5 minutes then beat in the eggs.

4 Soak the porcini in a little hot water until they are soft. Reserve the liquor and chop the porcini.

5 Fry the porcini with the sliced mushrooms and garlic in the olive oil for about 3 minutes. Season well, stir in the liquor and reduce down. Add the parsley.

6 Spoon a layer of pasta in the dish. Sprinkle over the mushrooms then more pasta and so on, finishing with pasta. Cover with greased foil. Heat the oven to 190°C/375°F/Gas 5 and bake for about 25–30 minutes. Allow to stand for 5 minutes before turning out to serve.

Aubergine Boats

These can be prepared ahead and baked prior to eating. The hazelnut topping contrasts nicely with the smooth aubergine filling.

SERVES 4
115 g/4 oz/⅔ cup brown basmati rice
2 medium size aubergines, halved lengthways
1 onion, chopped
2 garlic cloves, crushed
1 small green pepper, chopped
115 g/4 oz mushrooms, sliced
45 ml/3 tbsp olive oil
75 g/3 oz Cheddar cheese, grated
1 egg, beaten
2.5 ml/½ tsp marjoram
salt and ground black pepper
30 ml/2 tbsp hazelnuts, chopped

1 Boil the rice according to the instructions on the pack, drain and then cool. Scoop out the flesh from the aubergines and chop. Blanch the shells in boiling water for 2 minutes then drain upside down.

2 Fry the aubergine flesh, onion, garlic, pepper and mushrooms in the oil, for about 5 minutes.

3 Mix in the rice, cheese, egg, marjoram and seasoning. Arrange the aubergine shells in an ovenproof dish. Spoon the filling inside. Sprinkle over the nuts. Chill until ready to bake.

4 Heat the oven to 190°C/375°F/Gas 5 and bake the aubergines for about 25 minutes until the filling is set and the nuts are golden brown.

Crêpe Galette

Make a stack of light pancakes and layer them together with a tasty lentil filling for an impressive dinner party main course. Serve with a homemade tomato sauce.

SERVES 6
115 g/4 oz/1 cup plain flour
good pinch of salt
1 egg
300 ml/½ pint/1¼ cups buttermilk, or milk and water, mixed
oil, for cooking

FILLING
2 leeks, thinly sliced
1 small fennel bulb, thinly sliced
60 ml/4 tbsp olive oil
150 g/6 oz/¾ cup red lentils
150 ml/¼ pint/⅔ cup dry white wine
1 × 400 g/14 oz can chopped tomatoes
300 ml/½ pint/1¼ cups stock
5 ml/1 tsp dried oregano
salt and ground black pepper
1 onion, sliced
225 g/8 oz mushrooms, sliced
225 g/8 oz frozen leaf spinach, thawed and squeezed dry
200 g/7 oz low fat cream cheese
50 g/2 oz Parmesan cheese, freshly grated

1 Make the pancake batter by mixing the flour, salt, egg and buttermilk or milk and water in a blender until smooth. Set aside while you prepare the filling.

2 Gently fry the leeks and fennel in half the olive oil for 5 minutes, then add the lentils and wine. Cook for a minute until reduced down then stir in the tomatoes and stock.

3 Bring the leek/fennel mixture to a boil, add the oregano and seasoning then simmer for 20 minutes, stirring it occasionally until it thickens.

4 Fry the onion and mushrooms in the remaining olive oil for 5 minutes, stir in the spinach and heat. Season well then mix in the cream cheese.

5 Make about 12–14 pancakes with the batter in a well heated non-stick frying pan. Lightly grease a 20 cm/8 in round deep spring-form cake tin and line the base and sides with some of the pancakes, overlapping them as necessary.

6 Layer the remaining pancakes with the two fillings, sprinkling Parmesan in between and pressing them down well. Finish with a pancake on top.

7 Cover with foil and set aside to rest. Preheat the oven to 190°C/375°F/Gas 5. Bake for about 40 minutes, then turn out and allow to firm up for 10 minutes before cutting into wedges.

COOK'S TIP

This can be frozen ready made up, but it is probably nicer if frozen in parts – the pancakes interleaved with greaseproof paper and then wrapped in foil and the sauce frozen separately.

Polenta Fingers with Beans and Tomatoes

Polenta, or cornmeal, is a popular family favourite in Italy. It is eaten either hot from a bowl or allowed to set, cut into fingers, and grilled.

SERVES 6
1.75 litres/3 pints/7½ cups milk and water, mixed
10 ml/2 tsp salt
275 g/10 oz/1½ cups polenta
25 g/1 oz/2 tbsp butter, plus extra for spreading
50 g/2 oz Parmesan cheese, freshly grated
ground black pepper

SAUCE
1 onion, chopped
2 garlic cloves, crushed
30 ml/2 tbsp olive oil
1 × 400 g/14 oz can chopped tomatoes
salt and ground black pepper
good pinch of dried sage
225 g/8 oz frozen broad beans

1 In a large saucepan, bring the milk and water to a boil. Stir in the salt. While stirring with a wooden spoon trickle the polenta into the boiling liquid in a steady stream and continue stirring until the mixture has thickened.

2 Lower the heat and simmer for about 20 minutes, stirring frequently. Add the butter, cheese and seasoning.

3 Lightly grease a shallow roasting pan and pour in the polenta mixture. Cool, then chill overnight.

4 For the sauce, fry the onion and garlic in the oil for 5 minutes. Add the tomatoes, seasoning and sage and cook for a further 10 minutes. Stir in the broad beans and cook for 5 minutes more.

5 Turn out the polenta and cut into fingers. Grill both sides until brown and crisp. Spread with a little butter and serve accompanied by the tomato and beans.

Paprika and Parmesan Tartlets

Pretty pink pastry tarts with a tangy cream filling are ideal for handing round at drinks parties. Make the cases ahead of the party and fill them just before serving.

MAKES 18
225 g/8 oz/2 cups plain flour
10 ml/2 tsp paprika
150 g/5 oz/10 tbsp butter or sunflower margarine
40 g/1½ oz Parmesan cheese, freshly grated
cold water, to bind

FILLING
350 g/12 oz goats' cheese
50 g/2 oz rocket leaves, or watercress, chopped
30 ml/2 tbsp fresh chives, chopped
salt and ground black pepper
450 g/1 lb tomatoes, sliced

1 Sift the flour with the paprika and rub in the butter or margarine. Stir in the Parmesan and mix to a firm dough with cold water.

2 Roll out the pastry and stamp out 18 rounds, large enough to fit into bun tins. Prick the bases well with a fork and chill while you preheat the oven to 190°C/375°F/Gas 5.

3 Bake the tartlets for 15 minutes until crisp. Cool them on a wire rack.

4 Beat the cheese with the rocket or cress, chives and seasoning. Slice the tomatoes, allowing roughly two slices per tart.

5 When ready to serve, spoon the filling into the tarts. Top each one with some tomato and garnish with extra rocket or cress leaves.

Basmati and Blue Lentil Salad

Puy lentils from France (sometimes known as blue lentils) are small, deliciously nutty pulses, highly prized by gourmets. They blend beautifully with aromatic basmati rice.

SERVES 6
115 g/4 oz/⅔ cup puys de dome lentils, soaked
225 g/8 oz/1¼ cups basmati rice, rinsed well
2 carrots, coarsely grated
⅓ cucumber, halved, seeded and coarsely grated
3 spring onions, sliced
45 ml/3 tbsp fresh parsley, chopped

DRESSING
30 ml/2 tbsp sunflower oil
30 ml/2 tbsp extra virgin olive oil
30 ml/2 tbsp wine vinegar
30 ml/2 tbsp fresh lemon juice
good pinch of granulated sugar
salt and ground black pepper

1 Soak the lentils for 30 minutes. Meanwhile, make the dressing by shaking all the ingredients together in a screw-topped jar. Set aside.

2 Boil the lentils in plenty of unsalted water for 20–25 minutes or until soft. Drain thoroughly.

3 Boil the basmati rice for 10 minutes, then drain.

4 Mix together the rice and lentils in the dressing and season well. Leave to cool.

5 Add the carrots, cucumber, onions and parsley. Spoon into an attractive serving bowl and chill before serving.

Wild Rice with Julienne Vegetables

Make an accompanying dish more interesting with some exquisite wild rice. For the best flavour, buy a good quality wild rice (which is actually a cereal!) and, to shorten the cooking time, soak it overnight.

SERVES 4
115 g/4 oz/½ cup wild rice
1 red onion, sliced
2 carrots, cut in julienne sticks
2 celery sticks, cut in julienne sticks
50 g/2 oz/4 tbsp butter
150 ml/¼ pint/⅔ cup stock or water
salt and ground black pepper
2 medium courgettes, cut in thicker sticks
a few toasted almond flakes, to serve

1 Drain the soaked rice, then boil in plenty of unsalted water for 15–20 minutes, until it is soft and many of the grains have burst open. Drain.

2 In another saucepan, gently fry the onion, carrots and celery in the butter for 2 minutes then pour in the stock or water and season well.

3 Bring to a boil, simmer for 2 minutes then stir in the courgettes. Cook for 1 more minute then mix in the rice. Reheat and serve hot sprinkled with the almonds.

Oven-Crisp Asparagus Rolls

A lovely treat when fresh asparagus is in season is to wrap blanched spears in slices of thin bread and bake in a buttery glaze until crisp. Out of season, use canned or frozen spears.

SERVES 8
8 thick spears of fresh asparagus
salt
115 g/4 oz/8½ tbsp butter, softened
15 ml/1 tbsp coarse grained mustard
grated rind of 1 lemon
ground black pepper
8 slices thin white bread, crusts removed

1 Trim the asparagus stalks, peeling the tough woody skin at the base. Blanch until just tender in a shallow pan of boiling, salted water. Drain and refresh in cold water. Pat dry.

2 Blend two-thirds of the butter with the mustard, lemon rind and seasoning. Spread over the slices of bread.

3 Lay an asparagus spear on the edge of each bread slice and roll it up tightly. Place the rolls join side down on a lightly greased baking sheet.

4 Melt the remaining butter and brush over the rolls. Heat the oven to 190°C/375°F/Gas 5 and bake for 12–15 minutes until golden and crisp. Cool slightly before serving.

VARIATION

Asparagus has always been something of a luxury as its season is so short, but imports from across the world mean that it is available almost all year round, albeit at a price!

Thin baby asparagus, known as sprue, can be eaten raw in salads or stir-fried quickly. Opinions differ about the merits of green or white asparagus spears. The latter are forced in the dark (hence their white colour), but some people consider them to have a better flavour and texture.

Ratatouille Tart

Serve this pretty tart warm so the cheese is easy to cut and eat. For the best results, make the base and filling separately then heat and combine just before serving.

SERVES 6
115 g/4 oz/1 cup plain flour
115 g/4 oz/¾ cup wholemeal flour
5 ml/1 tsp dried mixed herbs
salt and ground black pepper
115 g/4 oz/½ cup sunflower margarine
45–60 ml/3–4 tbsp cold water

FILLING
1 small aubergine, thickly sliced
salt
45 ml/3 tbsp olive oil
1 onion, sliced
1 red or yellow pepper, sliced
2 garlic cloves, crushed
2 courgettes, thickly sliced
2 tomatoes, skinned and sliced
ground black pepper
30 ml/2 tbsp fresh basil, chopped
150 g/5 oz Mozzarella cheese, sliced
30 ml/2 tbsp pine nuts

1 Mix the two flours with the herbs and seasoning then rub in the margarine until it resembles fine crumbs. Mix to a firm dough with water.

2 Roll out the pastry and line a 23 cm/ 9 in round flan tin. Prick the base, line with foil and baking beans then allow to rest in the fridge.

3 Meanwhile, sprinkle the aubergine lightly with salt and leave to drain for 30 minutes in a colander. Rinse and pat dry.

4 Heat the oil in a frying pan and fry the onion and pepper for 5 minutes, then add the garlic, courgettes and aubergine. Fry for a further 10 minutes, stirring the mixture occasionally.

5 Stir in the tomatoes and seasoning, cook for a further 3 minutes, add the basil then remove the pan from the heat and allow to cool.

6 Heat the oven to 200°C/400°F/Gas 6. Place the flan on a baking sheet and bake for 25 minutes, removing the foil and baking beans for the last 5 minutes. Cool and then, if possible, remove the case from the tin.

7 When ready to serve, spoon the vegetables into the case using a slotted spoon so any juices drain off and don't soak into the pastry. Top with the cheese slices and pine nuts. Toast under a preheated grill until golden and bubbling. Serve warm.

Filo Baskets with Ginger Dill Vegetables

Make up some elegant filo baskets, then fill with some crisply steamed vegetables tossed in an interesting and tasty sauce.

SERVES 4
4 sheets of filo pastry
40 g/1½ oz/3 tbsp butter, melted
FILLING
30 ml/2 tbsp olive oil
15 ml/1 tbsp fresh root ginger, grated
2 garlic cloves, crushed
3 shallots, sliced
225 g/8 oz mushrooms, chestnut or brown, sliced
115 g/4 oz oyster mushrooms, sliced
1 courgette, sliced
200 g/7 oz crème fraîche
30 ml/2 tbsp fresh dill, chopped
salt and ground black pepper
dill and parsley sprigs, to serve

1 Cut the filo sheets into four. Line four Yorkshire pudding tins, angling the layers so that the corners form a pretty star shape. Brush between each layer with butter. Set aside.

2 Heat the oven to 190°C/375°F/Gas 5. Bake the cases for about 10 minutes until golden brown and crisp. Remove and cool.

3 For the filling, heat the oil and sauté the ginger, garlic and shallots for 2 minutes, then add the mushrooms and courgette. Cook for another 3 minutes.

4 Mix in the crème fraîche, chopped dill and seasoning. Heat until just bubbling then spoon into the filo cases. Garnish with the dill and parsley and serve.

Gado Gado Salad with Peanut Sambal

Indonesians enjoy a salad of lightly-steamed vegetables topped with a peanut sauce. It is ideal for a colourful summer buffet dish.

SERVES 6
225 g/8 oz new potatoes, halved
2 carrots, cut in sticks
115 g/4 oz green beans
½ small cauliflower, broken into florets
¼ firm white cabbage, shredded
200 g/7 oz bean or lentil sprouts
4 eggs, hard-boiled and quartered
bunch watercress, trimmed
SAUCE
90 ml/6 tbsp crunchy peanut butter
300 ml/½ pint/1¼ cups cold water
1 garlic clove, crushed
30 ml/2 tbsp dark soy sauce
15 ml/1 tbsp dry sherry
10 ml/2 tsp caster sugar
15 ml/1 tbsp fresh lemon juice
5 ml/1 tsp anchovy essence

1 Fit a steamer or metal colander over a pan of gently boiling water. Cook the potatoes for 10 minutes.

2 Add the rest of the vegetables and sprouts and steam for a further 10 minutes until tender. Cool and serve on a platter with the egg quarters surrounded by the watercress.

3 Beat all the sauce ingredients together until smooth. Put the sauce in a small bowl and drizzle over each individual serving of salad.

Vegetable Fritters with Tzatziki

Spicy deep-fried aubergine and courgette slices served with a creamy Greek yogurt and dill dip make a good, simple party starter or an excellent side dish.

SERVES 4–6
½ cucumber, coarsely grated
225 g/8 oz Greek natural yogurt
15 ml/1 tbsp extra virgin olive oil
10 ml/2 tsp fresh lemon juice
30 ml/2 tbsp fresh dill, chopped
15 ml/1 tbsp fresh mint, chopped
1 garlic clove, crushed
salt and ground black pepper
1 large aubergine, thickly sliced
2 courgettes, thickly sliced
1 egg white, beaten
40 g/1½ oz/4 tbsp plain flour
10 ml/2 tsp ground coriander
ground cumin

1 For the dip, mix the cucumber, yogurt, oil, lemon juice, dill, mint, garlic and seasoning. Spoon into a bowl then set aside.

2 Layer the aubergine and courgettes in a colander and sprinkle them with salt. Leave for 30 minutes. Rinse in cold water then pat dry.

3 Put the egg white into a bowl. Mix the flour, coriander and cumin with seasoning and put into another bowl.

4 Dip the vegetables first into the egg white then into the seasoned flour and set aside.

5 Heat about 2.5 cm/1 in of oil in a deep frying pan until quite hot, then fry the vegetables a few at a time until they are golden and crisp.

6 Drain and keep warm while you fry the remainder. Serve warm on a platter with a bowl of the tzatziki dip lightly sprinkled with paprika.

Mushroom Saucers

Recipes which are already portioned are a great boon for the host, as guests can help themselves without feeling they are taking more than their fair share. Large flat mushrooms are great for this reason.

SERVES 8
8 large flat mushrooms with stalks removed, wiped clean and chopped
45 ml/3 tbsp olive oil
salt and ground black pepper
1 onion, sliced
5 ml/1 tsp cumin seeds
450 g/1 lb leaf spinach, stalks trimmed, and shredded
1 × 425 g/15 oz can red kidney beans, drained
1 × 200 g/7 oz pack soft cheese with garlic and herbs
2 medium tomatoes, halved, seeded and sliced in strips

1 Heat the oven to 190°C/375°F/Gas 5. Lightly grease a large, shallow ovenproof dish. Brush the mushrooms with some oil, place them in the dish and season well. Cover with foil and bake for 15–20 minutes. Uncover, drain and reserve the juices.

2 Fry the onion and chopped mushroom stalks in the remaining oil for 5 minutes until soft. Then add the cumin seeds and mushroom juices and cook for a minute longer until reduced down.

3 Stir in the spinach and fry until the leaves begin to wilt, then mix in the beans and heat well. Add the cheese, stirring until melted and season again.

4 Divide the mixture between the mushroom cups and return to the oven to heat through. Serve garnished with tomato slices.

Marbled Quails' Eggs

Hard-boiled quails' eggs re-boiled in smoky China tea assume a pretty marbled skin. It's quite a treat to dip them into a fragrant spicy salt and hand them round with drinks. Szechuan peppercorns can be bought from Oriental food stores.

SERVES 4–6
12 quails' eggs
600 ml/1 pint/2½ cups strong lapsang souchong tea
15 ml/1 tbsp dark soy sauce
15 ml/1 tbsp dry sherry
2 star anise pods
lettuce leaves, to serve
milled Szechuan red peppercorns
sea salt, to mix

1 Place the quails' eggs in cold water and bring to the boil. Time them for 2 minutes from when the water boils.

2 Remove the eggs from the pan and run them under cold water to cool. Tap the shells all over so they are crazed, but do not peel yet.

3 In a saucepan, bring the tea to the boil and add the soy sauce, sherry and star anise. Re-boil the eggs for about 15 minutes, partially covered, so the liquid does not boil dry.

4 Cool the eggs, then peel them and arrange on a small platter lined with lettuce leaves. Mix the ground red peppercorns with equal quantities of salt and place in a small side dish.

Beetroot Roulade

This roulade is simple to make, yet will create a stunning impression. Prepare it in the autumn when beetroots are at their best.

SERVES 6
225 g/8 oz fresh beetroot, cooked and peeled
2.5 ml/½ tsp ground cumin
25 g/1 oz/2 tbsp butter
10 ml/2 tsp grated onion
4 eggs, separated
salt and ground black pepper
FILLING
150 ml/¼ pint/⅔ cup crème fraîche or double cream
10 ml/2 tsp white wine vinegar
good pinch dry mustard powder
5 ml/1 tsp sugar
45 ml/3 tbsp fresh parsley, chopped
30 ml/2 tbsp fresh dill, chopped
45 ml/3 tbsp horseradish relish

1 Line and grease a Swiss roll tin. Preheat the oven to 190°C/375°F/ Gas 5.

2 Roughly chop the beetroot then blend to a purée in a food processor and beat in the cumin, butter, onion, egg yolks and seasoning. Turn the beetroot purée into a large bowl.

3 In another bowl, that is spotlessly clean, whisk the egg whites until they form soft peaks. Fold them into the beetroot mixture carefully.

4 Spoon the mixture into the Swiss roll tin, level and bake for about 15 minutes until just firm to touch.

5 Have ready a clean tea towel laid over a wire rack. Turn the beetroot out onto the towel, and remove the paper carefully in strips.

6 Beat the crème fraîche or cream until lightly stiff, then fold in the remaining ingredients. Spread this mixture onto the beetroot. Roll up the roulade in the towel and allow it to cool.

Pasta and Beetroot Salad

Colour is vital at a party table, and this salad is certainly eye catching. Serve the egg and avocado at the last moment to avoid discoloration.

SERVES 8
2 uncooked beetroots, scrubbed
225 g/8 oz pasta shells or twists
45 ml/3 tbsp vinaigrette dressing
salt and ground black pepper
2 celery sticks, thinly sliced
3 spring onions, sliced
75 g/3 oz/⅔ cup walnuts or hazelnuts, roughly chopped
1 dessert apple, cored, halved and sliced
DRESSING
60 ml/4 tbsp mayonnaise
45 ml/3 tbsp natural yogurt or fromage frais
30 ml/2 tbsp milk
10 ml/2 tsp horseradish relish
TO SERVE
curly lettuce leaves
3 eggs, hard boiled and chopped
2 ripe avocadoes
box of salad cress

1 Boil the beetroots, without peeling them, in lightly salted water until they are just tender. Drain, cool, peel and chop. Set aside.

2 Cook the pasta according to the instructions on the pack then drain and toss in the vinaigrette and season well. Cool. Mix the pasta with the beetroot, celery, onions, nuts and apple.

3 Stir all the dressing ingredients together and mix into the pasta bowl. Chill well.

4 To serve, line a pretty salad bowl with the lettuce leaves and pile the salad in the centre. When ready to serve, scatter over the chopped egg. Peel and slice the avocadoes and arrange them on top then sprinkle over the cress.

Gazpacho

This classic Spanish no-cook soup is ideal for taking on picnics as it can be packed straight from the refrigerator. Keep the chopped vegetables in separate pots and hand them round as an accompaniment.

SERVES 6
1 slice white bread, crusts removed
cold water, to soak
1 garlic clove, crushed
30 ml/2 tbsp extra virgin olive oil
30 ml/2 tbsp white wine vinegar
6 large ripe tomatoes, skinned and finely chopped
1 small onion, finely chopped
2.5 ml/½ tsp paprika
good pinch ground cumin
150 ml/¼ pint/⅔ cup tomato juice
salt and ground black pepper
TO GARNISH
1 green pepper, chopped
⅓ cucumber, peeled, seeded and chopped
CROÛTONS
2 slices bread, cubed and deep fried

1 Soak the bread slice in enough cold water just to cover and leave for about 5 minutes, then mash with a fork.

2 Pound the garlic, oil and vinegar with a pestle and mortar or blend in a food processor. Mix this into the bread.

3 Spoon the mixture into a bowl and stir in the tomatoes, onion, spices and tomato juice. Season well and store in the refrigerator. Prepare the garnishes and store these in separate containers.

4 For a picnic, pour the chilled soup into a flask. Otherwise, pour into a chilled glass salad bowl and hand the garnishes round in smaller bowls.

Sesame Egg Roll

A Japanese-inspired idea. An egg pancake is rolled up with a creamy watercress filling and served cut in thick slices.

SERVES 3–4
3 eggs
15 ml/1 tbsp soy sauce
15 ml/1 tbsp sesame seeds
5 ml/1 tsp sesame seed oil
salt and ground black pepper
15 ml/1 tbsp sunflower oil
75 g/3 oz cream cheese with garlic
1 bunch watercress, chopped

1 Beat the eggs with the soy sauce, sesame seeds, sesame seed oil and seasoning.

2 Heat the sunflower oil in a large frying pan until quite hot, then pour in the egg mixture, tilting the pan so it covers the whole base. Cook until firm.

3 Allow the pancake to stand in the pan for a few minutes then turn out onto a chopping board and cool completely.

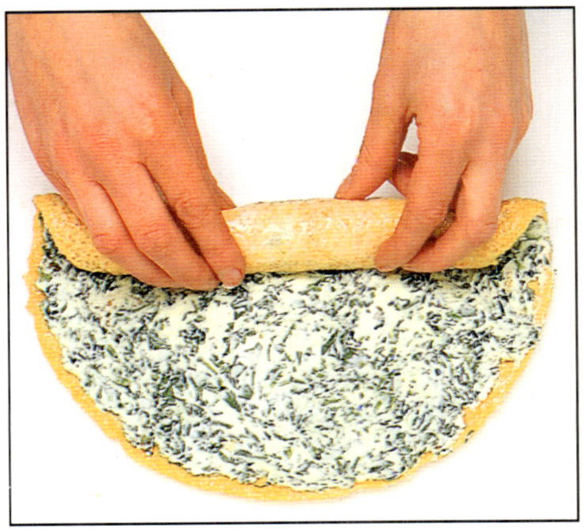

4 Beat the cream cheese until soft, season well then mix in the chopped watercress. Spread this over the egg pancake then roll it up quite firmly. Wrap in cling film and chill.

Homemade Coleslaw

Forget shop-bought coleslaw! Making your own at home is quite quick and easy to do – and it tastes fresh, crunchy and wonderful.

SERVES 4–6
¼ firm white cabbage
1 small onion, finely chopped
2 celery sticks, thinly sliced
2 carrots, coarsely grated
5–10 ml/1–2 tsp caraway seeds (optional)
1 dessert apple, cored and chopped (optional)
50 g/2 oz/½ cup walnuts, chopped (optional)
salt and ground black pepper
DRESSING
45 ml/3 tbsp mayonnaise
30 ml/2 tbsp single cream or natural yogurt
5 ml/1 tsp lemon rind, grated
salt and ground black pepper

1 Cut and discard the core from the cabbage quarter then shred the leaves finely. Place this in a large bowl.

2 Into the cabbage, toss the onion, celery and carrot, plus the caraway seeds, apple and walnuts, if using. Season well.

3 Mix the dressing ingredients together and stir into the vegetables. Cover and allow to stand for 2 hours, stirring occasionally, then chill the coleslaw lightly before serving.

Malfatti with Red Sauce

If you ever felt dumplings were a little heavy, try making these light Italian spinach and ricotta malfatti instead. Serve them with a simple tomato and red pepper sauce.

SERVES 4–6
450 g/1 lb fresh leaf spinach, stalks trimmed
1 small onion, chopped
1 garlic clove, crushed
15 ml/1 tbsp olive oil
400 g/14 oz ricotta cheese
75 g/3 oz/⅔ cup dried breadcrumbs
50 g/2 oz/½ cup plain flour
5 ml/1 tsp salt
50 g/2 oz Parmesan cheese, freshly grated
fresh nutmeg, grated, to taste
3 eggs, beaten
25 g/1 oz/2 tbsp butter, melted
SAUCE
1 large, red pepper, chopped
1 small red onion, chopped
30 ml/2 tbsp olive oil
1 × 400 g/14 oz can chopped tomatoes
150 ml/¼ pint/⅔ cup water
good pinch dried oregano
salt and ground black pepper
30 ml/2 tbsp single cream

1 Blanch the spinach in the tiniest amount of water until it is limp, then drain well, pressing it through a sieve with the back of a ladle or spoon. Chop very finely.

2 Lightly fry the onion and garlic in the oil for 5 minutes then mix with the spinach together with the ricotta, breadcrumbs, flour, salt, most of the Parmesan and nutmeg.

3 Allow the mixture to cool, add the eggs and melted butter, then mould into 12 small 'sausage' shapes.

4 Meanwhile, make the sauce by lightly sautéeing the pepper and onion in the oil for 5 minutes. Add the tomatoes, water, oregano and seasoning. Bring to a boil, then simmer for 5 minutes.

5 When cooked, remove from the heat and blend to a purée in a food processor. Return to the pan, then stir in the cream. Check the seasoning.

6 Bring a shallow pan of salted water to a gentle boil and drop the malfatti into it a few at a time and poach them for about 5 minutes. Drain them well and keep them warm.

7 Arrange the malfatti on warm plates and drizzle over the sauce. Serve topped with the remaining Parmesan.

COOK'S TIP

Quenelles are oval-shaped dumplings. To shape the Malfatti into quenelles you need two dessertspoons. Scoop up the mixture with one spoon, making sure it is mounded up, then, using the other spoon, scoop the mixture off the first spoon, twisting the top spoon into the bowl of the second.

Repeat this action two or three times until the quenelle is smooth, and then gently knock it off onto a plate ready to cook.

Curried Mango Chutney Dip

A quickly made, tangy and spicy dip or dressing, ideal as a dip for strips of pitta bread, grissini or sticks of fresh chopped vegetables.

SERVES 4–6
1 onion, chopped
1 garlic clove, crushed
30 ml/2 tbsp sunflower oil
10 ml/2 tsp mild curry powder
225 g/8 oz natural Greek yogurt
30 ml/2 tbsp mango chutney
salt and ground black pepper
30 ml/2 tbsp fresh parsley, chopped

1 Gently fry the onion and garlic in the oil for 5 minutes until they are soft. Add the curry powder and cook for a further minute then allow the mixture to cool.

2 Spoon into a food processor with the yogurt, chutney and seasoning and blend until smooth.

3 Stir in the parsley and chill before serving with a variety of vegetable crudités and strips of bread.

Nutty Mushroom Paté

Spread this delicious, medium-texture paté on chunks of crusty French bread and eat with crisp leaves of lettuce and sweet cherry tomatoes.

SERVES 4–6
1 onion, chopped
1 garlic clove, crushed
15 ml/1 tbsp sunflower oil
30 ml/2 tbsp water
15 ml/1 tbsp dry sherry
225 g/8 oz button mushrooms, chopped
salt and ground black pepper
75 g/3 oz/¾ cup cashew nuts or walnuts, chopped
150 g/5 oz low fat soft cheese
15 ml/1 tbsp soy sauce
few dashes Worcestershire sauce
fresh parsley, chopped, and a little paprika, to serve

1 Gently fry the onion and garlic in the oil for 3 minutes then add the water, sherry and mushrooms. Cook, stirring for about 5 minutes. Season to taste and allow to cool a little.

2 Put the mixture into a food processor with the nuts, cheese and sauces. Blend to a rough purée – do not allow it to become too smooth.

3 Check the seasoning then spoon into a serving dish. Swirl the top and serve lightly chilled sprinkled with parsley and paprika.

Antipasti with Aioli

For a simple starter or hand-around cocktail canapé, make a bowl of the classic French/Spanish garlic sauce – aioli – and serve it with a selection of attractively prepared vegetables and breads.

SERVES 4–6
4 garlic cloves
2 egg yolks
2.5 ml/½ tsp salt
ground black pepper
300 ml/½ pint/1¼ cups extra virgin olive oil
TO SERVE
red or yellow pepper, cut in thick strips
fennel, cut in slivers
radishes, halved if large
button mushrooms
broccoli florets
grissini sticks
French bread, thinly sliced

1 Crush the garlic into a bowl then beat in the egg yolks, salt and some ground black pepper.

2 Stand the bowl on a damp cloth and slowly trickle in the oil, drip by drip, whisking with a balloon whisk until you have a thick, creamy sauce. As the sauce thickens, you can add the oil in slightly larger amounts.

3 Spoon the aioli into a bowl. Arrange the dipping food around the bowl and serve lightly chilled.

Camembert Fritters

A popular starter or savoury course at the end of a leisurely dinner. These deep-fried cheeses are quite simple to do. They are served with a red onion marmalade which can be made in advance and stored in the refrigerator.

SERVES 4
MARMALADE
1 kg/2 lb red onions, sliced
45 ml/3 tbsp sunflower oil
45 ml/3 tbsp olive oil
15 ml/1 tbsp coriander berries, crushed
2 large bay leaves
45 ml/3 tbsp granulated sugar
90 ml/6 tbsp red wine vinegar
10 ml/2 tsp salt
CHEESE
8 individual portions of Camembert
1 egg, beaten
125 g/4 oz/1 cup natural colour dried breadcrumbs, to coat
oil, for deep fat frying

1 Make the marmalade first. In a large saucepan, gently fry the onions in the oil, covered, for 20 minutes or so or until they are soft.

2 Add the remaining marmalade ingredients, stir well and cook uncovered for a further 10–15 minutes until most of the liquid has been absorbed. Cool and then set aside.

VARIATION

You could make these fritters with fingers of firm Brie, or try it using baby goats' cheese.

3 Prepare the cheese by first scratching the mould rind lightly with a fork. Dip first in egg then in breadcrumbs to coat well. Dip and coat a second time if necessary. Store on a plate.

4 Pour oil into a deep fat fryer so it is one-third full; heat to 190°C/375°F.

5 Carefully lower the coated cheeses into the hot oil three or four at a time and fry until golden and crisp, about 2 minutes or less.

6 Drain well on kitchen paper and fry the rest, reheating the oil in between. Serve hot with some of the marmalade.

Tabbouleh

Almost the ultimate quick grain salad that simply needs soaking, draining and mixing. Bulgur is par-boiled wheat. Make this a day ahead, if possible, so that the flavours have time to develop.

SERVES 4
115 g/4 oz/¾ cup bulgur wheat
90 ml/6 tbsp fresh lemon juice
75 ml/5 tbsp extra virgin olive oil
90 ml/6 tbsp fresh parsley, chopped
60 ml/4 tbsp fresh mint, chopped
3 spring onions, finely chopped
4 firm tomatoes, skinned and chopped
salt and ground black pepper

1 Cover the bulgur with cold water and soak for 20 minutes, then drain well and squeeze out even more water from it with your hands.

2 Put the bulgur into another bowl and add all the other ingredients, stirring and seasoning well.

3 Cover and chill for a few hours, overnight, if possible.

Crudités with Houmous

Always a great family favourite, homemade houmous is speedily made with the help of a blender. The tahini paste is the secret of houmous and it is readily available in delicatessens or larger supermarkets.

SERVES 2–3
1 × 425 g/15 oz can chick peas, drained
30 ml/2 tbsp tahini paste
30 ml/2 tbsp fresh lemon juice
1 garlic clove, crushed
salt and ground black pepper
olive oil and paprika pepper, to garnish
TO SERVE
Selection of salad vegetables, e.g. cucumber, chicory, baby carrots, pepper strips, radishes
Bite size chunks of bread, e.g. pitta, walnut, naan, bruscheta, or grissini sticks

1 Put the chick peas, tahini paste, lemon juice, garlic and plenty of seasoning into a food processor or blender and mix to a smooth paste.

2 Spoon the houmous into a bowl and swirl the top with the back of a spoon. Trickle over a little olive oil and sprinkle with paprika.

3 Prepare a selection of fresh salad vegetables and chunks of your favourite fresh bread or grissini sticks into finger size pieces.

4 Set out in a colourful jumble on a large plate with the bowl of houmous in the centre. Then dip and eat!

Index

CUISINER LE
GRAND GIBIER

SANGLIER, CERF, CHEVREUIL

Valéry Drouet et Pierre-Louis Viel

CUISINER LE GRAND GIBIER

SANGLIER, CERF, CHEVREUIL

GERFAUT

SOMMAIRE

LE SANGLIER

LE CERF

LE CHEVREUIL

FONDS ET ACCOMPAGNEMENTS

LE SANGLIER

SANGLIER EN COCOTTE AUX FRUITS SECS ET AUX ÉPICES

Pour **4 personnes** / Préparation **30 min** / Cuisson **2 h 45**

1,2 KG D'ÉPAULE DE SANGLIER COUPÉE EN GROS MORCEAUX
3 CM DE GINGEMBRE FRAIS
2 OIGNONS JAUNES
3 GOUSSES D'AIL
1 C. À S. DE GRAINES DE CORIANDRE
1 C. À S. DE GINGEMBRE EN POUDRE
2 PINCÉES DE CURCUMA
½ C. À C. DE CANNELLE EN POUDRE
1 C. À C. DE CUMIN EN POUDRE
5 CL D'HUILE D'OLIVE
2 GROSSES C. À S. DE MIEL LIQUIDE
50 G DE GROS RAISINS SECS BLONDS
4 ABRICOTS SECS MOELLEUX
4 FIGUES SÉCHÉES MOELLEUSES
4 PRUNEAUX DÉNOYAUTÉS
100 G D'AMANDES ENTIÈRES
2 BRANCHES DE CORIANDRE
SEL, POIVRE DU MOULIN

À DÉGUSTER

avec un coteaux-d'aix-en-provence

1 Préchauffez le four à 160 °C (th. 5-6). Épluchez et râpez le gingembre frais. Épluchez et hachez les oignons et les gousses d'ail. Broyez grossièrement les graines de coriandre en les écrasant dans un bol avec un pilon. Ajoutez ensuite le gingembre en poudre, le gingembre râpé, le curcuma, la cannelle et le cumin.

2 Saisissez les morceaux de sanglier dans l'huile d'olive 5 minutes sur toutes leurs faces, dans une grande cocotte sur feu vif. Salez et poivrez.

3 Retirez la viande de la cocotte. Baissez le feu et mettez les oignons et l'ail. Faites-les rissoler 6 à 8 minutes en remuant régulièrement. Ajoutez le mélange d'épices. Laissez roussir 2 minutes, puis remettez la viande. Arrosez le tout de miel.

4 Augmentez le feu. Laissez légèrement caraméliser, puis ajoutez de l'eau froide à hauteur de la viande. Portez à ébullition, couvrez la cocotte et enfournez pendant 1 heure 30 sans l'ouvrir.

5 Sortez la cocotte du four. Ajoutez tous les fruits secs et mélangez. Enfournez à nouveau pendant 45 minutes.

6 Pendant ce temps, torréfiez les amandes quelques minutes dans une poêle chaude sans matière grasse. Ciselez la coriandre.

7 Retirez le couvercle de la cocotte et poursuivez la cuisson pendant 15 minutes.

8 Sortez la cocotte du four. Couvrez et laissez reposer 15 minutes. Parsemez d'amandes et de coriandre et servez accompagné d'une semoule.

GRATIN DE PATATES DOUCES ET DE SANGLIER AU VIN ROUGE

Pour **4 personnes** / Préparation **20 min** / Cuisson **2 h 15**

1 KG DE VIANDE DE SANGLIER
2 OIGNONS
1 GROSSE CAROTTE
5 CL D'HUILE D'OLIVE
1 C. À S. DE FARINE
75 CL DE VIN ROUGE
30 CL DE FOND DE VEAU
800 G DE PATATES DOUCES
15 CL DE LAIT CHAUD
90 G DE BEURRE
1 C. À S. DE CRÈME FRAÎCHE ÉPAISSE
2 C. À S. DE CHAPELURE
2 BRANCHES DE THYM
SEL, POIVRE DU MOULIN

—

À DÉGUSTER

avec un fronsac rouge

1 Coupez la viande en gros morceaux. Épluchez et émincez les oignons. Épluchez, lavez et coupez la carotte en petits morceaux.

2 Saisissez la viande dans l'huile d'olive 5 minutes dans une cocotte sur feu vif. Ajoutez les oignons et la carotte. Laissez-les fondre 10 minutes sur feu moyen en remuant. Ajoutez la farine, du sel et du poivre, et laissez roussir 2 minutes en remuant. Versez le vin, puis portez à ébullition. Ajoutez le fond de veau, le thym du sel et du poivre. Portez à nouveau à ébullition. Baissez ensuite le feu, couvrez la cocotte, et laissez mijoter 2 heures sur feu doux.

3 Épluchez, lavez les patates douces, puis coupez-les en morceaux. Faites-les ensuite cuire 30 minutes dans une grande casserole d'eau bouillante salée.

4 Égouttez les patates douces. Ajoutez le lait, 60 g de beurre et mixez le tout à l'aide d'un robot plongeant. Ajoutez la crème fraîche, du sel et du poivre. Mélangez pour obtenir une purée onctueuse.

5 Préchauffez le four à 190 °C (th. 6-7). Vérifiez la cuisson de la viande (elle doit être filandreuse) et égouttez-la. Laissez-la tiédir, puis effilochez-la à la main. Sortez les oignons et mélangez-les avec la viande en ajoutant un peu de sauce.

6 Disposez la viande et les oignons dans le fond d'un plat à gratin. Étalez la purée par-dessus, puis parsemez la surface de chapelure et du beurre restant en copeaux. Enfournez pendant 20 minutes, jusqu'à ce que la surface soit gratinée.

7 Servez bien chaud. Vous pouvez également réaliser cette recette avec un reste de civet.

Filets de sanglier en croûte de poivre et au sirop d'érable,

mousseline de céleri au beurre salé

Pour **4 personnes** / Préparation **40 min** / Cuisson **55 min**

700 G DE FILETS DE SANGLIER
15 G DE POIVRE DU SICHUAN BROYÉ
5 CL D'HUILE DE TOURNESOL
20 TRANCHES DE POITRINE FUMÉE
800 G DE CÉLERI-RAVE
10 CL DE SIROP D'ÉRABLE
80 G DE BEURRE SALÉ
1 C. À S. DE CRÈME FRAÎCHE ÉPAISSE
4 BRINS DE CIBOULETTE
SEL

À DÉGUSTER

avec un saumur rouge

1 Nettoyez les filets. Salez-les, roulez-les dans le poivre, puis faites-les saisir dans une cuillère à soupe d'huile de tournesol 1 minute dans une poêle sur feu vif. Enroulez les tranches de poitrine fumée autour des filets entiers en les chevauchant puis ficelez-les en serrant légèrement.

2 Préchauffez le four à 200 °C (th. 6-7). Épluchez et lavez le céleri, puis coupez-le en morceaux. Faites-le ensuite cuire 30 minutes dans une grande casserole d'eau bouillante salée.

3 Déposez les filets dans un plat en métal allant au four et sur la flamme. Versez dessus le reste d'huile et le sirop d'érable. Enfournez pendant 10 minutes.

4 Baissez la température du four à 180 °C (th. 6) et poursuivez la cuisson pendant 15 minutes.

5 Égouttez le céleri. Mettez les morceaux dans la cuve d'un robot, ajoutez le beurre et réduisez le tout jusqu'à l'obtention d'une purée onctueuse. Débarrassez la purée dans un récipient, ajoutez la crème fraîche épaisse et mélangez. Réservez ensuite la purée au chaud en la plaçant au bain-marie.

6 Sortez les filets du four. Enveloppez-les dans une feuille de papier aluminium et laissez-les reposer 10 minutes.

7 Dégraissez légèrement le plat de cuisson en le faisant chauffer 3 minutes sur feu moyen, en prenant soin de ne pas faire brûler le sirop d'érable.

8 Versez ensuite 15 cl d'eau et faites réduire en grattant bien le fond avec une spatule en bois.

9 Ciselez la ciboulette. Retirez les ficelles des morceaux de filets, coupez le filet en tranches épaisses. Ajoutez un peu de mousseline, versez le jus et parsemez de ciboulette.

Cuissot de sanglier de sept heures aux aromates

Pour **6 personnes** / Préparation **30 min** / Cuisson **7 h**

2 KG DE CUISSOT DE SANGLIER SANS L'OS
2 CAROTTES
1 BRANCHE DE CÉLERI
2 TOMATES
2 OIGNONS
1 TÊTE D'AIL
1 C. À S. D'HUILE D'OLIVE
1 BOUQUET GARNI
3 BAIES DE GENIÈVRE
1 C. À C. DE GRAINES DE CORIANDRE
1 BRANCHE DE ROMARIN
50 CL DE BOUILLON DE VOLAILLE
40 CL DE VIN BLANC
SEL, POIVRE DU MOULIN

1 Préchauffez le four à 110 °C (th. 3-4). Épluchez les carottes, puis lavez-les et coupez-les en petits cubes. Lavez la branche de céleri et détaillez-la en petits cubes. Rincez les tomates. Pelez-les, épépinez-les, puis coupez-les en quartiers. Épluchez et hachez les oignons. Détachez les gousses d'ail sans les éplucher.

2 Dans une grande cocotte allant au four, faites chauffer l'huile d'olive. Saisissez le cuissot sur toutes ses faces 10 minutes sur feu vif. Ajoutez tous les légumes, le bouquet garni, les gousses d'ail, les baies de genièvre, la coriandre et le romarin. Salez, poivrez, puis versez le bouillon et le vin blanc. Couvrez et enfournez pendant environ 7 heures en arrosant régulièrement.

3 La cuisse est prête lorsqu'elle est bien confite. Servez-la arrosée de jus de cuisson et accompagnée d'un écrasé de pommes de terre (voir page 80).

À DÉGUSTER

avec un pommard

PARMENTIER DE SANGLIER AU GENIÈVRE

Pour **4-6 personnes** / Préparation **30 min** / Cuisson **4 h 30**

800 G DE VIANDE DE SANGLIER
2 GOUSSES D'AIL
1 OIGNON
1 C. À C. DE PAPRIKA
8 BAIES DE GENIÈVRE
15 CL DE KETCHUP
1 C. À S. DE MOUTARDE FORTE
8 CL DE VINAIGRE DE VIN ROUGE
50 G DE SUCRE CASSONADE
5 CL D'HUILE D'OLIVE
40 CL DE VIN ROUGE
1 KG DE POMMES DE TERRE
15 CL DE CRÈME LIQUIDE
15 CL DE LAIT
80 G DE BEURRE
4 C. À S. DE CHAPELURE
SEL, POIVRE DU MOULIN

À DÉGUSTER

avec un côtes-du-roussillon rouge

1. Préchauffez le four à 180 °C (th. 6). Épluchez et hachez les gousses d'ail et l'oignon. Réservez.
2. Mélangez le paprika dans un bol avec les baies de genièvre écrasées, le ketchup, la moutarde, le vinaigre, le sucre, du sel et du poivre. Réservez.
3. Coupez la viande en morceaux. Saisissez les morceaux de viande 5 minutes de chaque côté dans une cocotte, avec l'huile d'olive, sur feu vif. Une fois dorés, ajoutez l'oignon et l'ail et laissez mijoter 5 minutes sur feu moyen. Versez ensuite le contenu du bol d'épices dans la cocotte, ainsi que le vin rouge. Couvrez la cocotte et laissez mijoter 3 heures 30 sur feu très doux, en mélangeant régulièrement pendant la cuisson ; vous pouvez ajouter un peu de vin pendant la cuisson si nécessaire.
4. Pendant la cuisson de la viande, épluchez, lavez et coupez les pommes de terre en morceaux. Faites-les cuire 20 minutes dans l'eau salée. Faites chauffer la crème, le lait et 50 g de beurre dans une casserole. Une fois les pommes de terre cuites, égouttez-les et passez-les au presse-purée. Mélangez les pommes de terre et le contenu de la casserole, de manière à obtenir une purée onctueuse et assaisonnez.
5. Arrêtez la cuisson de la viande : elle doit être très fondante et le jus réduit et sirupeux. Laissez reposer la viande 15 minutes, puis effilochez-la à l'aide une fourchette.
6. Répartissez la viande et son jus dans le fond d'un plat à gratin. Déposez la purée dessus et lissez la surface avec une cuillère. Saupoudrez la purée de chapelure et parsemez avec le reste du beurre en petits morceaux. Mettez le parmentier à gratiner 30 à 35 minutes au four. Servez le parmentier aussitôt sorti du four.

BAECKEOFFE DE SANGLIER AUX POMMES DE TERRE

Pour **4 personnes** / Préparation **30 min** / Marinade **12 h** / Cuisson **3 h 30**

POUR LA MARINADE :
1,2 KG D'ÉPAULE DE SANGLIER COUPÉE EN CUBES DE 2 CM DE CÔTÉ ENVIRON
1 C. À S. DE GRAINES DE CARVI
1 C. À S. DE GINGEMBRE EN POUDRE
2 PINCÉES DE CANNELLE
1 C. À C. RASE DE POUDRE DE QUATRE-ÉPICES
½ C. À C. DE PAPRIKA
2 FEUILLES DE LAURIER
2 BRANCHES DE THYM
75 CL DE VIN BLANC
SEL, POIVRE DU MOULIN

2 OIGNONS JAUNES
3 GOUSSES D'AIL
600 G DE POMMES DE TERRE
SEL, POIVRE DU MOULIN

POUR LA PÂTE :
400 G DE FARINE
25 CL D'EAU

1 La veille, dans un grand récipient, mélangez la viande, toutes les épices, le laurier, le thym et le vin blanc. Salez et poivrez. Couvrez de film alimentaire et placez le tout 12 heures au réfrigérateur.

2 Le jour même, épluchez les oignons et les gousses d'ail. Épluchez les pommes de terre et coupez-les en rondelles.

3 Dans une très grande terrine en terre, disposez les oignons, les pommes de terre et la viande par couches. Versez la marinade par-dessus en complétant avec un peu d'eau si nécessaire (les ingrédients doivent être à peine recouverts de liquide). Couvrez la terrine avec son couvercle.

4 Préparez la pâte : mélangez la farine avec l'eau. Formez un boudin avec la pâte et posez-le sur le couvercle en suivant son contour afin de le souder.

5 Enfournez la terrine et allumez le four à 180 °C (th. 6). Laissez cuire 3 heures 30.

6 Sortez la terrine du four et laissez reposer 15 minutes avant de servir.

À DÉGUSTER
avec un pinot noir d'Alsace

Brochettes de sanglier mariné au paprika et compotée de tomates

Pour **4 personnes** / Préparation **40 min** / Marinade **6 h** / Cuisson **50 min**

750 G DE FILET DE SANGLIER COUPÉ EN CUBES DE 2 CM DE CÔTÉ
1 GROS POIVRON JAUNE
2 OIGNONS JAUNES
1 C. À S. DE PAPRIKA
1 C. À C. D'AIL DÉSHYDRATÉ
10 CL D'HUILE D'OLIVE
8 TOMATES MOYENNES
2 GOUSSES D'AIL
1 C. À C. DE SUCRE
2 BRANCHES DE THYM
SEL, POIVRE DU MOULIN

À DÉGUSTER

avec un côtes-de-provence rouge

1 Nettoyez et coupez le poivron en petits morceaux en carrés de 2 cm de côté. Épluchez un des deux oignons, puis détaillez-le en morceaux de la même taille.

2 Dans un grand récipient, mélangez le paprika, l'ail déshydraté et les deux tiers de l'huile d'olive. Salez, puis ajoutez les morceaux de sanglier, le poivron et l'oignon. Montez les brochettes en alternant viande et légumes. Placez-les dans un plat et mettez-les à mariner 6 heures au réfrigérateur.

3 Plongez les tomates 20 secondes dans une casserole d'eau bouillante, puis égouttez-les à l'aide d'une écumoire. Pelez-les, épépinez-les et concassez-les grossièrement. Épluchez et hachez le second oignon et les gousses d'ail.

4 Faites fondre l'oignon et l'ail dans le reste d'huile d'olive 5 minutes dans une casserole sur feu moyen. Ajoutez les tomates, le sucre et le thym. Salez et poivrez, puis poursuivez la cuisson 30 minutes sur feu moyen.

5 Au dernier moment, faites griller les brochettes au barbecue ou à la poêle 5 à 8 minutes, selon la cuisson désirée. Servez avec la compotée de tomate (voir page 80).

Carbonade de sanglier

Pour **4 personnes** / Préparation **30 min** / Cuisson **3 h 15**

1,2 KG DE VIANDE DE SANGLIER COUPÉE EN MORCEAUX
2 GROS OIGNONS JAUNES
3 TRANCHES DE PAIN D'ÉPICES SANS LA CROÛTE
3 C. À S. DE MOUTARDE FORTE
5 CL D'HUILE DE PÉPINS DE RAISIN
30 G DE BEURRE
75 G DE SUCRE VERGEOISE
50 CL DE BIÈRE BRUNE
30 CL DE FOND DE VEAU
SEL, POIVRE DU MOULIN

À DÉGUSTER

avec une bière ambrée ou un bourgueil rouge

1. Préchauffez le four à 140 °C (th. 4-5). Épluchez et émincez les oignons. Badigeonnez les tranches de pain d'épices de moutarde.
2. Saisissez les morceaux de sanglier dans l'huile 5 minutes dans une grande cocotte sur feu vif. Égouttez la viande et mettez le beurre et les oignons à la place. Laissez-les fondre 10 minutes sur feu moyen. Ajoutez la vergeoise et laissez légèrement caraméliser 5 minutes sur feu moyen.
3. Remettez les morceaux de viande dans la cocotte. Versez la bière, portez à ébullition, puis ajoutez le fond de veau. Salez et poivrez. Déposez les tranches de pain d'épices, puis portez à nouveau à ébullition. Couvrez la cocotte et enfournez-la pendant 3 heures, en mélangeant deux ou trois fois pendant la cuisson.
4. Sortez la carbonnade du four et servez avec des frites maison bien croustillantes ou des endives caramélisées.

POMMES DE TERRE FARCIES AU SANGLIER

ET AUX CHAMPIGNONS, GRATINÉES AU COMTÉ

Pour **4 personnes** / Préparation **50 min** / Cuisson **2 h 45**

400 G DE VIANDE DE SANGLIER
1 PETIT OIGNON
2 ÉCHALOTES
8 CL D'HUILE D'OLIVE
25 CL DE VIN ROUGE
25 CL DE FOND DE VEAU
2 BRANCHES DE THYM
4 GROSSES POMMES DE TERRE BINTJE
150 G DE CHAMPIGNONS DE PARIS
20 G DE BEURRE
60 G DE COMTÉ RÂPÉ
SEL, POIVRE DU MOULIN

—

À DÉGUSTER

avec un saumur rouge

1 Coupez la viande en cubes de 3 cm de côté. Épluchez et émincez l'oignon et les échalotes.

2 Saisissez la viande dans la moitié de l'huile d'olive 5 minutes dans une cocotte sur feu fort. Ajoutez l'oignon et les échalotes, et laissez-les fondre 5 minutes sur feu moyen. Versez le vin, puis portez à ébullition. Ajoutez le fond de veau et le thym. Laissez cuire 1 heure 30 à 1 heure 45 sur feu doux, jusqu'à ce que la viande soit filandreuse.

3 Pendant ce temps, préchauffez le four à 180 °C (th. 6). Lavez les pommes de terre avec leur peau. Découpez quatre carrés de papier aluminium, puis déposez un peu de sel et une pomme de terre au centre. Enveloppez chaque pomme de terre de sa feuille d'aluminium, puis placez-les dans un plat. Enfournez pendant 50 minutes.

4 Nettoyez et hachez grossièrement les champignons. Faites-les ensuite revenir avec le beurre 5 minutes dans une poêle sur feu moyen. Salez et poivrez.

5 Égouttez, puis effilochez la viande. Mélangez-la avec un peu de jus de cuisson et les champignons dans un récipient.

6 Sortez les pommes de terre du four. Laissez-les tiédir 10 minutes, puis évidez-les à l'aide d'une petite cuillère sur une profondeur de 1 cm (conservez la chair pour préparer un écrasé de pommes de terre à l'huile d'olive). Garnissez les pommes de terre avec la farce, puis déposez-les dans un plat. Parsemez de comté râpé, arrosez du reste d'huile d'olive et mettez le tout à gratiner 20 minutes au four. Servez bien chaud.

Colombo de sanglier à la patate douce

Pour **4 personnes** / Préparation **30 min** / Marinade **12 h** / Cuisson **3 h 45**

1,5 KG DE VIANDE DE SANGLIER
2 OIGNONS JAUNES
6 GOUSSES D'AIL
2 PETITS PIMENTS ROUGES
10 CL D'HUILE D'OLIVE
LE JUS DE **2** CITRONS VERTS
2 C. À S. BOMBÉE DE POUDRE DE COLOMBO
1 C. À S. BOMBÉE DE FARINE
800 G DE PATATE DOUCE
50 G DE BEURRE
3 BRINS DE CORIANDRE
SEL, POIVRE DU MOULIN

À DÉGUSTER

avec un cornas rouge

1 La veille, coupez la viande en cubes de 3 cm environ. Épluchez et hachez les oignons et les gousses d'ail, nettoyez et hachez les piments. Mettez la viande dans un grand récipient avec l'oignon, l'ail, le piment, l'huile d'olive, le jus des citrons, du sel et du poivre. Couvrez la préparation avec du film alimentaire et mettez-la à mariner au moins 12 heures au réfrigérateur.

2 Le jour même, égouttez la viande, en prenant soin de bien retirer tous les morceaux d'oignon, d'ail et de piment. Saisissez les morceaux de viande dans une grande cocotte, sans huile : celle de la marinade suffit. Ajoutez la garniture égouttée de la marinade, la poudre de colombo et la farine. Mélangez et laissez roussir le tout sur feu moyen pendant 5 minutes.

3 Couvrez largement la viande d'eau à hauteur, salez, poivrez. Portez à ébullition, écumez la surface, couvrez la cocotte et laissez mijoter 3 heures sur feu doux, en remuant de temps en temps.

4 Épluchez, lavez et coupez les patates douces en gros cubes. Faites-les légèrement dorer 3 minutes dans une poêle avec le beurre, puis salez et poivrez.

5 Une fois la viande cuite, ajoutez les patates douces dans la cocotte et un peu d'eau si nécessaire. Laissez mijoter 30 minutes sur feu doux.

6 Au moment de servir, parsemez de coriandre fraîche et ciselée.

POMMES RÔTIES ET FARCIES À L'EFFILOCHÉ DE SANGLIER AUX AIRELLES

Pour **4 personnes** / Préparation **45 min** / Cuisson **3 h**

600 G D'ÉPAULE DE SANGLIER DÉSOSSÉE
1 OIGNON
1 CAROTTE
8 CL D'HUILE D'OLIVE
40 CL DE VIN ROUGE
20 CL DE FOND DE VEAU
4 POMMES GOLDEN
1 C. À S. DE GELÉE DE GROSEILLE
60 G D'AIRELLES
2 BRANCHES DE PERSIL CISELÉES
5 CL DE CRÈME OU DE SIROP DE CASSIS
SEL, POIVRE DU MOULIN

À DÉGUSTER

avec un minervois blanc

1 Coupez la viande en gros morceaux. Épluchez et hachez l'oignon. Épluchez, lavez et coupez la carotte en petits cubes.

2 Saisissez la viande dans 5 cl d'huile d'olive 5 minutes dans une cocotte sur feu vif. Ajoutez l'oignon et la carotte, et laissez-les fondre 10 minutes sur feu moyen en remuant. Versez le vin sur la viande et portez à ébullition. Ajoutez ensuite le fond de veau, la crème de cassis, du sel et du poivre. Portez à ébullition, puis couvrez la cocotte. Baissez le feu et laissez mijoter 2 heures 30 sur feu doux.

3 Préchauffez le four à 190 °C (th. 6-7). Lavez les pommes et coupez-les en deux dans l'épaisseur. Retirez délicatement la chair à l'aide d'une cuillère en laissant 1 cm de bord environ.

4 Vérifiez la cuisson de la viande, elle doit être filandreuse. Égouttez-la, laissez-la tiédir, puis effilochez-la à la main.

5 Filtrez la sauce et faites-la réduire avec la gelée de groseille sur feu doux jusqu'à obtenir 15 cl environ. Mélangez-la ensuite avec la viande effilochée et les airelles.

6 Mettez les demi-pommes dans un plat à rôti. Salez, poivrez, arrosez d'huile d'olive, puis garnissez-les de viande. Enfournez pendant 20 à 25 minutes.

7 Sortez le plat du four. Parsemez de persil et dégustez. Vous pouvez également réaliser cette recette avec un reste de civet.

Civet de sanglier au chocolat et aux airelles

Pour **4 personnes** / Préparation **30 min** / Marinade **12 h** / Cuisson **3 h**

1,5 KG D'ÉPAULE DE SANGLIER
1 OIGNON JAUNE
1 CAROTTE
2 BAIES DE GENIÈVRE
1 BOUQUET GARNI
1 L DE VIN ROUGE
5 CL D'HUILE DE TOURNESOL
5 CL DE COGNAC
60 G DE FARINE
5 CL DE CRÈME DE CASSIS
50 CL DE FOND DE VEAU
100 G D'AIRELLES AU SIROP
3 CARRÉS DE CHOCOLAT NOIR À 70 % DE CACAO
SEL, POIVRE DU MOULIN

À DÉGUSTER

avec un corbières rouge

1 La veille, épluchez l'oignon et la carotte, puis coupez-les en petits morceaux. Écrasez grossièrement les baies de genièvre. Coupez la viande en morceaux. Dans un grand récipient, mettez la viande, l'oignon, la carotte, les baies de genièvre et le bouquet garni. Poivrez, puis versez le vin rouge. Couvrez avec du film alimentaire et placez au frais pendant 12 heures.

2 Le jour même, sortez la viande de la marinade, puis faites-la saisir dans l'huile de tournesol 5 minutes dans une cocotte sur feu vif. Une fois la viande dorée, versez le cognac et faites flamber. Versez la farine, mélangez et laissez roussir 3 minutes. Ajoutez le vin rouge et la garniture de la marinade ainsi que la crème de cassis. Portez à ébullition 3 minutes, puis ajoutez le fond de veau. Salez.

3 Couvrez la cocotte et laissez cuire 2 heures 30 sur feu doux en remuant régulièrement. Ajoutez un peu d'eau pendant la cuisson si nécessaire.

4 Sortez la viande à l'aide d'une écumoire et filtrez la sauce. Mixez celle-ci avec un robot plongeant pour la lisser.

5 Remettez la viande et la sauce dans la cocotte, et laissez mijoter encore 15 à 20 minutes sur feu doux. Ajoutez les airelles et les carrés de chocolat, puis mélangez délicatement pendant 5 minutes pour les faire fondre. Accompagnez avec un gratin de blettes au vieux comté (voir page 78).

SALTIMBOCCA DE SANGLIER AU JAMBON DE PARME

Pour **4 personnes** / Préparation **20 min** / Cuisson **15 min**

8 TRANCHES FINES (3 À 4 MM D'ÉPAISSEUR) ET ASSEZ LARGES DE FILET DE SANGLIER
4 TRANCHES FINES (1 MM D'ÉPAISSEUR) DE JAMBON DE PARME COUPÉES EN DEUX
80 G DE PARMESAN
8 FEUILLES DE SAUGE
5 CL D'HUILE DE TOURNESOL
15 CL DE JUS DE VEAU
20 G DE BEURRE
SEL, POIVRE DU MOULIN

—

À DÉGUSTER

avec un volnay

1. Râpez le parmesan en fins copeaux. Émincez finement les feuilles de sauge.

2. Étalez les tranches de filet de sanglier sur le plan de travail, salez-les et poivrez-les. Déposez une demi-tranche de jambon de Parme sur chaque escalope, puis répartissez les copeaux de parmesan et la sauge par-dessus. Roulez les tranches en les serrant légèrement et plantez une pique en bois pour les maintenir roulées.

3. Dans une poêle, faites cuire les saltimbocca dans l'huile 8 à 10 minutes sur feu moyen en les tournant régulièrement. Retirez-les de la poêle, posez-les sur une assiette et couvrez-les avec une feuille de papier aluminium.

4. Dégraissez et déglacez la poêle avec le jus de veau. Faites-le réduire de moitié, puis ajoutez le beurre en fouettant. Vérifiez l'assaisonnement de la sauce. Remettez les saltimbocca à chauffer 2 minutes dans la sauce et servez aussitôt avec un écrasé de pommes de terre à l'huile d'olive. (voir page 80)

ÉPAULE DE MARCASSIN RÔTIE AU PIMENT D'ESPELETTE, POIRES ET GROSEILLES

Pour **4-6 personnes** / Préparation **30 min** / Marinade **6 h** / Cuisson **1 h**

1 ÉPAULE DE MARCASSIN DÉSOSSÉE
2 C. À S. RASES DE PIMENT D'ESPELETTE
10 CL D'HUILE D'OLIVE
1 GROSSE CAROTTE
1 GROS OIGNON JAUNE
1 GOUSSE D'AIL
1 PETITE BRANCHE DE CÉLERI
3 PETITES POIRES À CHAIR FERME
15 CL DE VIN BLANC
30 CL DE FOND DE GIBIER OU DE FOND DE VEAU
100 G DE GELÉE DE GROSEILLE
30 G DE BEURRE
150 G DE GROSEILLES FRAÎCHES OU SURGELÉES
SEL, POIVRE DU MOULIN

À DÉGUSTER

avec un beaumes-de-venise rouge

1 Un peu avant de cuisiner, assaisonnez l'intérieur et l'extérieur de l'épaule désossée avec le piment d'Espelette, du sel et 1/3 de l'huile d'olive, en massant bien avec vos mains pour faire pénétrer le piment dans la chair. Roulez ensuite l'épaule et ficelez-la fermement. Enveloppez-la dans deux ou trois couches de film alimentaire, toujours en serrant bien, puis placez-la 6 heures au réfrigérateur.

2 Préchauffez le four à 200 °C (th. 6-7). Épluchez, lavez et coupez en petits morceaux la carotte, l'oignon, l'ail et le céleri.

3 Retirez le film alimentaire de l'épaule et déposez-la sur une plaque à rôtir. Répartissez la garniture autour de l'épaule et arrosez le tout avec le reste de l'huile d'olive. Mettez l'épaule à cuire 45 minutes à 1 heure dans le four selon la cuisson désirée, en la tournant et en l'arrosant toutes les 15 minutes et en y ajoutant les poirées coupées en deux après 30 minutes de cuisson.

4 Lorsque vous sortez l'épaule du four, enveloppez-la dans une grande feuille de papier aluminium et laissez-la reposer 15 à 20 minutes. Retirez les poires et maintenez-les au chaud.

5 Dégraissez la plaque de cuisson en laissant la garniture aromatique dedans. Mettez la plaque sur le feu, déglacez avec le vin blanc en grattant le fond de la plaque avec une spatule. Ajoutez le fond de gibier, du sel et du poivre et faites réduire la sauce de moitié sur feu moyen. Ajoutez la gelée de groseille et le beurre et mélangez au fouet, puis ajoutez les groseilles fraîches et les poires.

6 Tranchez l'épaule de marcassin et servez avec la sauce. Accompagnez avec une purée de céleri (voir page 84) ou des légumes-racines.

Effiloché de sanglier façon "pulled pork"

Pour **4 personnes** / Préparation **30 min** / Cuisson **3 h 30**

800 G D'ÉPAULE DE SANGLIER COUPÉE EN GROS CUBES
3 GOUSSES D'AIL
1 OIGNON
1 C. À C. DE PAPRIKA
1 C. À C. DE CUMIN EN POUDRE
2 C. À S. DE KETCHUP
5 CL DE SAUCE WORCESTERSHIRE
5 CL DE VINAIGRE DE VIN ROUGE
30 G DE SUCRE CASSONADE BRUN
5 CL D'HUILE DE TOURNESOL
1 GROSSE C. À S. DE MOUTARDE FORTE
SEL, POIVRE DU MOULIN

À DÉGUSTER

avec un chinon rouge

1 Préchauffez le four à 140 °C (th. 4-5). Épluchez et émincez les gousses d'ail et l'oignon.

2 Dans un bol, mélangez les épices avec le ketchup, la sauce Worcestershire, la moutarde, le vinaigre, le sucre, du sel et du poivre.

3 Saisissez les morceaux de sanglier dans l'huile 5 minutes dans une cocotte sur feu vif. Ajoutez l'oignon et l'ail, et poursuivez la cuisson 5 minutes sur feu moyen. Ajoutez ensuite la préparation aux épices et 20 cl d'eau, puis portez à ébullition en mélangeant. Couvrez la cocotte et enfournez pendant 3 heures 30 en mélangeant toutes les 30 minutes et en ajoutant un peu d'eau pendant la cuisson si nécessaire.

4 Sortez la cocotte du four. Laissez tiédir, puis effilochez la viande avec une fourchette. Servez avec des tranches de pain grillé ou dans un pain à hamburger, accompagné de salade, de cornichons et des pickles d'oignons rouges (voir page 88).

Carré de sanglier rôti aux champignons et sa sauce au romarin

Pour **4 personnes** / Préparation **30 min** / Cuisson **1 h 30**

POUR LE BEURRE DE ROMARIN :
1 GOUSSE D'AIL
1 BRANCHE DE ROMARIN
90 G DE BEURRE MOU
SEL, POIVRE DU MOULIN

1 CARRÉ DE SANGLIER DE 8 CÔTES
1 BRANCHE DE ROMARIN
50 G DE BEURRE
3 C. À S. D'HUILE D'OLIVE
4 ÉCHALOTES
1 BRANCHE DE ROMARIN
500 G DE CHAMPIGNONS SAUVAGES OU DE CHAMPIGNONS DE PARIS
20 CL DE VIN BLANC
SEL, POIVRE DU MOULIN

À DÉGUSTER

avec un cahors

1. Préparez le beurre de romarin : épluchez et hachez l'ail finement. Hachez les feuilles de romarin. Dans un bol, mélangez avec une cuillère le beurre ramolli avec l'ail, le romarin, du sel et du poivre.
2. Préchauffez le four à 200 °C (th. 6-7). Faites une entaille de 2 cm de long entre les côtes du carré de sanglier et garnissez l'intérieur avec le beurre de romarin. Refermez et ficelez fermement le carré de porc.
3. Placez le carré dans un plat allant au four et sur la flamme. Salez, poivrez et répartissez le reste du beurre dessus. Arrosez d'huile d'olive. Épluchez les échalotes et disposez-les entières autour du carré. Ajoutez le romarin et enfournez pendant 20 minutes.
4. Baissez le four à 170 °C (th. 5-6) et laissez cuire encore 45 minutes à 1 heure, selon la cuisson désirée. Tournez le carré à mi-cuisson et arrosez régulièrement.
5. Pendant ce temps, nettoyez et coupez les champignons en quartiers. Faites-les ensuite revenir dans 25 g de beurre 4 à 5 minutes (10 minutes si ce sont des champignons de Paris) dans une poêle sur feu vif. Salez et poivrez.
6. Sortez le carré du four. Enveloppez-le dans une grande feuille de papier aluminium, puis laissez reposer 15 à 20 minutes. Retirez les échalotes et réservez-les.
7. Sans enlever le romarin, faites chauffer le plat de cuisson sur feu vif. Déglacez avec le vin blanc, laissez réduire de moitié, puis versez 15 cl d'eau. Laissez réduire 5 minutes sur feu vif en grattant le fond. Ajoutez le reste du beurre froid coupé en petits morceaux et fouettez. Filtrez ensuite la sauce dans un bol pour dégustation immédiate ou dans une petite casserole pour réchauffer au moment voulu.
8. Découpez le carré et servez aussitôt avec les échalotes confites et la sauce au romarin, et accompagné d'un gratin de pommes de terre (voir page 78).

PALLARES
SOLSONA

TOURNEDOS DE SANGLIER AUX TROMPETTES ET AUX POIRES

Pour **4 personnes** / Préparation **45 min** / Cuisson **40 min**

4 TOURNEDOS DE SANGLIER DE **180** G ENVIRON
30 CL DE FOND DE VEAU
1 FEUILLE DE LAURIER
1 BRANCHE DE THYM
400 G DE TROMPETTES-DES-MORTS FRAÎCHES
1 ÉCHALOTE
60 G DE BEURRE
1 C. À S. DE CRÈME FRAÎCHE ÉPAISSE
2 POIRES COMICES À CHAIR FERME
1 C. À S. DE SUCRE CASSONADE
2 C. À S. D'ALCOOL DE POIRE OU DE CALVADOS
5 CL D'HUILE VÉGÉTALE
SEL, POIVRE DU MOULIN

À DÉGUSTER

avec un côtes-du-rhône village blanc

1. Dans une casserole, mettez le fond de veau, le laurier, le thym, du sel et du poivre, et faites réduire de moitié sur feu moyen.
2. Nettoyez les trompettes, puis rincez-les rapidement à l'eau froide. Épluchez et hachez l'échalote.
3. Faites fondre les échalotes dans 30 g de beurre 5 minutes dans une grande poêle sur feu doux. Augmentez le feu et ajoutez les trompettes. Poursuivez la cuisson 5 à 6 minutes en remuant.
4. Égouttez les trompettes dans une passoire en récupérant le jus de cuisson, et versez celui-ci dans la casserole avec le fond de veau. Retirez le laurier et le thym, ajoutez la crème, puis faites légèrement réduire sur feu moyen. Salez et poivrez. Mixez la sauce avec un robot plongeant. Ajoutez les trompettes et réservez la sauce au chaud.
5. Épluchez et coupez les poires en quartiers. Faites-les ensuite dorer dans le reste du beurre 5 minutes dans une poêle sur feu moyen. Saupoudrez-les de cassonade, laissez-les caraméliser encore 3 minutes, puis flambez-les avec l'alcool de poire.
6. Dans une sauteuse, faites cuire les tournedos de sanglier dans l'huile 4 à 6 minutes de chaque côté, selon la cuisson désirée, sur feu doux moyen. Retirez-les ensuite de la sauteuse et réservez-les dans une assiette.
7. Dégraissez la sauteuse, puis versez la sauce aux trompettes dans la sauteuse en mélangeant sur feu doux. Déposez les tournedos dans la sauce, laissez mijoter 1 minute sur feu doux et servez avec les poires accompagnés d'une compotée d'aubergines et de tomates cerises (voir page 80) ou de potiron rôti (voir page 92).

EN -
111-GE

CÔTELETTES DE SANGLIER À LA LIE DE VIN

Pour **4 personnes** / Préparation **20 min** / Cuisson **1 h**

8 CÔTELETTES DE SANGLIER
1 CAROTTE
70 G DE CÉLERI-RAVE
½ OIGNON
½ GOUSSE D'AIL
1 BRANCHE DE CÉLERI
1 L DE VIN ROUGE
1 FEUILLE DE LAURIER
5 CL DE FOND DE VEAU CORSÉ
20 G DE SUCRE CASSONADE
20 G DE BEURRE
1 C. À S. D'HUILE DE TOURNESOL
SEL, POIVRE DU MOULIN

À DÉGUSTER

avec un pommard

1. Épluchez la carotte, le céleri-rave, l'oignon et l'ail. Nettoyez la branche de céleri. Hachez l'oignon et l'ail. Taillez tous les autres légumes en petits cubes.
2. Mettez tous les légumes dans une casserole avec le vin, la feuille de laurier, du sel et du poivre. Portez à ébullition et faites réduire le vin aux trois quarts sur feu moyen. Ajoutez le fond de veau et le sucre, puis laissez réduire encore 10 minutes.
3. Filtrez la sauce dans une casserole propre à l'aide d'une passoire fine. Faites-la chauffer sur feu doux, puis ajoutez le beurre en fouettant.
4. Salez et poivrez les côtelettes, puis faites-les cuire dans l'huile 3 à 6 minutes de chaque côté dans une poêle sur feu moyen, ou sur un gril.
5. Servez les côtelettes accompagnées de la sauce à la lie de vin et d'une purée de céleri (voir page 84).

Rôti de sanglier au cabécou et aux pleurotes

Pour **4-6 personnes** / Préparation **30 min** / Cuisson **50 min**

800 G DE FILET OU D'ÉPAULE DE SANGLIER
8 PETITS OIGNONS NOUVEAUX
2 GROSSES TOMATES
200 G DE PLEUROTES
20 G DE BEURRE
4 CABÉCOU
4 C. À S. D HUILE D'OLIVE
2 BRANCHES DE THYM
1 C. À C. DE PIMENT D'ESPELETTE
SEL, POIVRE DU MOULIN

À DÉGUSTER

avec un cornas

1 Préchauffez le four à 180 °C (th. 6). Épluchez les petits oignons. Mondez, épépinez et concassez les tomates. Nettoyez les pleurotes, puis hachez-les à l'aide d'un couteau.

2 Faites cuire les pleurotes dans le beurre 5 à 6 minutes dans une poêle sur feu moyen. Salez et poivrez.

3 Faites deux entailles profondes dans le morceau de viande dans le sens de la longueur, mais sans aller jusqu'au bout. Salez et poivrez l'intérieur, puis garnissez de pleurotes et de cabécou. Ficelez la viande fermement pour obtenir un rôti.

4 Saisissez ce rôti dans l'huile 5 minutes dans une cocotte sur feu moyen. Disposez les petits oignons et les tomates autour, salez, parsemez de brindilles de thym et de piment d'Espelette. Enfournez pendant 20 minutes.

5 Sortez la cocotte. Versez le vin blanc et enfournez à nouveau pendant 20 minutes.

6 Sortez le rôti. Enveloppez-le de papier aluminium et laissez-le reposer 15 minutes.

7 Mettez la cocotte sur feu doux et faites légèrement réduire le jus de cuisson jusqu'à ce que la sauce épaississe.

8 Servez avec la garniture et le jus de cuisson, et accompagné d'une purée de pommes de terre (voir page 84).

CIVET DE SANGLIER MARINÉ AU GENIÈVRE, AU VIN ET À L'OIGNON CONFIT

Pour **4 personnes** / Préparation **30 min** / Marinade **24 h** / Cuisson **3 h 30**

1,5 KG DE VIANDE DE SANGLIER
1 GROSSE CAROTTE
2 GOUSSES D'AIL
5 OIGNONS JAUNES MOYENS
8 BAIES DE GENIÈVRE
1 FEUILLE DE LAURIER
10 CL D'HUILE D'OLIVE
75 CL DE VIN BLANC SEC
1 C. À C. BOMBÉE DE FARINE
30 CL DE FOND DE GIBIER OU DE FOND DE VEAU
40 G DE BEURRE
25 G DE SUCRE CASSONADE
SEL, POIVRE DU MOULIN

À DÉGUSTER

avec un gigondas

1 La veille, épluchez, lavez et coupez la carotte en morceaux, épluchez les gousses d'ail, épluchez et émincez un oignon. Coupez la viande en gros morceaux, mettez-la dans un grand récipient creux avec la carotte et l'oignon, les gousses d'ail, les baies de genièvre écrasées, la feuille de laurier, 5 cl d'huile d'olive et le vin blanc. Mélangez puis couvrez le tout avec un film alimentaire et mettez la préparation à mariner 24 heures au réfrigérateur.

2 Le jour même, égouttez la viande. Saisissez-la 6 à 8 minutes dans une grande cocotte avec le reste de l'huile d'olive sur feu vif. Salez, poivrez, saupoudrez-la de farine, mélangez et laissez roussir 3 minutes sur feu vif. Versez le reste de la marinade dans la cocotte. Portez à ébullition, puis ajoutez le fond de gibier ou de veau. Couvrez la cocotte et laissez mijoter 2 heures 30 sur feu très doux, en remuant de temps en temps.

3 Épluchez le reste des oignons et coupez-les en petits quartiers. Faites-les fondre 10 minutes dans une poêle avec le beurre, sur feu moyen. Salez, poivrez, ajoutez le sucre et laissez les oignons confire à feu très doux pendant 10 minutes, ou jusqu'à ce qu'ils soient à peine caramélisés.

4 Une fois que la viande est cuite, égouttez-la. Filtrez la sauce. Remettez la sauce et la viande dans la cocotte, ajoutez les oignons confits et un peu d'eau si nécessaire. Couvrez la cocotte et laissez mijoter 30 minutes sur feu doux.

5 Servez le civet avec une poêlée de champignons (voir page 92).

CHOU FARCI AU SANGLIER

Pour **4-6 personnes** / Préparation **45 min** / Cuisson **2 h**

600 G D'ÉPAULE DE SANGLIER HACHÉ
1 CHOU POMMÉ
1 GROS OIGNON JAUNE
2 CAROTTES
1 BOUQUET DE PERSIL
150 G DE CHAMPIGNONS DE PARIS
1 TRANCHE DE PAIN DE MIE ÉPAISSE SANS LA CROÛTE
½ VERRE DE LAIT
3 C. À S. D'HUILE D'OLIVE
1 ŒUF
1 MORCEAU DE CRÉPINE DE 40 X 40 CM ENVIRON
40 CL DE VIN BLANC
20 CL DE FOND DE VEAU
2 BRANCHES DE THYM FRAIS
SEL, POIVRE DU MOULIN

À DÉGUSTER

avec un beaujolais rouge

1 Préparez le chou : après avoir retiré les premières feuilles, détachez délicatement les suivantes en retirant les côtes. Blanchissez-les 3 à 4 minutes dans une grande casserole d'eau bouillante salée. Égouttez-les, puis plongez-les aussitôt dans un grand saladier d'eau froide.

2 Épluchez et hachez l'oignon. Épluchez, lavez et coupez les carottes en petits cubes. Lavez, équeutez et hachez le persil. Nettoyez et coupez les champignons en quartiers. Mettez le pain à tremper avec le lait dans un bol.

3 Faites fondre la moitié des oignons dans l'huile d'olive 5 minutes dans une poêle sur feu moyen. Ajoutez les champignons, poursuivez la cuisson pendant 5 minutes. Salez et poivrez.

4 Dans un saladier, mélangez la viande avec les oignons et les champignons, le persil, l'œuf et le pain de mie imbibé de lait. Salez et poivrez.

5 Préchauffez le four à 170 °C (th. 5-6). Préparez le chou farci : lavez et rincez la crépine. Prenez un saladier (sa forme va vous aider à réaliser un chou farci régulier), tapissez ses parois avec la crépine, puis, par-dessus, les deux tiers des feuilles de chou. Ajoutez ensuite la farce et le reste des feuilles de chou. Refermez le tout en rabattant les feuilles de chou situées en dessous et la crépine de sorte à former une boule. Retournez le saladier délicatement et ficelez le chou.

6 Mettez le reste des oignons et les carottes dans une grande cocotte. Ajoutez le vin blanc, le fond de veau et le thym. Salez et poivrez. Faites chauffer la cocotte sur feu moyen 10 minutes, puis placez le chou dans la cocotte. Couvrez et enfournez pendant 1 heure 15.

7 Retirez le couvercle et augmentez le four à 190 °C (th. 6-7). Laissez cuire encore 20 minutes.

8 Sortez le chou farci de la cocotte et placez-le dans une feuille de papier aluminium, afin de le garder au chaud. Faites réduire le jus de cuisson de la cocotte 10 minutes sur feu moyen. Servez le chou farci découpé en parts et accompagné de sa sauce.

CHAMBORD

Côtelettes de marcassin rôties à la moutarde et à l'estragon

Pour **4 personnes** / Préparation **20 min** / Cuisson **20 min**

12 BELLES CÔTELETTES DE MARCASSIN
2 PETITES ÉCHALOTES
1 GROS BOUQUET D'ESTRAGON
150 G DE BEURRE MOU
1 C. À C. DE MOUTARDE DOUCE
1 C. À S. DE PASTIS
500 G DE PETITS POIS
2 C. À S. D'HUILE D'OLIVE
SEL, POIVRE DU MOULIN

À DÉGUSTER

avec un beaumes-de-venise rouge

1 Préchauffez le gril du four. Épluchez et hachez finement les échalotes. Effeuillez et hachez l'estragon. Mélangez le beurre mou dans un récipient avec les échalotes hachées, l'estragon, la moutarde, le pastis, du sel et du poivre. Réservez.

2 Faites cuire les petits pois 10 à 12 minutes dans une casserole d'eau bouillante salée. Égouttez-les et rafraîchissez-les à l'eau très froide. Réservez.

3 Assaisonnez les côtelettes de marcassin et saisissez-les 1 à 2 minutes de chaque côté dans une poêle avec l'huile d'olive. Déposez-les sur une grille et laissez-les tiédir, puis transférez-les sur une grande plaque allant au four et badigeonnez-les généreusement de beurre à l'estragon. Répartissez les petits pois autour des côtelettes. Placez la plaque sous le gril du four et laissez cuire le tout 6 à 8 minutes. Quand vous sortez la plaque, servez aussitôt.

CÔTELETTES DE SANGLIER À LA CRÈME D'AIL

Pour **4 personnes** / Préparation **20 min** / Cuisson **50 min**

8 CÔTELETTES DE SANGLIER
3 GROSSES TÊTES D'AIL
30 CL DE CRÈME LIQUIDE
8 CL D'HUILE D'OLIVE
4 BRANCHES DE THYM FRAIS
SEL, POIVRE DU MOULIN

À DÉGUSTER

avec un luberon blanc

1. Préchauffez le four à 180 °C (th. 6). Détachez et épluchez les gousses d'une des trois têtes et placez-les dans une casserole d'eau. Portez à ébullition, laissez blanchir 1 minute, puis égouttez. Renouvelez deux fois l'opération, départ eau froide à chaque fois.
2. Dans une casserole, mettez les gousses blanchies, la crème, 5 cl d'eau, du sel et du poivre. Portez à ébullition, puis laissez cuire 20 minutes sur feu moyen.
3. Coupez les autres têtes d'ail en deux dans l'épaisseur. Déposez-les dans un plat allant au four, arrosez avec 5 cl d'huile d'olive, parsemez de thym, salez, poivrez, et enfournez pendant 20 minutes.
4. Pendant ce temps, mixez la crème avec un robot plongeant. Réservez au chaud.
5. Salez et poivrez les côtelettes et badigeonnez-les d'huile d'olive. Faites-les ensuite griller 3 à 6 minutes de chaque côté sur un gril en fonte ou au barbecue.
6. Sortez les têtes d'ail. Servez aussitôt avec les côtelettes et la crème d'ail.

ÉPAULE DE SANGLIER CONFITE AUX AGRUMES ET AUX PETITES CAROTTES

Pour **4 personnes** / Préparation **30 min** / Marinade **6 h** / Cuisson **3 h**

1,2 KG D'ÉPAULE DE SANGLIER DÉSOSSÉE ET EN UN SEUL MORCEAU
2 ORANGES À JUS BIO
1 CITRON JAUNE BIO
1 CITRON VERT BIO
8 CL D'HUILE D'OLIVE
1 OIGNON
1 TÊTE D'AIL
1 BOTTE DE PETITES CAROTTES FANES
2 C. À S. DE MIEL LIQUIDE
30 CL DE FOND DE VEAU
SEL, POIVRE DU MOULIN

—

À DÉGUSTER

avec un chorey-lès-beaune

1. Lavez et zestez les agrumes à l'aide d'une râpe fine. Pressez-en ensuite le jus.
2. Dans un bol, mélangez les zestes avec la moitié de l'huile d'olive et 2 cuillères à soupe de jus d'agrumes.
3. Salez et poivrez l'épaule, puis badigeonnez-la de la préparation aux zestes. Enveloppez-la de film alimentaire et placez-la 6 heures au réfrigérateur.
4. Épluchez et hachez l'oignon. Détachez les gousses d'ail sans les éplucher. Épluchez et lavez les carottes.
5. Préchauffez le four à 160 °C (th. 5-6). Sortez l'épaule, retirez le film alimentaire et faites-la saisir dans le reste d'huile d'olive 5 minutes dans une cocotte sur feu vif. Ajoutez l'oignon et le miel, baissez le feu et laissez cuire encore 5 minutes. Versez le reste de jus d'agrumes et le fond de veau, salez, poivrez et portez le tout à ébullition. Couvrez la cocotte, puis enfournez pendant 1 heure 30.
6. Sortez la cocotte. Retournez l'épaule, ajoutez les carottes et les gousses d'ail et enfournez à nouveau pendant 1 heure 30, jusqu'à ce qu'elle soit bien confite.
7. Laissez reposer la viande 15 minutes avant de servir accompagné d'un gratin de courgettes au parmesan (voir page 86).

Brochettes de marcassin laquées au romarin et au soja

Pour **4 personnes** / Préparation **20 min** / Marinade **4 h** / Cuisson **20 min**

600 G DE VIANDE DE MARCASSIN
3 CM DE GINGEMBRE FRAIS
3 GOUSSES D'AIL
1 BRANCHE DE ROMARIN
8 CL D'HUILE D'OLIVE
1 GROS OIGNON ROUGE
3 PINCÉES DE PAPRIKA EN POUDRE
10 CL DE SAUCE SOJA SUCRÉE
SEL, POIVRE DU MOULIN

—

À DÉGUSTER

avec un madiran rouge, un grignan-les-adhémar rouge

1. Coupez la viande en petits cubes de 1,5 cm environ.
2. Épluchez et râpez le gingembre, épluchez et hachez les gousses d'ail, hachez finement les brindilles de romarin. Mélangez le tout dans un bol avec l'huile d'olive, le paprika, du sel et du poivre. Mélangez la marinade et les morceaux de marcassin dans un récipient. Couvrez la viande avec du film alimentaire et placez-la 4 heures au réfrigérateur.
3. Épluchez et coupez l'oignon en petits morceaux. Sortez la viande et montez les brochettes en intercalant les morceaux de viande et d'oignon.
4. Faites griller les brochettes sur un gril en fonte ou sur une plancha 10 à 12 minutes, en les tournant régulièrement. Baissez ensuite le feu, arrosez les brochettes de sauce soja et laissez cuire encore 5 à 6 minutes en tournant régulièrement les brochettes de manière à les faire légèrement laquer.
5. Servez les brochettes avec des pommes de terre rôties au carvi.

Cuissot de sanglier rôti à la moutarde ancienne au miel et à la bière

Pour **6-8 personnes** / Préparation **30 min** / Cuisson **55 min**

1 MORCEAU DE CUISSOT DE SANGLIER DE **1,5** KG ENVIRON DÉSOSSÉ
2 GROSSES C. À S. DE MOUTARDE À L'ANCIENNE
30 CL DE BIÈRE BRUNE
2 GROSSE C. À S. DE MIEL LIQUIDE
5 CL D'HUILE D'OLIVE
1 C. À C. RASE DE PIMENT D'ESPELETTE
2 BOTTES D'OIGNONS NOUVEAUX
SEL

1 Préchauffez le four à 220 °C (th. 7-8). Dans un récipient, mélangez la moutarde, la bière et le miel.

2 Badigeonnez la viande d'huile d'olive, de sel et de piment d'Espelette à la main, pour bien les faire pénétrer dans la chair. Déposez le cuissot dans un grand plat à rôti, puis enfournez pendant 15 minutes.

3 Sortez le plat. Étalez le mélange à la moutarde sur le cuissot et enfournez à nouveau pendant 20 minutes.

4 Pendant ce temps, nettoyez les petits oignons en gardant un peu de leurs tiges.

5 Baissez la température du four à 190 °C (th. 6-7). Répartissez les petits oignons autour du cuissot et remettez-le à cuire pendant 20 minutes.

6 Sortez le cuissot. Couvrez-le d'une feuille de papier aluminium et laissez-le reposer 10 minutes avant de le servir coupé en tranches accompagné d'une purée de panais au wasabi (voir page 84).

À DÉGUSTER

avec un saint-émilion

CIVET DE MARCASSIN À LA GELÉE DE GROSEILLE,
POIRES RÔTIES AUX BAIES ROSES

Pour **4 personnes** / Préparation **30 min** / Marinade **24 h** / Cuisson **3 h**

1,5 KG DE VIANDE DE MARCASSIN
1 OIGNON
1 CAROTTE
4 BAIES DE GENIÈVRE
2 BRANCHES DE THYM
5 CL DE COGNAC
1 L DE VIN ROUGE
5 CL D'HUILE D'OLIVE
1 C. À S. BOMBÉE DE FARINE
8 CL DE CRÈME DE CASSIS
50 CL DE FOND DE GIBIER OU DE FOND DE VEAU DÉSHYDRATÉ
4 PETITES POIRES À CHAIR FERME
30 G DE BEURRE
120 G DE GELÉE DE GROSEILLE
SEL, POIVRE DU MOULIN, BAIES ROSES

À DÉGUSTER

avec un chinon rouge

1 La veille, épluchez la carotte et l'oignon et coupez-les en petits morceaux. Coupez la viande en gros cubes et mettez-la dans un grand récipient avec l'oignon, la carotte, les baies de genièvre écrasées, le thym, le cognac, du sel et du poivre. Recouvrez le tout avec le vin rouge, puis couvrez avec un film alimentaire et mettez la préparation à mariner 24 heures au réfrigérateur.

2 Le jour même, égouttez la viande. Saisissez-la dans une cocotte avec l'huile. Saupoudrez-la de farine, laissez roussir 2 minutes sur feu vif puis versez le reste de la marinade (avec les légumes) en y ajoutant la crème de cassis. Portez à ébullition 5 minutes puis ajoutez le fond de gibier ou de veau. Couvrez la cocotte et laissez mijoter 2 heures 30 sur feu très doux, en remuant de temps en temps.

3 Épluchez et coupez les poires en deux. Faites-les dorer 5 minutes dans une poêle avec le beurre, puis parsemez-les de baies roses.

4 Sortez la viande de la cocotte puis filtrez la sauce dans un récipient. Remettez la sauce dans la cocotte, ajoutez la gelée de groseille, faites bouillir le tout 8 à 10 minutes sur feu vif pour obtenir une sauce légèrement épaisse. Remettez ensuite la viande dans la sauce, ajoutez les poires aux baies roses et laissez mijoter 15 minutes avant de servir.

5 Vous pouvez rajouter encore un peu de gelée de groseille dans la sauce au moment de servir. Accompagnez d'un gratin de cardons à l'emmental (voir page 86).

Daube de marcassin à l'orientale

Pour **4 personnes** / Préparation **30 min** / Marinade **6 h** / Cuisson **2 h 15**

800 G DE VIANDE DE MARCASSIN
2 GOUSSES D'AIL
2 OIGNONS JAUNES MOYENS
1 GROS PIMENT ROUGE
10 CL D'HUILE D'OLIVE + **1** C. À S.
1 C. À S. RASE DE POUDRE DE CUMIN
1 C. À S. DE GINGEMBRE FRAIS RÂPÉ
3 ORANGES BIO
60 CL DE VIN BLANC
1 C. À S. DE MIEL LIQUIDE
1 BOTTE DE CORIANDRE FRAÎCHE
SEL, POIVRE DU MOULIN

—

À DÉGUSTER

avec un cahors

1 Coupez la viande de marcassin en cubes de 2 cm environ. Épluchez et écrasez les gousses d'ail. Épluchez et émincez les oignons. Nettoyez, épépinez et hachez le piment. Mettez la viande dans un grand récipient avec 10 cl d'huile d'olive, le cumin en poudre, les gousses d'ail, les oignons, le piment, le gingembre, du sel et du poivre. Lavez deux oranges, zestez-les sur la viande puis pressez-les et mettez le jus d'orange dans le récipient avec les autres ingrédients. Mélangez. Couvrez le tout avec un film alimentaire et laissez-le mariner 6 heures au réfrigérateur.

2 Égouttez la viande et la garniture aromatique, tout en veillant à conserver le liquide de la marinade. Faites rissoler les morceaux de viande dans une grande cocotte 6 à 8 minutes sur feu vif. Ajoutez ensuite la garniture de la marinade (oignon, ail, piment, etc.) et laissez cuire 6 à 8 minutes sur feu moyen. Versez le liquide de la marinade dans la cocotte avec le vin blanc et portez à ébullition. Couvrez d'eau à hauteur, salez, poivrez, puis couvrez la cocotte et laissez mijoter 1 heure 45 à 2 heures sur feu doux en remuant régulièrement et en écumant la surface.

3 Lavez et coupez la troisième orange en huit quartiers. Faites griller les quartiers d'orange 2 minutes de chaque côté dans une poêle avec une cuillère à soupe d'huile d'olive. Ajoutez le miel dans la poêle et faites légèrement caraméliser les quartiers. Mettez-les dans la cocotte 15 minutes avant la fin de cuisson avec le caramel de la poêle.

4 En fin de cuisson de la daube, ajoutez la coriandre ciselée, mélangez et servez accompagné de chou rouge confit à l'orange (voir page 90).

ROUELLE DE SANGLIER AU VINAIGRE ET AUX OIGNONS GRELOTS

Pour **4 personnes** / Préparation **20 min** / Cuisson **2 h 45**

1,2 KG DE ROUELLE DE SANGLIER AVEC L'OS ET DE PRÉFÉRENCE FICELÉE
10 CL DE VINAIGRE DE CIDRE
2 C. À S. DE MIEL LIQUIDE
50 CL DE FOND DE VEAU
300 G DE PETITS OIGNONS GRELOTS AU VINAIGRE
1 BOUQUET DE THYM FRAIS
5 CL D'HUILE D'OLIVE
30 G DE BEURRE FROID
SEL, POIVRE DU MOULIN

À DÉGUSTER

avec un bandol rouge

1 Préchauffez le four à 160 °C (th. 5-6). Saisissez la rouelle dans l'huile d'olive 5 minutes de chaque côté dans une cocotte sur feu vif, jusqu'à ce qu'elle soit bien dorée. Salez et poivrez.

2 Retirez la rouelle de la cocotte. Baissez légèrement le feu et déglacez la cocotte avec le vinaigre. Ajoutez le miel, portez à ébullition, puis faites réduire de moitié. Versez ensuite le fond de veau dans la cocotte. Remettez la rouelle dans la cocotte, répartissez les oignons autour et ajoutez le thym. Couvrez la cocotte et enfournez pendant 2 heures 30 en tournant la viande à mi-cuisson.

3 Après avoir vérifié la cuisson de la viande (elle doit être moelleuse), sortez-la de la cocotte et laissez-la reposer sur une assiette.

4 Faites légèrement réduire le jus de cuisson sur feu doux, puis ajoutez le beurre en fouettant.

5 Remettez la viande dans la cocotte et servez aussitôt avec une purée de pommes de terre maison (voir page 84) ou de poireaux grillés (voir page 90).

TERRINE DE FOIE DE SANGLIER AU GENIÈVRE ET AUX HERBES DE PROVENCE

Pour **6-8 personnes** / Préparation **30 min** / Cuisson **2 h**

600 G DE FOIE DE SANGLIER
200 G D'ÉPAULE OU DE CUISSOT DE SANGLIER (VIANDE MAIGRE)
600 G DE POITRINE DE PORC
1 MORCEAU DE CRÉPINE DE 40 X 40 CM ENVIRON
2 C. À S. DE VINAIGRE D'ALCOOL
12 BAIES DE GENIÈVRE
1 GROSSE C. À S. D'HERBES DE PROVENCE SÉCHÉES
1 ŒUF
5 CL DE COGNAC
15 G DE SEL
10 G DE POIVRE

1 Mettez la crépine à tremper dans l'eau froide avec le vinaigre 10 minutes. Rincez-la, puis pressez-la entre vos mains. Chemisez une terrine de 20 x 8 cm environ avec la crépine.

2 Préchauffez le four à 170 °C (th. 5-6). Coupez les viandes en morceaux, puis hachez-les avec les graines de genièvre à l'aide d'une grille moyenne. Dans un récipient, mélangez la viande hachée avec les herbes de Provence, l'œuf, le cognac, le sel et le poivre.

3 Garnissez la terrine de ce mélange. Rabattez la crépine par-dessus en l'enfonçant bien sur les bords. Mettez ensuite la terrine à cuire 2 heures dans le four au bain-marie.

4 Sortez la terrine. Laissez-la refroidir, puis placez-la au réfrigérateur au moins 2 jours avant de la déguster. Servez avec du pain de campagne grillé, de la confiture d'oignons et des pickles d'oignons rouges (voir page 88)

À DÉGUSTER

avec un fitou

Rillettes de sanglier au madère

Pour **4-6 personnes** / Préparation **20 min** / Cuisson **4 h** / Réfrigération **12 h**

300 G DE VIANDE DE SANGLIER MAIGRE
250 G DE POITRINE DE PORC
250 G DE SAINDOUX
10 CL DE MADÈRE
2 FEUILLES DE LAURIER
2 BRANCHES DE THYM
SEL, POIVRE DU MOULIN

À DÉGUSTER

avec un saint-julien

1 Coupez les viandes de sanglier et de porc en petits morceaux.

2 Faites bouillir 15 cl d'eau dans une cocotte en fonte. À l'ébullition, ajoutez 150 g de saindoux, puis laissez fondre sur feu moyen. Ajoutez ensuite les morceaux de viande. Salez, poivrez et laissez rissoler doucement les morceaux de porc 10 minutes sur feu doux (ils ne doivent pas colorer). Couvrez d'eau à hauteur, ajoutez le thym et le laurier, fermez la cocotte et laissez mijoter 4 heures sur feu très doux, en mélangeant régulièrement et en rajoutant un peu d'eau si besoin. Éteignez le feu et laissez tiédir.

3 Dans une casserole, faites réduire de deux tiers le madère sur feu doux. Dans une autre casserole, faites fondre le reste du saindoux sur feu doux.

4 Égouttez la viande, qui doit maintenant être confite. Mettez-la dans un récipient et écrasez-la à l'aide d'une fourchette. Versez ensuite le saindoux et le madère dessus et mélangez vivement à l'aide d'une spatule en bois.

5 Mettez les rillettes dans un récipient propre et préalablement stérilisé de préférence. Couvrez avec un film alimentaire et laissez-les reposer au moins 12 heures avant de les déguster accompagnées de pain grillé.

TERRINE DE MARCASSIN AUX PRUNEAUX ET À L'ARMAGNAC

Pour **4-6 personnes** / Préparation **30 min** / Cuisson **1 h 45** / Réfrigération **2 jours**

500 G DE VIANDE DE MARCASSIN HACHÉE GROS
300 G DE GORGE DE PORC HACHÉE GROS
150 G DE FOIE DE MARCASSIN OU À DÉFAUT DE PORC, HACHÉ GROS
1 ŒUF
1 OIGNON MOYEN
150 G DE PRUNEAUX DÉNOYAUTÉS ET COUPÉS EN MORCEAUX
5 CL D'ARMAGNAC
1 C. À C. DE GINGEMBRE FRAIS RÂPÉ
1 BARDE DE PORC POUR CHEMISER LA TERRINE
10 CL DE GELÉE
10 G DE SEL
1 C. À C. RASE DE PIMENT D'ESPELETTE

1. Préchauffez le four à 160 °C (th. 5-6). Mettez toutes les viandes hachées dans un grand récipient avec l'œuf, l'oignon haché, les morceaux de pruneaux, l'armagnac, le gingembre, le sel et le piment d'Espelette. Mélangez pendant 5 minutes avec vos mains pour obtenir une farce homogène.
2. Chemisez une terrine de 20 cm environ avec la barde. Remplissez largement la terrine de farce, rabattez la barde sur la farce et posez le couvercle dessus. Mettez la terrine à cuire 1 heure 15 au four au bain-marie.
3. Retirez le couvercle, faites cuire la terrine encore 30 minutes. Lorsque vous sortez la terrine, laissez-la refroidir puis placez-la une nuit au frais en posant une presse dessus.
4. Le lendemain, retirez la presse, retirez l'excédent de graisse, puis faites couler un peu de gelée sur le dessus. Placez de nouveau la terrine au frais et laissez-la reposer au moins 2 jours avant de la déguster. Servez la terrine avec un pain aux noix ou un pain aux céréales et des pickles d'oignons rouges (voir page 88)

À DÉGUSTER

avec un saint-joseph rouge ou un cahors

Terrine de campagne au sanglier

Pour **6-8 personnes** / Préparation **20 min** / Cuisson **2 h 30** / Repos **12 h**

400 G D'ÉPAULE DE SANGLIER HACHÉ
200 G DE GORGE DE SANGLIER HACHÉ
100 G DE FOIE DE SANGLIER HACHÉ
300 G DE POITRINE DE PORC HACHÉE
1 GRAND MORCEAU DE CRÉPINE
1 C. À S. DE VINAIGRE D'ALCOOL
2 TRANCHES DE PAIN DE MIE SANS LA CROÛTE
8 CL DE LAIT
1 OIGNON
1 ŒUF
5 CL DE CALVADOS
15 G DE SEL
1 C. À S. RASE DE POIVRE MOULU
10 CL DE GELÉE

—

À DÉGUSTER

avec un madiran

1 Préchauffez le four à 160 °C (th. 5-6). Faites tremper la crépine dans un grand bol d'eau froide avec le vinaigre. Faites également tremper le pain de mie dans un bol avec le lait. Épluchez et hachez finement l'oignon.

2 Dans un grand saladier, mélangez à la main toutes les viandes hachées avec le pain imbibé de lait, l'oignon, l'œuf, le calvados, le sel et le poivre. La farce doit être homogène.

3 Rincez et égouttez la crépine en la pressant entre vos mains, puis tapissez-en une terrine de 18 x 10 cm. Ajoutez la farce et rabattez la crépine par-dessus. Couvrez la terrine avec son couvercle et faites-la cuire 2 heures dans le four au bain-marie.

4 Retirez le couvercle et prolongez la cuisson de 30 minutes.

5 Sortez la terrine et laissez-la tiédir. Placez une planche de la taille de la terrine dessus, puis, par-dessus, un poids de 2 kg. Laissez refroidir complètement avant de la placer 12 heures au frais.

6 Le lendemain, retirez la presse, nettoyez les bords de la terrine, puis versez la gelée préalablement réchauffée. Placez à nouveau la terrine au frais.

7 Si possible, attendez au moins 2 jours avant de déguster la terrine, elle n'en sera que meilleure. Accompagnez-la d'une tranche de pain de campagne, de cornichons, de pickles de légumes ou de confiture d'oignons (voir page 88).

TERRINE DE SANGLIER AUX TROMPETTES ET AUX NOISETTES

Pour **6-8 personnes** / Préparation **30 min** / Cuisson **2 h** / Repos **3 jours**

500 G DE VIANDE DE SANGLIER MAIGRE HACHÉE GROS
300 G DE GORGE DE PORC HACHÉE GROS
150 G DE FOIE DE PORC OU DE SANGLIER HACHÉ GROS
150 G DE TROMPETTES-DES-MORTS FRAÎCHES
1 OIGNON
2 GOUSSES D'AIL
2 C. À S. D'HUILE DE NOIX
1 ŒUF
100 G DE NOISETTES ENTIÈRES
5 CL DE PORTO OU DE MADÈRE
1 BARDE DE PORC
10 CL DE GELÉE
SEL, POIVRE DU MOULIN

—

À DÉGUSTER

avec un pomerol

1. Préchauffez le four à 160 °C (th. 5-6). Nettoyez et lavez les trompettes. Épluchez et hachez finement l'oignon et l'ail.
2. Faites revenir les trompettes dans l'huile de noix 3 à 4 minutes dans une poêle sur feu moyen. Salez et poivrez. Égouttez-les dans une passoire, puis hachez-les grossièrement.
3. Dans un grand récipient, mélangez les viandes, l'œuf, l'oignon, l'ail, les noisettes, le porto et les trompettes. Ajoutez 15 g de sel et 10 g de poivre. Mélangez pendant 5 minutes à la main pour obtenir une farce homogène.
4. Chemisez une terrine avec la barde. Remplissez largement la terrine de farce, puis rabattez la barde par-dessus. Refermez la terrine avec son couvercle et mettez-la à cuire 1 heure 30 dans le four au bain-marie.
5. Retirez le couvercle de la terrine et poursuivez la cuisson pendant 30 minutes.
6. Sortez la terrine. Laissez-la refroidir, puis déposez une presse dessus. Placez le tout au frais pendant une nuit.
7. Le lendemain, retirez la presse. Nettoyez les bords de la terrine pour retirer l'excédent de graisse et versez la gelée. Replacez la terrine au frais et laissez-la reposer au moins 2 jours avant de la déguster. Accompagnez de confiture d'oignons et de pickles d'oignons rouges (voir page 88).

Terrine de sanglier au pain d'épices

Pour **6-8 personnes** / Préparation **40 min** / Marinade **6 h** / Cuisson **2 h** / Repos **3 jours**

600 G DE VIANDE DE SANGLIER MAIGRE HACHÉ GROS
150 G DE FOIE DE SANGLIER OU DE PORC HACHÉ GROS
100 G DE GORGE DE PORC HACHÉ GROS
200 G DE LARD DE PORC HACHÉ GROS
4 TRANCHES DE PAIN D'ÉPICES SANS LA CROÛTE
10 CL DE LAIT
3 ÉCHALOTES
1 GOUSSE D'AIL
5 CL DE VIN BLANC
5 CL DE COGNAC
1 C. À C. BOMBÉE DE POUDRE DE QUATRE-ÉPICES
½ C. À C. DE CANNELLE
1 MORCEAU DE CRÉPINE DE 40 X 40 CM
2 C. À S. DE VINAIGRE D'ALCOOL
1 GROSSE C. À S. DE CRÈME FRAÎCHE
1 ŒUF
12 GROS PRUNEAUX DÉNOYAUTÉS
SEL, POIVRE DU MOULIN

À DÉGUSTER

avec un collioure rouge

1 Épluchez et hachez les échalotes et l'ail.

2 Dans un grand récipient, mélangez les viandes hachées, l'ail, les échalotes, le vin blanc, le cognac, le quatre-épices et la cannelle. Ajoutez 15 g de sel et 10 g de poivre. Couvrez de film alimentaire et placez 6 heures au réfrigérateur.

3 Faites tremper la crépine de porc dans un récipient d'eau froide avec le vinaigre pendant 10 minutes. Rincez-la, puis pressez-la entre vos mains. Faites tremper le pain d'épices dans le lait.

4 Sortez la viande de la marinade ou retirez la marinade. Ajoutez la crème fraîche, le pain d'épices imbibé de lait et l'œuf. Mélangez vivement à la main pour obtenir une farce homogène.

5 Préchauffez le four à 160 °C (th. 5-6). Tapissez le fond et les bords d'une terrine de 20 x 8 cm environ avec la crépine, en la laissant dépasser sur les bords. Garnissez de farce, puis rabattez la crépine par-dessus. Couvrez la terrine avec son couvercle et mettez-la à cuire 1 heure 30 au four au bain-marie.

6 Retirez le couvercle de la terrine. Augmentez la température à 170 °C (si possible) et laissez cuire encore 30 minutes. Sortez la terrine, retirez-la du bain-marie et laissez-la refroidir.

7 Posez une presse sur la terrine, puis placez-la 12 heures au réfrigérateur.

8 Retirez la presse et laissez reposer encore 2 jours au réfrigérateur. Vous pouvez verser un filet de gelée sur la terrine pour un aspect plus brillant. Dégustez accompagné d'une confiture d'oignons et de pickles d'oignons rouges (voir page 88).

Par commodité, nous avons choisi d'utiliser le mot « cerf » pour toutes les recettes. Cependant il est possible de remplacer la viande de cerf par de la viande de biche ou de faon, il n'y aura pas de différence notable de temps de cuisson comme de goût.

La viande de cerf est très appréciée pour son goût raffiné, son grain fin proche de celle du bœuf et sa tendreté, surtout s'il s'agit de sujets jeunes. Sa qualité nutritionnelle est exceptionnelle, elle est très digeste car peu grasse. Riche en fer, phosphore et potassium, c'est une viande saine, maigre et peu calorique.

Régalez-vous !

L'éditeur

LE CERF

CARBONADE DE CERF AUX MYRTILLES ET AUX CHAMPIGNONS

Pour **4 personnes** / Préparation **30 min** / Cuisson **3 h 15**

1,2 KG D'ÉPAULE DE CERF EN MORCEAUX
5 CL D'HUILE DE TOURNESOL
2 GROS OIGNONS JAUNES
40 G DE VERGEOISE BRUNE
40 CL DE BIÈRE BRUNE
30 CL DE FOND DE VEAU
2 TRANCHES DE PAIN D'ÉPICES
1 C. À S. DE MOUTARDE FORTE
2 C. À S. DE CONFITURE DE MYRTILLES
600 G DE CHAMPIGNONS DE PARIS
20 G DE BEURRE
200 G DE MYRTILLES
SEL ET POIVRE DU MOULIN

—

À DÉGUSTER

avec une bière brune ou un anjou-villages

1. Préchauffez le four à 150 °C (th. 5). Épluchez et émincez les oignons.

2. Dans une cocotte, saisissez les morceaux de cerf 5 minutes de chaque côté sur feu vif avec l'huile. Réservez les morceaux dans une assiette, mettez les oignons à leur place dans la cocotte et faites-les fondre 10 minutes sur feu moyen. Saupoudrez de vergeoise, laissez légèrement caraméliser. Ajoutez les morceaux de cerf sur le lit d'oignons, salez, poivrez. Versez la bière, portez à ébullition, ajoutez le fond de veau, les tranches de pain d'épices badigeonnées de moutarde et de confiture de myrtilles.

3. Couvrez la cocotte, placez-la dans le four, faites cuire 2 h 30 en mélangeant la viande toutes les 45 minutes environ.

4. Nettoyez les champignons, coupez-les en quartiers. Faites-les sauter 5 minutes dans une poêle sur feu vif avec le beurre. Salez et poivrez.

5. Après 2 h 30 de cuisson, ajoutez les champignons et les myrtilles dans la cocotte et laissez cuire encore 30 minutes. Servez bien chaud accompagné de frites ou de purée de pommes de terre (voir p. 88).

RÔTI DE CERF À LA BORDELAISE

Pour **4 personnes** / Préparation **45 min** / Cuisson **1 h 15**

1 RÔTI DE CERF, BARDÉ DE PRÉFÉRENCE, DANS LE FILET DE 800 G ENVIRON
5 BELLES ÉCHALOTES
60 CL DE VIN ROUGE DE BORDEAUX
15 CL DE FOND DE VEAU CORSÉ
50 G DE BEURRE
5 CL D'HUILE DE TOURNESOL
SEL ET POIVRE DU MOULIN

À DÉGUSTER

avec un pomerol

1. Épluchez et hachez les échalotes, mettez-les dans une casserole avec le vin rouge. Portez à ébullition, laissez cuire sur feu moyen jusqu'à ce que le vin soit réduit des ¾.
2. Préchauffez le four à 210 °C (th. 7).
3. Ajoutez le fond de veau dans la réduction de vin rouge, laissez cuire encore 15 à 20 minutes sur feu doux pour obtenir une sauce légèrement épaisse puis ajoutez 20 g de beurre froid en morceaux en fouettant. Gardez la sauce au chaud au bain-marie.
4. Assaisonnez le rôti, mettez-le dans un plat à four, déposez le reste du beurre en morceaux dessus et arrosez-le d'huile. Mettez le plat dans le four, faites cuire le rôti 20 à 25 minutes pour une cuisson rosée, ajoutez 5 minutes pour une cuisson à point en le tournant et en l'arrosant de gras à mi-cuisson.
5. Sortez le plat du four enveloppez le rôti dans une feuille de papier aluminium, laissez-le reposer 10 minutes puis tranchez-le et servez-le avec la sauce bordelaise, accompagné d'un gratin de cardon ou de pommes de terre (voir p. 92), d'oignons rôtis dans leur peau au thym (voir p. 86) ou encore d'une poêlée de champignons.

Parmentier de cerf au céleri et au carvi

Pour **4 personnes** / Préparation **45 min** / Cuisson **2 h 15**

1 KG DE VIANDE DE CERF (ÉPAULE)
1 CAROTTE
1 OIGNON
1 BRANCHE DE CÉLERI
5 CL D'HUILE D'OLIVE
40 CL DE VIN ROUGE
30 CL DE FOND DE VEAU
600 G DE CÉLERI BOULE
1 GROSSE POMME DE TERRE
80 G DE BEURRE
1 C. À S. BOMBÉE DE GRAINES DE CARVI
90 G DE CHAPELURE
SEL ET POIVRE DU MOULIN

—

À DÉGUSTER

avec un côtes-du-rhône-villages

1. Épluchez et coupez en morceaux la carotte, l'oignon et la branche de céleri. Dans une grande casserole, faites saisir les morceaux de cerf de tous côtés dans l'huile d'olive. Versez le vin rouge, portez à ébullition 5 minutes. Ajoutez les légumes, le fond de veau, du sel et du poivre. Couvrez la casserole, laissez cuire 1 h 30 sur feu doux en écumant la surface régulièrement. La viande doit être fondante et s'effilocher après cuisson.

2. Épluchez, lavez et coupez en morceaux le céleri boule et la pomme de terre. Mettez-les dans une casserole. Couvrez largement d'eau, salez, portez à ébullition, laissez cuire 20 minutes sur feu moyen.

3. Égouttez les légumes puis mixez le tout avec 70 g de beurre avec un mixeur plongeant pour obtenir une purée lisse. Ajoutez les graines de carvi dans la purée, mélangez.

4. Laissez tiédir la viande dans son jus de cuisson, égouttez-la et effilochez-la dans un plat à gratin. Filtrez 15 cl de jus de cuisson, mélangez-le avec la viande, du sel et du poivre si nécessaire. Étalez bien la viande dans le fond du plat.

5. Préchauffez le four à 180 °C (th. 6). Couvrez la viande avec la purée de céleri. Parsemez la surface de chapelure et du reste du beurre en petits morceaux. Placez le plat dans le four, faites cuire le gratin 20 à 30 minutes jusqu'à ce qu'il soit bien doré. Servez aussitôt.

Bourguignon de cerf aux petits oignons acidulés et caramélisés

Pour **4 personnes** / Préparation **40 min** / Cuisson **2 h**

1,2 KG DE VIANDE DE CERF (ÉPAULE, CUISSOT)
1 OIGNON JAUNE
1 CAROTTE
5 CL D'HUILE VÉGÉTALE
40 G DE FARINE
75 CL DE VIN ROUGE DE BOURGOGNE
50 CL DE FOND DE VEAU
2 BRANCHES DE THYM
1 FEUILLE DE LAURIER
400 G DE PETITS OIGNONS AU VINAIGRE
50 G DE BEURRE
2 C. À S. DE SUCRE CASSONADE
2 TRANCHES DE LARD FUMÉ DE 8 À 10 MM D'ÉPAISSEUR
SEL ET POIVRE DU MOULIN

—

À DÉGUSTER

avec un mercurey

1. Épluchez et émincez l'oignon et la carotte. Coupez la viande en gros morceaux. Dans une grande cocotte, faites-les saisir 5 minutes avec l'huile sur feu vif. Ajoutez l'oignon et la carotte, laissez rissoler 3 minutes puis saupoudrez de farine. Salez, poivrez, laissez cuire 3 minutes sur feu vif en faisant bien rissoler les morceaux de viande dans la farine. Versez le vin rouge dans la cocotte, portez à ébullition, laissez bouillir 5 minutes. Ajoutez le fond de veau, le thym et le laurier. Couvrez la cocotte, laissez cuire 1 h 30 sur feu doux en écumant la surface régulièrement.
2. Égouttez les petits oignons. Dans une poêle, faites-les rissoler 5 minutes sur feu vif avec le beurre. Saupoudrez-les de sucre, laissez-les caraméliser 5 minutes sur feu vif en remuant sans cesse. Salez et poivrez.
3. Taillez le lard en lardons. Dans une poêle, faites-les rissoler 5 minutes sur feu vif sans matière grasse.
4. Au bout de 1 h 30 de cuisson du bourguignon, vérifiez l'assaisonnement, salez et poivrez de nouveau si nécessaire puis ajoutez les petits oignons et les lardons dans la cocotte. Laissez cuire encore 15 minutes sans couvrir sur feu moyen. Servez bien chaud avec des endives braisées ou des carottes rôties.

TOURTE DE POMME DE TERRE À LA FARCE DE CERF

Pour **4 à 6 personnes** / Préparation **45 min** / Cuisson **1 h 15**

400 G DE VIANDE DE CERF HACHÉE
600 G DE POMMES DE TERRE
2 GOUSSES D'AIL
1 GROSSE ÉCHALOTE
1 BOUQUET DE PERSIL
1 ROULEAU DE PÂTE BRISÉE
20 CL DE CRÈME LIQUIDE ENTIÈRE
1 ROULEAU DE PÂTE FEUILLETÉE
1 JAUNE D'ŒUF
SEL ET POIVRE DU MOULIN

À DÉGUSTER

avec un fitou

1 Épluchez, lavez et émincez les pommes de terre en tranches de 2 à 3 mm d'épaisseur. Épluchez et hachez les gousses d'ail ainsi que l'échalote, lavez et hachez le persil. Mélangez la viande de cerf dans un récipient avec l'ail, l'échalote, le persil, du sel et du poivre.

2 Préchauffez le four à 220 °C (th. 7-8). Chemisez un moule à manqué beurré de 22 cm environ avec la pâte brisée.

3 Déposez une couche de pommes de terre, salez, poivrez, étalez la farce et la moitié de la crème fraîche. Couvrez avec le reste des pommes de terre, salez, poivrez et mettez le reste de crème fraîche. Couvrez avec la pâte feuilletée et soudez les bords avec un peu de jaune d'œuf mélangé avec 1 cuillerée à soupe d'eau.

4 Faites un petit trou au milieu et enfoncez un petit cône en papier sulfurisé ou en papier d'aluminium pour former une cheminée.

5 Dessinez quelques traits sur le dessus de la pâte avec la pointe d'un couteau et badigeonnez de jaune d'œuf. Placez la tourte dans le four pendant 15 minutes, baissez la température à 180 °C (th. 6), prolongez la cuisson pendant 1 heure. Servez avec une salade verte.

MIJOTÉ DE CERF AUX CHAMPIGNONS ET AU JAMBON DE BAYONNE

Pour **4 personnes** / Préparation **40 min** / Cuisson **2 h**

1,2 KG DE VIANDE DE CERF (ÉPAULE, CUISSOT)
1 OIGNON JAUNE
1 CAROTTE
5 CL D'HUILE VÉGÉTALE + 1 C. À S.
60 G DE FARINE
75 CL DE VIN ROUGE
40 CL DE FOND DE VEAU
4 BAIES DE GENIÈVRE
600 G DE CHAMPIGNONS DE PARIS
60 G DE BEURRE
1 GROSSE BOTTE DE PETITS OIGNONS
1 C. À S. DE SUCRE
2 TRANCHES DE JAMBON DE BAYONNE DE 4 À 5 MM D'ÉPAISSEUR
SEL ET POIVRE DU MOULIN

—

À DÉGUSTER

avec un irouléguy ou un côte-de-beaune

1. Épluchez et émincez l'oignon et la carotte. Dans une grande cocotte, faites saisir les morceaux de viande dans l'huile sur feu vif. Ajoutez l'oignon et la carotte, laissez rissoler 3 minutes puis saupoudrez de farine. Salez, poivrez, laissez cuire 3 minutes sur feu vif en mélangeant les morceaux de viande dans la farine.

2. Versez le vin rouge dans la cocotte, portez à ébullition, laissez bouillir 5 minutes. Ajoutez le fond de veau et les baies de genièvre, couvrez la cocotte, laissez cuire 1 h 30 sur feu doux en écumant la surface régulièrement.

3. Pendant ce temps, lavez et coupez les champignons en quartiers. Dans une poêle, faites-les sauter 10 minutes avec 40 g de beurre, salez et poivrez.

4. Épluchez les petits oignons. Dans une casserole, faites-les rissoler 5 minutes dans le reste du beurre, ajoutez le sucre, mouillez d'eau à hauteur. Salez, poivrez, puis couvrez-les avec une feuille de papier sulfurisé posée sur le liquide et laissez cuire 10 minutes sur feu moyen.

5. Coupez le jambon en petits cubes. Dans une poêle, faites-les rissoler 5 minutes sur feu vif avec 1 cuillerée à soupe d'huile.

6. Au bout de 1 h 30 de cuisson, vérifiez l'assaisonnement, ajoutez les petits oignons et les champignons dans la cocotte. Laissez cuire encore 15 minutes sans couvrir, sur feu doux, en mélangeant régulièrement. Ajoutez les cubes de jambon, laissez mijoter encore 5 minutes et servez aussitôt.

PAVÉS DE CERF AUX FIGUES ET AU MIEL

Pour **4 personnes** / Préparation **20 min** / Cuisson **30 min**

4 PAVÉS DE CERF DANS LE FILET DE 180 G ENVIRON
2 C. À S. D'HUILE D'OLIVE
40 G DE BEURRE
6 FIGUES FRAÎCHES
8 CL DE FERNET-BRANCA
2 GROSSES C. À S. DE MIEL LIQUIDE
SEL, POIVRE DU MOULIN

À DÉGUSTER

avec un saint-joseph

1 Salez et poivrez les pavés de cerf. Saisissez-les de chaque côté dans une poêle sur feu vif dans l'huile d'olive. Baissez ensuite le feu et laissez-les cuire 3 à 5 minutes de chaque côté pour une cuisson à point. Enveloppez-les ensuite dans une feuille de papier aluminium et laissez-les reposer le temps de réaliser la sauce.

2 Dégraissez la poêle, puis mettez la moitié du beurre dedans. Coupez les figues en deux et faites-les dorer 2 minutes de chaque côté dans le beurre. Réservez.

3 Versez le Fernet-Branca dans la poêle, faites réduire de moitié puis ajoutez le miel. Laissez mijoter 3 minutes sur feu vif, puis ajoutez 10 cl d'eau, le reste du beurre, du sel et du poivre. Faites réduire le tout pour obtenir une sauce sirupeuse. Remettez les figues à chauffer 2 minutes dans la sauce.

4 Coupez les pavés en tranches, puis servez avec les figues et la sauce bien chaude. Accompagnez avec des brocolis, un gratin de blettes ou de pommes de terre (voir p. 92), des carottes rôties au miel et à l'orange (voir p. 86) ou des oignons rôtis dans leur peau au thym (voir p. 86).

Boulettes de cerf au bacon et au parmesan

Pour **4 personnes** / Préparation **30 min** / Cuisson **15 min**

500 G DE VIANDE DE CERF HACHÉE (FILET, CUISSOT)
30 G DE BEURRE
10 TRANCHES DE BACON
5 CL D'HUILE D'OLIVE
1 PETIT OIGNON JAUNE
10 FEUILLES DE BASILIC
100 G DE LARD HACHÉ
80 G DE CHAPELURE
2 ŒUFS
80 G DE PARMESAN RÂPÉ
1 C. À S. D'AIL EN POUDRE
4 BRANCHES DE THYM
SEL ET POIVRE DU MOULIN

1 Placez le beurre au congélateur 2 heures avant de réaliser la recette.

2 Dans une poêle, faites rissoler les tranches de bacon sur feu vif avec quelques gouttes d'huile d'olive. Laissez-le refroidir puis hachez-le avec un couteau.

3 Épluchez et hachez l'oignon, ciselez le basilic. Mettez la viande de cerf et le lard haché dans un récipient. Ajoutez l'oignon haché, le bacon haché, la chapelure, les œufs, le parmesan, l'ail en poudre, les brindilles de thym, le basilic, du sel et du poivre. Râpez le beurre dans le récipient puis malaxez le tout aussitôt pour obtenir une farce homogène. Avec vos mains, formez des boulettes de la taille d'une grosse noix.

4 Dans une grande poêle, faites rissoler les boulettes sur feu moyen pendant 10 à 12 minutes en les tournant régulièrement. Servez aussitôt avec des spaghettis à l'huile d'olive et au basilic ou au pesto vert ou rouge.

À DÉGUSTER

avec un bourgueil ou un côtes-du-rhône blanc (viognier)

Côtelettes de cerf à la réduction de vin cuit, mousseline de carotte

Pour **4 personnes** / Préparation **20 min** / Cuisson **1 h**

8 CÔTELETTES DE CERF
1 CAROTTE
70 G DE CÉLERI-RAVE
½ OIGNON
½ GOUSSE D'AIL
1 BRANCHE DE CÉLERI
1 FEUILLE DE LAURIER
1 L DE VIN ROUGE
20 G DE SUCRE CASSONADE
10 CL DE FOND DE GIBIER (VOIR P. 80) OU DE FOND DE VEAU
15 G DE BEURRE
SEL ET POIVRE DU MOULIN

POUR LA MOUSSELINE DE CAROTTE :

700 G DE CAROTTE
3 CM DE RACINE DE GINGEMBRE
1 CITRON NON TRAITÉ
100 G DE BEURRE
SEL ET POIVRE DU MOULIN

1. Épluchez la carotte, le céleri-rave, l'oignon et l'ail. Nettoyez le céleri-branche. Hachez l'oignon et l'ail, taillez tous les autres légumes en petits cubes. Mettez tous les légumes dans une casserole avec la feuille de laurier, du sel et du poivre. Versez le vin, ajoutez le sucre, portez à ébullition, faites réduire le vin des ¾ sur feu moyen.

2. Pendant ce temps, préparez la mousseline. Épluchez, lavez et coupez les carottes en morceaux, plongez-les dans une casserole d'eau bouillante salée, faites-les cuire 30 minutes sur feu moyen.

3. Épluchez et râpez le gingembre, lavez et zestez le citron. Égouttez les carottes, mettez-les dans un récipient avec le gingembre, les zestes de citron, le beurre froid en petits morceaux. Salez, poivrez puis mixez avec un mixeur plongeant. Gardez la mousseline au chaud au bain-marie.

4. Ajoutez le fond de gibier dans la réduction de vin, faites réduire 10 minutes. Passez la sauce dans une passoire fine, mettez-la dans une casserole propre et faites chauffer sur feu doux. Ajoutez le beurre en fouettant.

5. Assaisonnez les côtelettes. Dans une poêle, faites-les cuire sur feu moyen 1 à 2 minutes de chaque côté, selon la cuisson souhaitée. Vous pouvez aussi utiliser un gril. Servez avec la sauce et la mousseline de carotte.

À DÉGUSTER

avec un saint-joseph

CHILI DE HARICOTS ROUGES PIMENTÉ AU CERF

Pour **4 personnes** / Préparation **20 min** / Cuisson **2 h**

700 G DE VIANDE DE CERF HACHÉE
400 G DE HARICOTS ROUGES SECS OU, À DÉFAUT, CUITS EN CONSERVE
1 GROS OIGNON JAUNE
3 GOUSSES D'AIL
1 POIVRON ROUGE
1 PIMENT ROUGE DOUX FRAIS
5 CL D'HUILE D'OLIVE
2 C. À S. BOMBÉES DE POUDRE DE CHILI
1 C. À C. DE CONCENTRÉ DE TOMATE
40 CL DE COULIS DE TOMATE
25 CL DE BOUILLON DE BŒUF
SEL

1 La veille, faites tremper les haricots rouges dans un récipient rempli d'eau froide.

2 Le lendemain, égouttez et rincez les haricots, mettez-les dans une casserole, couvrez-les très largement d'eau froide. Portez à ébullition, faites cuire 1 h 15 à 1 h 30 sur feu doux. Salez en fin de cuisson.

3 Épluchez et hachez l'oignon et les gousses d'ail. Nettoyez, épépinez et coupez le poivron et le piment en petits cubes. Égouttez et rincez les haricots rouges.

4 Dans une cocotte sur feu moyen, faites fondre l'oignon et l'ail 5 minutes dans l'huile d'olive. Ajoutez la viande de cerf hachée, laissez-la saisir 5 minutes sur feu vif. Ajoutez le poivron et le piment hachés, la poudre de chili et le concentré de tomate. Laissez rissoler 5 minutes sur feu vif en mélangeant.

5 Versez le coulis de tomate et le bouillon de bœuf dans la cocotte, salez et laissez mijoter 30 minutes. Ajoutez les haricots rouges égouttés dans la cocotte, mélangez, laissez mijoter le tout encore 30 minutes sur feu moyen. Servez bien chaud, accompagné de pain au maïs.

À DÉGUSTER

avec un madiran
ou un cahors

Lasagnes de cerf au vin rouge

Pour **4 à 6 personnes** / Préparation **40 min** / Cuisson **2 h 30**

800 G DE VIANDE DE CERF HACHÉE
4 GOUSSES D'AIL
1 GROS OIGNON JAUNE
10 FEUILLES DE BASILIC
200 G DE LARD HACHÉ
5 CL D'HUILE D'OLIVE
1 C. À C. DE GRAINES DE FENOUIL
2 C. À S. D'ORIGAN SÉCHÉ
30 CL DE VIN ROUGE
1 C. À C. DE SUCRE
40 CL DE COULIS DE TOMATE
1 BOUQUET DE PERSIL
350 G DE RICOTTA
20 PLAQUES DE PÂTES À LASAGNE
150 G DE MOZZARELLA RÂPÉE
90 G DE PARMESAN RÂPÉ
SEL ET POIVRE DU MOULIN

À DÉGUSTER

avec un bandol rouge ou rosé

1 Épluchez et hachez les gousses d'ail et l'oignon. Ciselez le basilic. Dans une cocotte sur feu vif, faites saisir la viande de cerf et le lard 6 à 8 minutes dans l'huile d'olive.

2 Retirez la viande de la cocotte, mettez l'ail et l'oignon à la place, laissez fondre 5 minutes. Remettez les viandes dans la cocotte, ajoutez les graines de fenouil, l'origan, le basilic, du sel et du poivre, mélangez.

3 Versez le vin dans la cocotte avec le sucre, portez à ébullition, ajoutez le coulis de tomate, couvrez la cocotte. Faites cuire 1 h 15 sur feu doux.

4 Préchauffez le four à 180 °C (th. 6). Lavez et hachez le persil. Mélangez le persil avec la ricotta dans un bol.

5 Tapissez le fond d'un plat à gratin huilé avec des pâtes à lasagne. Étalez une couche de viande et de sauce dessus, remettez une couche de pâte à lasagne et la moitié du mélange de ricotta au persil. Remettez une couche de pâte, une couche de viande, terminez avec une couche de pâte puis un peu de sauce à la viande et le reste de ricotta. Parsemez la surface de mozzarella et de parmesan. Couvrez le plat avec une feuille de papier aluminium. Placez le plat dans le four, faites cuire 30 minutes. Retirez le papier aluminium, faites cuire encore 20 à 25 minutes.

6 Sortez les lasagnes, couvrez-les avec la feuille de papier aluminium, laissez reposer 10 à 15 minutes avant de les déguster.

RÔTI DE CERF AU POIVRE VERT

Pour **4 personnes** / Préparation **20 min** / Cuisson **40 min**

1 RÔTI DE CERF, BARDÉ DE PRÉFÉRENCE, DANS LE FILET DE 700-800 G
2 GROSSES C. À S. DE POIVRE VERT EN CONSERVE
5 CL DE COGNAC
25 CL DE FOND DE VEAU OU DE FOND DE GIBIER (VOIR P. 78)
5 CL D'HUILE D'OLIVE
1 GROSSE C. À S. DE CRÈME FRAÎCHE ÉPAISSE
SEL ET POIVRE DU MOULIN

—

À DÉGUSTER

avec un gigondas

1 Préchauffez le four à 200 °C (th. 6-7).

2 Préparez la sauce. Égouttez le poivre vert. Dans une casserole, faites-le rissoler 3 minutes sur feu moyen sans matière grasse. Versez le cognac dessus, faites-le flamber et réduire de moitié. Ajoutez le fond de veau ou de gibier, salez, poivrez, laissez réduire la sauce 15 minutes sur feu très doux.

3 Dans une poêle, assaisonnez le rôti, faites-le saisir 2 minutes sur feu vif dans l'huile d'olive.

4 Mettez le rôti et le gras de cuisson dans un plat à four. Placez le plat dans le four, faites cuire le rôti 15 à 20 minutes selon la cuisson désirée. Sortez le rôti, enveloppez-le dans une feuille de papier aluminium, laissez-le reposer 10 minutes.

5 Terminez la sauce : ajoutez la crème dans la casserole, faites bouillir 5 minutes sur feu moyen puis mixez la sauce avec un mixeur plongeant. Tranchez le rôti, servez avec la sauce. Accompagnez avec une poêlée de champignons, une purée ou un gratin de légumes (voir p. 88 et 92).

Filet de cerf rôti aux figues, sauce pain d'épices

Pour **4 personnes** / Préparation **20 min** / Cuisson **30 min**

800 G DE FILET DE CERF
4 GROSSES FIGUES MOELLEUSES
2 C. À S. D'HUILE D'OLIVE
2 TRANCHES DE PAIN D'ÉPICES
1 GROSSE C. À S. DE CONFIT DE FIGUE OU DE CONFITURE DE FIGUE EN POT
2 C. À S. DE MIEL
600 G DE CHOUX DE BRUXELLES
20 CL DE BANYULS ROUGE
20 CL DE FOND DE GIBIER (VOIR P. 80) OU DE FOND DE VEAU
60 G DE BEURRE
SEL ET POIVRE DU MOULIN

À DÉGUSTER

avec un pauillac

1. Préchauffez le four à 200 °C (th. 6-7). Coupez les figues en petits morceaux. Dans une poêle sur feu vif, saisissez le filet de cerf 2 minutes dans l'huile d'olive. Retirez la croûte des tranches de pain d'épices, puis émiettez-le et mélangez-le dans un bol avec les morceaux de figue et le confit de figue.
2. Ouvrez le filet de cerf en portefeuille, garnissez l'intérieur avec le mélange figue/pain d'épices, puis ficelez le filet. Déposez-le dans un plat à rôtir, puis arrosez-le d'huile d'olive, nappez-le de miel, salez et poivrez. Réservez au frais.
3. Nettoyez les choux de Bruxelles. Faites-les cuire 15 minutes dans une grande casserole d'eau bouillante salée.
4. Enfournez le filet de cerf 15 à 20 minutes (pour qu'il soit rosé), en le retournant et en l'arrosant avec de l'huile d'olive et du miel à mi-cuisson.
5. Sortez le filet du four, enveloppez-le dans une feuille de papier aluminium et laissez-le reposer 10 minutes. Découpez ensuite le filet en tranches de 2 cm d'épaisseur, puis servez-les avec les choux de Bruxelles et la sauce au pain d'épices.

Filet de cerf grillé, béarnaise à la menthe, frites de patate douce

Pour **4 personnes** / Préparation **40 min** / Cuisson **45 min**

POUR LA SAUCE PALOISE (BÉARNAISE À LA MENTHE) :

2 BELLES ÉCHALOTES
15 FEUILLES DE MENTHE
1 C. À S. RASE DE POIVRE MIGNONNETTE
8 CL DE VINAIGRE DE VIN BLANC
200 G DE BEURRE
3 JAUNES D'ŒUFS

800 G DE FILETS DE CERF
600 G DE PATATES DOUCES
1 C. À S. DE FÉCULE DE MAÏS
1 C. À S. DE PAPRIKA
5 CL D'HUILE D'OLIVE
SEL ET POIVRE DU MOULIN

À DÉGUSTER

avec un saint-émilion

1. Préparez la sauce paloise : épluchez et hachez les échalotes, hachez la moitié de la menthe. Dans une casserole, mettez les échalotes avec la menthe hachée, le poivre mignonnette et le vinaigre. Faites réduire le tout presque à sec sur feu moyen.

2. Faites fondre le beurre dans un récipient au bain-marie. Dans une casserole propre, mélangez la réduction au vinaigre légèrement refroidie avec les jaunes d'œufs et 3 cuillerées à soupe d'eau. Fouettez le tout sur feu très doux pendant 6 à 8 minutes pour obtenir un sabayon. Continuez de fouetter 2 minutes hors du feu pour arrêter la cuisson.

3. Clarifiez le beurre (faites-le chauffer et retirez le petit-lait). Versez le beurre clarifié en filet dans le sabayon en fouettant sans cesse. Passez la sauce dans une passoire fine. Hachez le reste des feuilles de menthe, mélangez-les avec la sauce, salez. Gardez la sauce paloise à température ambiante jusqu'au moment de servir.

4. Préchauffez le four à 210 °C (th. 7). Épluchez, lavez et coupez les patates douces en forme de frites. Mettez-les dans un grand récipient avec la fécule, le paprika, l'huile d'olive, du sel et du poivre. Mélangez bien le tout avec vos mains, étalez les frites sur une plaque de four sur une seule couche. Placez la plaque dans le four, faites cuire les frites 20 à 25 minutes selon leur grosseur.

5. Assaisonnez les filets de cerf. Sur un gril, au barbecue ou dans une poêle, faites-les griller 5 à 8 minutes selon la cuisson désirée. Servez avec la béarnaise à la menthe et les frites de patate douce.

BOLOGNAISE DE CERF À LA SAUCE WORCESTERSHIRE ET AUX OIGNONS

Pour **4 personnes** / Préparation **20 min** / Cuisson **1 h 45**

800 G DE VIANDE DE CERF HACHÉE
100 G DE CAROTTE
½ BRANCHE DE CÉLERI
200 G D'OIGNON
2 GOUSSES D'AIL
5 CL D'HUILE D'OLIVE
15 CL DE VIN BLANC
10 CL DE SAUCE WORCESTERSHIRE
400 G DE TOMATES PELÉES
2 BRANCHES DE THYM
2 FEUILLES DE LAURIER
SEL ET POIVRE DU MOULIN

1. Épluchez et taillez la carotte en brunoise (petits cubes de 2 mm environ). Nettoyez le céleri, coupez-le en brunoise également. Épluchez et hachez l'oignon et les gousses d'ail.
2. Dans une sauteuse, faites fondre l'oignon, le céleri, l'ail et la carotte 2 minutes dans l'huile d'olive sur feu moyen. Ajoutez la viande hachée, augmentez le feu, faites-la saisir 5 minutes. Salez, poivrez, ajoutez le vin blanc et la sauce Worcestershire. Laissez cuire 5 minutes puis ajoutez les tomates pelées, 15 cl d'eau, le thym et le laurier. Salez et poivrez.
3. Couvrez avec une feuille de papier sulfurisé et laissez mijoter 1 h 30 à 1 h 45 sur feu très doux en remuant régulièrement. Servez avec des spaghettis.

À DÉGUSTER

avec un côte-de-provence ou un chianti classico

BROCHETTES DE CERF MARINÉES AUX ÉPICES

Pour **4 personnes** / Préparation **40 min** / Marinade **6 h** / Cuisson **10 min**

750 G DE FILET DE CERF OU DE CUISSOT COUPÉ EN CUBES DE 3 CM
1 GROS POIVRON JAUNE
2 OIGNONS ROUGES MOYENS
½ C. À C. DE PAPRIKA
½ C. À C. DE CURRY
1 C. À C. DE CUMIN EN POUDRE
10 CL D'HUILE D'OLIVE
12 TOMATES CERISES
SEL ET POIVRE DU MOULIN

À DÉGUSTER

avec un tavel rosé

1 Nettoyez et coupez le poivron en morceaux de la même taille que les cubes de viande. Épluchez et coupez les oignons en morceaux de la même taille.

2 Dans un bol, préparez la marinade en mélangeant le paprika, le curry, le cumin, l'huile d'olive, du sel et du poivre.

3 Montez les brochettes en intercalant harmonieusement les morceaux de viande, de poivron, d'oignon et les tomates cerises. Déposez les brochettes dans un plat, versez la marinade dessus, enrobez bien les brochettes dedans, mettez-les à mariner au moins 6 heures au réfrigérateur.

4 Au dernier moment, faites griller les brochettes 6 à 8 minutes selon la cuisson désirée en les retournant régulièrement. Servez avec des légumes grillés ou une salade de légumes croquants.

Tournedos de cerf aux griottes, écrasé de panais

Pour **4 personnes** / Préparation **30 min** / Cuisson **50 min**

700-800 G DE FILET DE CERF
800 G DE PANAIS
50 G DE SUCRE
5 CL DE VINAIGRE
30 CL DE FOND DE GIBIER (VOIR P. 80) OU DE FOND DE VEAU
100 G DE BEURRE
16 GRIOTTES À L'ALCOOL
1 MORCEAU DE BARDE
2 C. À S. D'HUILE DE TOURNESOL
SEL ET POIVRE DU MOULIN

—

À DÉGUSTER

avec un bourgogne côte-de-nuits ou un irancy

1 Épluchez, lavez et coupez les panais en morceaux. Plongez-les dans une casserole d'eau bouillante salée, faites-les cuire 30 minutes sur feu moyen.

2 Mettez le sucre dans une casserole avec 3 cuillerées à soupe d'eau. Faites cuire sur feu moyen pour obtenir un caramel légèrement brun. Déglacez le caramel avec le vinaigre puis ajoutez le fond de gibier ou de veau, du sel et du poivre. Laissez cuire la sauce 15 minutes sur feu moyen pour qu'elle ait une consistance sirupeuse. Ajoutez 10 g de beurre en fouettant puis ajoutez les griottes. Gardez la sauce au chaud sans la faire bouillir.

3 Coupez 4 petites bandes de barde, formez 4 tournedos avec le filet de cerf, entourez-les de barde et ficelez-les pour la maintenir.

4 Égouttez les panais dans une passoire, remettez-les dans la casserole propre. Faites-les sécher 2 minutes sur feu moyen en mélangeant puis, hors du feu, écrasez-les avec une fourchette, ajoutez le reste du beurre, du sel et du poivre.

5 Dans une poêle, faites cuire les tournedos 2 à 4 minutes de chaque côté sur feu vif avec l'huile, salez et poivrez. Servez avec l'écrasé de panais et la sauce.

LAND-ROVER
EN-111-GE

FILET DE CERF POIVRÉ, LIE DE VIN AU CÉLERI ET CHANTERELLES

Pour **4 personnes** / Préparation **45 min** / Réfrigération **3 h** / Cuisson **1 h**

700 G DE FILET DE CERF
2 C. À S. DE POIVRE À QUEUE
400 G DE CHANTERELLES
½ OIGNON JAUNE
1 BRANCHE DE CÉLERI
75 CL DE BOURGOGNE ROUGE
40 G DE SUCRE CASSONADE
20 CL DE FOND DE GIBIER CORSÉ (VOIR P. 78) OU DE VEAU
50 G DE BEURRE
5 CL D'HUILE D'OLIVE
SEL

À DÉGUSTER

avec un bourgueil

1 Broyez le poivre. Coupez le filet de cerf en quatre pavés et roulez-les dans le poivre. Enveloppez-les de film alimentaire et placez-les 3 heures au frais.

2 Nettoyez les chanterelles, égouttez-les et séchez-les délicatement dans un torchon. Réservez-les au frais.

3 Épluchez et hachez l'oignon. Nettoyez et coupez la branche de céleri en petits cubes. Mettez-les dans une casserole avec le vin rouge, le sucre et du sel. Portez à ébullition et laissez mijoter 30 minutes sur feu moyen, jusqu'à ce que le vin soit réduit aux ¾. Ajoutez ensuite le fond de gibier ou de veau et laissez mijoter 10 minutes sur feu vif jusqu'à ce que la sauce soit légèrement épaisse. Ajoutez 20 g de beurre en fouettant. Gardez la sauce au chaud sur feu doux ou au bain-marie.

4 Faites chauffer le reste du beurre dans une poêle. Jetez les chanterelles dans la poêle très chaude, salez, poivrez et faites-les cuire 3 minutes sur feu vif en remuant.

5 Faites chauffer l'huile d'olive dans une grande poêle. Retirez le film alimentaire autour des pavés de cerf, puis saisissez-les 2 à 3 minutes de chaque côté sur feu vif. Baissez ensuite le feu et laissez cuire les pavés 6 à 10 minutes de chaque côté pour une cuisson à point.

6 Servez les pavés de cerf avec les chanterelles et la sauce à la lie de vin. Accompagnez de croquettes de pommes de terre à la mimolette (voir p. 90).

CIVET DE CERF À L'ORANGE ET À LA CANNELLE

Pour **4 personnes** / Préparation **40 min** / Cuisson **2 h**

1 KG DE VIANDE DE CERF COUPÉE EN GROS MORCEAUX
1 GROS OIGNON JAUNE
2 CAROTTES
1 ORANGE NON TRAITÉE
5 CL D'HUILE D'OLIVE
40 G DE FARINE
1 C. À C. DE CANNELLE EN POUDRE
1 C. À S. DE GRAINES DE CARVI
50 CL DE VIN ROUGE
30 CL DE FOND DE GIBIER (VOIR P. 78) OU DE FOND DE VEAU
1 BÂTON DE CANNELLE
2 BRANCHES DE THYM
1 FEUILLE DE LAURIER
SEL ET POIVRE DU MOULIN

1 Épluchez et émincez l'oignon. Épluchez, lavez et coupez les carottes en cubes. Lavez et zestez l'orange.

2 Dans une grande cocotte, faites saisir les morceaux de cerf dans l'huile 5 minutes sur feu vif. Ajoutez l'oignon et les carottes, laissez rissoler 3 minutes puis saupoudrez de farine et de cannelle. Laissez roussir 2 minutes en mélangeant, salez, poivrez et ajoutez le carvi.

3 Versez le vin rouge dans la cocotte, portez à ébullition puis laissez bouillir 5 minutes. Ajoutez le fond de gibier ou de veau, les zestes d'orange, le bâton de cannelle, le thym et le laurier.

4 Couvrez la cocotte, laissez cuire 1 h 45 sur feu doux en écumant la surface et en mélangeant régulièrement.

5 Servez avec une bonne purée au beurre (voir p. 88), du chou braisé au lard ou des pommes de terre Hasselback rôties au piment (voir p. 90).

À DÉGUSTER

avec un coteaux-du-languedoc

Goulasch de cerf à la groseille

Pour **4 personnes** / Préparation **30 min** / Marinade **24 h** / Cuisson **2 h**

POUR LA MARINADE :

8 BAIES DE GENIÈVRE
1 GROS OIGNON JAUNE
1 CAROTTE
2 FEUILLES DE LAURIER
1 C. À S. DE SUCRE CASSONADE
75 CL DE VIN CORSÉ

1 KG DE VIANDE DE CERF COUPÉE EN GROS MORCEAUX
5 CL D'HUILE DE TOURNESOL
50 G DE FARINE
100 G DE GELÉE DE GROSEILLE
2 CARRÉS DE CHOCOLAT NOIR
SEL ET POIVRE DU MOULIN

—

À DÉGUSTER

avec un terrasses-du-larzac

1 La veille, écrasez grossièrement les baies de genièvre. Épluchez et émincez l'oignon. Épluchez, lavez et coupez la carotte en brunoise (cubes de 2 mm environ). Mettez les morceaux de viande dans un grand récipient. Ajoutez l'oignon, la brunoise de carotte, les baies de genièvre, les feuilles de laurier et le sucre. Versez le vin sur la viande et mélangez. Couvrez le récipient avec un papier film et placez-le 24 heures au réfrigérateur.

2 Le lendemain, égouttez la viande, retirez les feuilles de laurier, filtrez la marinade. Dans une grande cocotte, faites saisir les morceaux de viande 5 minutes sur feu vif dans l'huile. Une fois les morceaux bien dorés, retirez-les de la cocotte.

3 Mettez l'oignon et la carotte de la marinade à leur place, faites fondre 5 minutes sur feu moyen, ajoutez le sucre cassonade. Remettez la viande dans la cocotte, ajoutez la farine et faites rissoler le tout 5 minutes en mélangeant. Versez le vin rouge dans la cocotte, ajoutez la gelée de groseille, salez et poivrez. Couvrez la cocotte, laissez mijoter 1 h 45 sur feu moyen en remuant régulièrement.

4 En fin de cuisson, ajoutez les carrés de chocolat, mélangez doucement et servez. Accompagnez avec un gratin de pâtes ou un tian de pomme de terre, oignon, fenouil et courgette au romarin (voir p. 91).

Pavés de cerf aux cèpes et foie gras chaud

Pour **4 personnes** / Préparation **20 min** / Cuisson **45 min**

4 PAVÉS DE FILET DE CERF DE 180 G ENVIRON (4 À 5 CM D'ÉPAISSEUR)
600 G DE CÈPES
1 GROSSE ÉCHALOTE
5 CL D'HUILE DE NOIX
2 C. À S. D'HUILE D'OLIVE
10 CL DE FOND DE GIBIER CORSÉ (VOIR P. 78)
15 CL DE CRÈME LIQUIDE
4 TRANCHES DE FOIE GRAS CRU DE 100 G ENVIRON
SEL ET POIVRE DU MOULIN

À DÉGUSTER

avec un madiran

1 Nettoyez et coupez les cèpes en morceaux. Épluchez et hachez finement l'échalote. Faites-la fondre dans une poêle 3 minutes sur feu moyen, dans l'huile de noix. Ajoutez les cèpes, salez, poivrez et faites-les sauter 5 minutes sur feu vif.

2 Dans une autre poêle, saisissez les pavés de cerf, dans l'huile d'olive, 3 minutes de chaque côté. Baissez ensuite légèrement le feu et faites-les cuire encore 6 à 10 minutes par côté selon la cuisson désirée. Salez, poivrez et enveloppez-les dans une feuille de papier aluminium. Réservez.

3 Dégraissez la poêle, déglacez-la avec le fond de gibier, laissez cuire 5 minutes sur feu vif puis ajoutez la crème, du sel et du poivre. Toujours sur feu vif, faites réduire la sauce en la fouettant de manière à obtenir une sauce légèrement épaisse. Ajoutez ensuite les cèpes dans la poêle et laissez mijoter 5 minutes sur feu doux.

4 Assaisonnez les tranches de foie gras. Faites-les cuire dans une autre poêle, sans matière grasse, 2 à 3 minutes de chaque côté.

5 Ouvrez les pavés de cerf en deux, glissez une tranche de foie gras chaud dans l'ouverture créée et déposez-les sur les assiettes. Répartissez les cèpes et la sauce autour et servez aussitôt. Accompagnez de pommes de terre Hasselback au piment (voir p. 90).

CÔTELETTES DE CERF EN CROÛTE D'OIGNON FRIT, CHOU GRILLÉ AUX CACAHUÈTES

Pour **4 personnes** / Préparation **30 min** / Cuisson **20 min**

12 CÔTELETTES DE CERF
10 FEUILLES D'ESTRAGON
2 C. À S. DE MOUTARDE
5 CL D'HUILE D'OLIVE
100 G D'OIGNONS FRITS (EN ÉPICERIE SOUS VIDE)
80 G DE CACAHUÈTES
1 CHOU CHINOIS
2 GOUSSES D'AIL
5 CL DE SAUCE SOJA SALÉE
SEL ET POIVRE DU MOULIN

À DÉGUSTER

avec un beaujolais saint-amour

1. Préchauffez le four à 210 °C (th. 7). Hachez les feuilles d'estragon, mélangez-les dans un bol avec la moutarde et la moitié de l'huile d'olive. Assaisonnez les côtelettes, badigeonnez-les de moutarde à l'estragon puis panez-les dans les oignons frits. Déposez les côtelettes sur une plaque de four recouverte d'une feuille de papier sulfurisé.
2. Concassez les cacahuètes avec un couteau, émincez le chou chinois, épluchez et hachez les gousses d'ail. Placez les côtelettes dans le four, faites-les cuire 10 à 12 minutes.
3. Faites chauffer le reste de l'huile dans un wok ou, à défaut, dans une poêle. Mettez le chou chinois émincé et l'ail haché dans l'huile chaude, fautes-le sauter 3 à 4 minutes sur feu vif en remuant. Ajoutez la sauce soja et les cacahuètes, continuez à faire sauter le chou pendant 2 minutes sur feu vif en remuant.
4. Sortez les côtelettes du four et servez aussitôt avec le chou aux cacahuètes.

Curry de cerf coco-coriandre

Pour **4 personnes** / Préparation **30 min** / Cuisson **1 h 30**

800 G DE FILET DE CERF
1 GROS OIGNON JAUNE
5 CL D'HUILE DE TOURNESOL
2 C. À S. DE PÂTE DE CURRY VERT
1 C. À S. DE GINGEMBRE FRAIS RÂPÉ
30 CL DE LAIT DE COCO
60 G DE NOIX DE COCO RÂPÉE
1 PETIT BOUQUET DE CORIANDRE FRAÎCHE
SEL

—

À DÉGUSTER
avec un bourgueil

1. Coupez la viande en cubes de 2 cm environ. Faites dorer les morceaux de cerf 5 minutes dans l'huile dans une grande cocotte sur feu vif. Sortez-les ensuite du feu et réservez.
2. Épluchez et hachez finement l'oignon. Faites-le fondre 6 à 8 minutes dans la cocotte sur feu doux en mélangeant. Ajoutez la pâte de curry vert et le gingembre et laissez roussir 5 minutes sur feu moyen. Versez ensuite le lait de coco et 40 cl d'eau. Salez, puis mettez les morceaux de cerf dans la sauce. Portez à ébullition, couvrez la cocotte et laissez mijoter 50 minutes à 1 heure sur feu doux en remuant régulièrement.
3. Faites griller la noix de coco 2 minutes dans une poêle sans matière grasse sur feu moyen, puis réservez.
4. En fin de cuisson du curry, ajoutez la coriandre ciselée et la moitié de la coco râpée dans la cocotte, mélangez et laissez cuire 3 minutes.
5. Parsemez le reste de noix de coco râpée dans les assiettes au moment de servir. Accompagnez avec du riz blanc ou grillé ou du potiron rôti à l'ail et au miel (voir p. 84).

Pavé de cerf aux cèpes et au porto, crumble noisette

Pour **4 personnes** / Préparation **30 min** / Cuisson **35 min**

4 BEAUX MORCEAUX DE CERF DE 200 G ENVIRON DANS LE FILET
½ CAROTTE
4 CM DE BRANCHE DE CÉLERI
25 CL DE PORTO
1 C. À C. DE SUCRE CASSONADE
15 CL DE FOND DE GIBIER (VOIR P. 78) OU DE FOND DE VEAU
80 G DE BEURRE
40 G DE NOISETTES
40 G DE FARINE
500 G DE CÈPES
2 C. À S. D'HUILE D'OLIVE
SEL ET POIVRE DU MOULIN

À DÉGUSTER

avec un cahors

1 Épluchez et coupez la carotte et le céleri en brunoise (petits cubes de 2 mm). Mettez-les dans une casserole avec le porto et le sucre cassonade. Portez à ébullition, faites réduire le porto de ⅔. Ajoutez le fond de gibier ou de veau. Salez, poivrez et faites réduire de moitié sur feu moyen pour obtenir une sauce sirupeuse et laquée. Filtrez la sauce dans une petite casserole propre, ajoutez 10 g de beurre en fouettant. Gardez la sauce au chaud.

2 Préchauffez le four à 180 °C (th. 6). Hachez grossièrement les noisettes avec un couteau. Mélangez-les dans un récipient avec 40 g de beurre mou et la farine pour obtenir une pâte légèrement friable.

3 Émiettez cette pâte sur une plaque de four recouverte d'une feuille de papier sulfurisé, placez-la dans le four et faites cuire 15 à 20 minutes pour obtenir un crumble doré.

4 Nettoyez les cèpes, coupez-les en morceaux. Dans une poêle, faites-les sauter 5 minutes sur feu vif avec 1 cuillerée à soupe d'huile et le reste du beurre. Salez, poivrez, débarrassez les cèpes sur une assiette.

5 Ajoutez 1 cuillerée à soupe d'huile d'olive dans la poêle, assaisonnez les filets de cerf, faites-les cuire 3 à 5 minutes de chaque côté selon la cuisson désirée, sur feu vif. Remettez les cèpes dans la poêle pour les réchauffer 30 secondes et servez avec la sauce au porto. Parsemez de crumble aux noisettes.

NOISETTES DE FILET DE CERF RÔTI AU POIVRE, TOPINAMBOURS AU VINAIGRE

Pour **4 personnes** / Préparation **30 min** / Cuisson **40 min**

700 G DE FILET DE CERF COUPÉ EN 8 MORCEAUX PAS TROP ÉPAIS
700 G DE TOPINAMBOURS
4 TRANCHES DE JAMBON FUMÉ
15 G DE POIVRE DOUX MOULU ASSEZ FINEMENT
50 G DE BEURRE
30 G DE SUCRE CASSONADE
10 CL DE VINAIGRE DE VIN
2 C. À S. D'HUILE D'OLIVE
SEL ET POIVRE DU MOULIN

À DÉGUSTER

avec un haut-médoc

1 Épluchez les topinambours. Dans une casserole remplie d'eau bouillante salée, faites-les cuire 20 minutes.

2 Coupez les tranches de jambon en deux. Enroulez chaque morceau de cerf avec ½ tranche de jambon, puis passez-les dans le poivre.

3 Égouttez et rafraîchissez les topinambours. Dans une grande poêle, faites fondre le beurre puis faites-y dorer les topinambours. Une fois dorés, saupoudrez-les de sucre, laissez-les caraméliser légèrement puis arrosez-les de vinaigre. Ajoutez 10 cl d'eau, salez, poivrez et laissez cuire les topinambours 10 minutes sur feu moyen.

4 Au dernier moment, dans une poêle propre, saisissez les noisettes de cerf dans l'huile d'olive bien chaude, 3 à 5 minutes de chaque côté, selon la cuisson désirée. Servez aussitôt avec les topinambours et leur jus de cuisson.

CIVET DE CERF AU VIN BLANC ET AUX CAROTTES

Pour **4 personnes** / Préparation **30 min** / Marinade **24 h** / Cuisson **1 h 45**

POUR LA MARINADE :

1 OIGNON JAUNE
2 GOUSSES D'AIL
4 GROSSES CAROTTES
1 BRANCHE DE CÉLERI
1 BRANCHE DE THYM
1 FEUILLE DE LAURIER
5 CL DE COGNAC
1 L DE VIN BLANC
POIVRE

1,2 KG DE VIANDE DE CERF COUPÉE EN GROS MORCEAUX
5 CL D'HUILE DE TOURNESOL
2 C. À S. DE FARINE
1 BOUQUET DE PERSIL PLAT

À DÉGUSTER

avec un nuits-saint-georges ou un côte-de-nuits-village blanc

1 La veille, épluchez et émincez l'oignon et les gousses d'ail. Épluchez, lavez et taillez les carottes en rondelles, nettoyez et émincez le céleri. Mettez dans un grand récipient la viande avec les carottes, l'oignon, le céleri, l'ail, le thym, le laurier, le cognac et du poivre. Versez le vin blanc dessus, mélangez, couvrez le récipient avec un papier film et placez-le 24 heures au réfrigérateur.

2 Le lendemain, égouttez la viande de la marinade. Filtrez la marinade.

3 Dans une grande cocotte, faites saisir les morceaux de viande 5 à 7 minutes sur feu vif dans l'huile. Saupoudrez les morceaux de farine, laissez roussir 2 minutes sur feu vif puis versez le liquide de la marinade dessus et remuez. Ajoutez les légumes de la marinade, couvrez la cocotte et laissez cuire 1 h 30 sur feu moyen en remuant régulièrement.

4 Lavez et ciselez le persil. Vérifiez la cuisson de la viande, parsemez de persil et servez.

STAUB

Rôti de cerf à la catalane

Pour **4 personnes** / Préparation **30 min** / Cuisson **45 min**

700-800 G DE FILET DE CERF
3 ORANGES
4 PIMENTS VERTS LONGS DOUX
5 CL D'HUILE D'OLIVE
15 CL DE VIN BLANC
8 GOUSSES D'AIL
SEL, PIMENT D'ESPELETTE

—

À DÉGUSTER

avec un côtes-du-marmandais rouge

1. Préchauffez le four à 190 °C (th. 6-7). Pressez une orange pour en extraire le jus, pelez les deux autres à vif et coupez la chair en demi-tranches épaisses d'1 cm environ. Nettoyez et coupez les piments en deux dans la longueur, retirez les pépins.

2. Enfoncez un pic à brochette en acier ou une petite broche dans le filet de cerf puis ficelez-le pour le maintenir et qu'il soit régulier en forme. Assaisonnez le filet de sel et de piment d'Espelette. Saisissez-le dans un plat à rôtir avec l'huile d'olive sur feu vif, en vous aidant du pic pour le tourner, afin qu'il soit bien doré sur toute la surface. Baissez ensuite le feu et déglacez le plat avec le vin blanc et le jus d'orange.

3. Répartissez les gousses d'ail avec leur peau, les piments et les morceaux d'orange autour du rôti. Enfournez et faites cuire le rôti 30 à 40 minutes selon la cuisson désirée, en le retournant à mi-cuisson.

4. Sortez le plat du four, couvrez-le avec une feuille de papier aluminium, laissez-le reposer 10 minutes puis coupez le rôti en tranches. Servez avec les morceaux d'orange, les gousses d'ail, les piments et la sauce de cuisson. Accompagnez d'un chou-fleur rôti entier (voir p. 87).

Pavé de cerf sauce chocolat

Pour **4 personnes** / Préparation **20 min** / Cuisson **30 min**

4 PAVÉS DE CERF DANS LE FILET
2 ÉCHALOTES
20 G DE BEURRE
5 CL DE SIROP DE FRAMBOISE
25 CL DE VIN ROUGE
15 CL DE FOND DE GIBIER (VOIR P. 78) OU DE FOND DE VEAU
30 G DE BON CHOCOLAT NOIR
3 C. À S. D'HUILE DE TOURNESOL
SEL ET POIVRE DU MOULIN

À DÉGUSTER

avec un gigondas
ou un vacqueyras

1 Épluchez et hachez finement les échalotes. Dans une casserole, faites-les fondre 3 minutes sur feu moyen dans l'huile. Ajoutez le sirop de framboise, laissez légèrement réduire puis ajoutez le vin rouge. Salez, poivrez, laissez réduire de moitié sur feu moyen. Ajoutez le fond de gibier ou de veau, faites encore réduire de moitié.

2 Filtrez la sauce dans une petite casserole propre, remettez-la à chauffer sur feu doux. Hors du feu, ajoutez les carrés de chocolat en fouettant. Ajoutez un peu d'eau si la sauce est trop épaisse. Gardez la sauce au chaud au bain-marie.

3 Au moment de servir, assaisonnez les pavés de cerf, faites-les cuire 3 à 5 minutes de chaque côté, selon la cuisson désirée. Servez les pavés avec la sauce chocolat, accompagnez avec un céleri cuit au sel ou une purée de céleri ou de panais (voir p. 88).

CÔTELETTES DE CERF GRILLÉES, CONDIMENT PIMENTÉ AU GINGEMBRE

Pour **4 personnes** / Préparation **30 min** / Marinade **4 h** / Cuisson **45 min**

12 CÔTELETTES DE CERF
6 CM DE RACINE DE GINGEMBRE
5 CL D'HUILE D'OLIVE
4 PINCÉES DE CURCUMA
4 GROSSES ÉCHALOTES
2 GOUSSES D'AIL
1 PIMENT DOUX ROUGE, FRAIS
2 TOMATES
2 PINCÉES DE PIMENT
5 CL DE VINAIGRE DE VIN
30 G DE SUCRE
SEL ET POIVRE DU MOULIN

À DÉGUSTER

avec un cassis

1 Épluchez et râpez le gingembre. Mélangez la moitié de l'huile d'olive dans un bol avec ⅓ du gingembre et le curcuma. Mettez les côtelettes dans un plat, badigeonnez-les avec l'huile au curcuma et au gingembre. Couvrez-les avec un papier film et placez-les 4 heures au réfrigérateur.

2 Épluchez et émincez les échalotes et les gousses d'ail. Nettoyez et hachez le piment (retirez les pépins si vous aimez moins piquant). Pelez, épépinez et coupez les tomates en cubes. Mettez les échalotes dans une casserole avec le piment frais, l'ail, le piment en poudre, le reste du gingembre, les cubes de tomate, le vinaigre, le sucre, du sel, du poivre et 15 cl d'eau. Faites cuire 45 minutes sur feu doux pour obtenir une sorte de chutney. Laissez refroidir.

3 Au moment de servir, faites griller les côtelettes 1 à 2 minutes de chaque côté sur le gril ou dans une poêle sur feu vif. Servez avec une salade de belles tomates anciennes ou des légumes racines rôtis (voir p. 87).

2017 28

Filet de cerf rôti à la moutarde, chou vert, compotée au lard

Pour **4 personnes** / Préparation **45 min** / Cuisson **1 h**

800 G DE FILET DE CERF
2 TRANCHES DE LARD FUMÉ DE 5 MM D'ÉPAISSEUR
1 GROS OIGNON
500 G DE CHOU VERT
40 G DE BEURRE
5 CL D'HUILE DE TOURNESOL
2 GROSSES C. À S. DE MOUTARDE DOUCE
50 G DE CHAPELURE
20 CL DE CRÈME LIQUIDE
SEL ET POIVRE DU MOULIN

À DÉGUSTER

avec un pinot noir d'Alsace

1. Coupez le lard en lardons. Épluchez et émincez l'oignon. Nettoyez et émincez le chou. Dans une cocotte, faites fondre l'oignon 5 minutes sur feu moyen avec le beurre. Ajoutez les lardons, faites-les rissoler 5 minutes puis ajoutez le chou et 15 cl d'eau. Salez, poivrez, couvrez la cocotte et laissez compoter 30 à 35 minutes sur feu moyen en remuant régulièrement.
2. Préchauffez le four à 210 °C (th. 7). Dans une poêle, faites rissoler le filet de cerf 30 secondes de chaque côté sur feu vif dans l'huile. Déposez-le sur un plat, laissez-le tiédir.
3. Dans un bol, mélangez la moutarde avec la chapelure, du sel et du poivre. Badigeonnez le filet de cerf du mélange à la moutarde, déposez le filet dans un plat de cuisson. Placez le filet dans le four, faites-le cuire 12 à 15 minutes selon la cuisson désirée.
4. Ajoutez la crème dans la compotée de chou, faites cuire encore 5 minutes sans couvrir. Sortez le rôti du four, laissez-le reposer 8 à 10 minutes avant de le trancher et de le servir avec le chou.

NOISETTES DE CERF AU JUS CORSÉ, LARD CROUSTILLANT ET ENDIVES GLACÉES

Pour **4 personnes** / Préparation **40 min** / Cuisson **50 min**

800 G DE FILET DE CERF COUPÉ EN MÉDAILLONS
10 FINES TRANCHES DE LARD FUMÉ
1 C. À C. DE CONCENTRÉ DE TOMATE
40 CL DE FOND DE GIBIER (VOIR P. 78) OU DE FOND DE VEAU
6 BELLES ENDIVES
40 G DE BEURRE
30 G DE SUCRE CASSONADE
30 CL DE BIÈRE BLONDE
5 CL D'HUILE DE TOURNESOL
SEL ET POIVRE CONCASSÉ
QUELQUES FEUILLES DE ROMARIN

À DÉGUSTER

avec une bière blonde ou un coteaux-du-languedoc

1. Coupez 2 tranches de lard en petits morceaux. Dans une casserole, faites-les rissoler 3 minutes sur feu vif avec quelques gouttes d'huile. Une fois le lard doré, ajoutez le concentré de tomate et le romarin, laissez roussir 30 secondes puis versez le fond de gibier ou de veau. Faites réduire sur feu moyen pour obtenir 10 cl de jus bien corsé et fumé.

2. Nettoyez les endives, coupez-les en deux et retirez leur trognon. Dans une sauteuse, faites-les dorer 2 minutes de chaque côté sur feu moyen dans 30 g de beurre. Saupoudrez-les de sucre, laissez-les légèrement caraméliser puis versez la bière dessus. Couvrez avec un papier sulfurisé posé sur les endives, laissez-les cuire 15 à 20 minutes sur feu moyen.

3. Dans une poêle, faites rissoler le reste des tranches de lard sur feu vif avec 1 cuillerée à soupe d'huile. Égouttez-les sur une feuille de papier absorbant, laissez-les refroidir puis hachez-les grossièrement avec un couteau.

4. Filtrez la sauce dans une petite casserole propre, remettez-la à chauffer sur feu doux et ajoutez le reste du beurre en fouettant.

5. Assaisonnez les médaillons de cerf. Dans une poêle, faites-les cuire sur feu vif dans le reste de l'huile 2 à 4 minutes de chaque côté, selon la cuisson désirée. Dressez les médaillons sur les assiettes avec les endives glacées, nappez de sauce, parsemez de lard croustillant, d'une branche de romarin et dégustez.

Filet de cerf roulé au lard, sauce fruits rouges au thym

Pour **4 personnes** / Préparation **30 min** / Cuisson **45 min**

800 G DE FILET DE CERF
2 GROSSES ÉCHALOTES
4 CM DE BRANCHE DE CÉLERI
20 G DE BEURRE
60 G DE GELÉE DE FRAMBOISE
5 CL DE VINAIGRE DE FRAMBOISE
15 CL DE VIN ROUGE
20 CL DE FOND DE GIBIER (VOIR P. 78) OU DE VEAU
5 BRANCHES DE THYM
12 TRANCHES DE LARD FUMÉ
5 CL D'HUILE D'OLIVE
50 G DE FRAMBOISES
50 G DE MYRTILLES
SEL ET POIVRE DU MOULIN

À DÉGUSTER

avec un crozes-hermitage

1 Épluchez et hachez finement les échalotes, nettoyez et taillez le céleri en brunoise (cubes de 2 mm). Dans une casserole, faites-les fondre 3 minutes sur feu moyen dans le beurre. Ajoutez la gelée de framboise et le vinaigre, faites cuire 3 minutes puis ajoutez le vin rouge. Laissez réduire de moitié, ajoutez le fond de gibier ou de veau, les feuilles de 2 branches de thym. Salez, poivrez et faites réduire pour obtenir une sauce sirupeuse.

2 Préchauffez le four à 210 °C (th. 7). Assaisonnez le filet de cerf de sel et de poivre, parsemez-le avec le reste des feuilles de thym. Entourez-le de tranches de lard en serrant bien. Ficelez au besoin.

3 Déposez le rôti dans un plat à four, arrosez-le d'huile d'olive. Placez la plaque dans le four et faites cuire 15 minutes.

4 Ajoutez les fruits rouges dans la sauce chaude, faites chauffer sur feu doux sans faire bouillir. Sortez le rôti, laissez-le reposer 8 à 10 minutes avant de le trancher et de le servir avec la sauce. Accompagnez avec un gratin de légumes ou de macaronis.

Filet de cerf pané crispy sauce barbecue, pommes gaufrettes

Pour **4 personnes** / Préparation **30 min** / Marinade **2 h** / Cuisson **45 min**

600 G DE FILET DE CERF COUPÉ EN PETITS MÉDAILLONS
1 PETIT PIMENT DOUX
1 C. À C. DE CUMIN EN POUDRE
1 C. À S. DE SAUCE SOJA SALÉE
500 G DE GROSSES POMMES DE TERRE
HUILE POUR FRITURE
2 ŒUFS
150 G DE CHAPELURE
SEL ET POIVRE DU MOULIN

POUR LA SAUCE BARBECUE :

70 G D'ÉCHALOTE
200 G DE KETCHUP
60 G DE SUCRE ROUX
100 G DE SAUCE SOJA SALÉE
10 CL D'EAU
5 CL DE WHISKY
SEL ET POIVRE DU MOULIN

1 Nettoyez et hachez finement le piment, mélangez-le dans un grand récipient avec le cumin, la sauce soja, du sel et du poivre. Ajoutez les morceaux de cerf, enrobez-les dans le mélange, couvrez-les avec un papier film puis mettez-les à mariner 2 heures au réfrigérateur.

2 Réalisez la sauce barbecue : épluchez et hachez finement l'échalote. Mettez-la dans une casserole avec le ketchup, le sucre roux, la sauce soja, l'eau, le whisky, du sel et du poivre. Faites cuire le tout 10 minutes sur feu moyen puis mixez la sauce avec un mixeur plongeant. Laissez refroidir.

3 Épluchez et lavez les pommes de terre, taillez-les en gaufrettes à l'aide d'une mandoline appropriée, rincez-les sous l'eau froide. Égouttez-les, faites-les frire par petites quantités dans un bain d'huile à 180 °C. Égouttez-les sur un papier absorbant, salez-les.

4 Battez les œufs dans une assiette creuse. Panez les médaillons de cerf en les passant dans les œufs puis dans la chapelure en appuyant bien dessus pour la faire adhérer.

5 Faites frire les médaillons de cerf 4 à 5 minutes dans l'huile chaude. Égouttez-les sur une feuille de papier absorbant. Servez aussitôt avec les pommes gaufrettes et la sauce barbecue.

À DÉGUSTER

avec un côtes-du-rhône-villages Massif d'Uchaux

RÔTI DE CERF EN CROÛTE AUX TROMPETTES ET AUX MARRONS

Pour **4 personnes** / Préparation **45 min** / Cuisson **50 min**

600 G DE FILET DE CERF
2 C. À S. D'HUILE DE TOURNESOL
250 G DE TROMPETTES DES MORTS FRAÎCHES
1 ÉCHALOTE
100 G DE MARRONS EN CONSERVE
30 G DE BEURRE
300 G DE PÂTE FEUILLETÉE FRAÎCHE OU SURGELÉE EN PÂTON
1 JAUNE D'ŒUF POUR LA DORURE
1 C. À S. RASE D'HERBES DE PROVENCE
SEL ET POIVRE DU MOULIN

À DÉGUSTER

avec un saint-julien

1. Préchauffez le four à 190 °C (th. 6-7). Coupez le filet de cerf dans sa longueur. Saisissez-le sur toutes ses faces 2 minutes dans une poêle dans l'huile sur feu vif. Salez, poivrez, puis laissez-le refroidir sur une grille.

2. Nettoyez les trompettes, épluchez et hachez l'échalote, hachez grossièrement les marrons. Faites fondre l'échalote 2 minutes dans une poêle avec le beurre sur feu doux. Augmentez le feu, ajoutez les trompettes, salez, poivrez et laissez-les cuire 5 minutes sur feu vif. Égouttez-les dans une passoire puis hachez-les grossièrement.

3. Étalez la pâte en rectangle un peu plus long et beaucoup plus large que la taille du filet de cerf. Déposez le rectangle de pâte sur une plaque de four recouverte d'une feuille de papier sulfurisé et badigeonnez-la de jaune d'œuf avec un pinceau, afin que la pâte adhère bien à la viande pendant la cuisson. Posez les deux morceaux de filet de cerf dessus, puis déposez le mélange de trompettes aux marrons au milieu. Enveloppez le tout avec la pâte feuilletée. Badigeonnez la pâte de jaune d'œuf et parsemez la surface d'herbes de Provence. Mettez le rôti feuilleté à cuire 35 à 40 minutes au four.

4. Après avoir sorti le rôti feuilleté du four, laissez-le reposer 5 minutes avant de couper des tranches épaisses et de le déguster.

Terrine de cerf au genièvre

Pour **6 à 8 personnes** / Préparation **40 min** / Marinade **12 h** /
Cuisson **2 h 35** / Réfrigération **48 h**

POUR LA MARINADE :

5 CL DE GIN
1 GOUSSE D'AIL
15 BAIES DE GENIÈVRE

500 G DE VIANDE DE CERF
250 G DE POITRINE DE PORC
250 G DE GORGE DE PORC
1 MORCEAU DE CRÉPINE DE 25 X 25 CM ENVIRON
1 C. À S. DE VINAIGRE BLANC
150 G D'OIGNON
50 G D'ÉCHALOTES
20 G DE BEURRE
100 G DE LAIT
1 ŒUF
1 C. À S. RASE DE SEL
1 C. À C. BOMBÉE DE POIVRE CONCASSÉ

—

À DÉGUSTER

avec un cornas

1. La veille, coupez les viandes en petits morceaux, mélangez-les dans un récipient avec le gin, l'ail haché et les baies de genièvre concassées grossièrement. Couvrez le récipient de film alimentaire et placez 12 heures au réfrigérateur.

2. Mettez la crépine à tremper dans un bol d'eau froide avec le vinaigre. Épluchez et hachez l'oignon et les échalotes. Faites-les fondre 5 minutes dans une casserole sur feu moyen avec le beurre. Éteignez le feu, ajoutez le lait.

3. Hachez les viandes au hachoir avec la grosse grille. Mettez les viandes hachées dans un saladier avec le mélange à l'oignon, échalote et lait, l'œuf, le sel et le poivre. Mélangez pendant 4 à 5 minutes avec la main pour obtenir une farce homogène.

4. Préchauffez le four à 160 °C (th. 5-6). Rincez et pressez la crépine entre vos mains.

5. Chemisez une terrine de 20 x 12 cm environ avec la crépine en la faisant largement dépasser des bords. Transvasez la farce dans la terrine en tassant bien avec une cuillère. Rabattez la crépine sur la farce, coupez l'excédent si nécessaire, couvrez la terrine avec son couvercle ou une feuille de papier aluminium. Déposez la terrine dans un bain-marie au four, faites cuire la terrine 1 h 30. Retirez le couvercle de la terrine ou le papier aluminium, augmentez la température du four à 190 °C (th. 6-7), prolongez la cuisson 30 minutes.

6. Laissez refroidir la terrine, posez son couvercle dessus, placez-la 48 heures au réfrigérateur avant de la déguster accompagnée de pickles (voir p. 82) ou de confiture d'oignons (voir p. 82).

Terrine de cerf aux noisettes et aux pruneaux

Pour **6 à 8 personnes** / Préparation **40 min** / Marinade **12 h** / Cuisson **2 h 40** / Réfrigération **48 h**

POUR LA MARINADE :

5 CL DE COGNAC
1 BRIN DE THYM
1 BRANCHE DE ROMARIN

500 G DE VIANDE DE CERF
200 G DE POITRINE DE PORC
200 G DE GORGE DE PORC
120 G DE FOIE DE CERF (OU À DÉFAUT DE FOIE DE PORC)
1 OIGNON MOYEN
1 GROSSE ÉCHALOTE
20 G DE BEURRE
10 CL DE FOND DE VEAU
8 PRUNEAUX MOELLEUX
60 G DE NOISETTES ENTIÈRES DÉCORTIQUÉES
1 C. À S. DE CRÈME FRAÎCHE
30 CM DE BARDE
15 CL DE GELÉE (RÉALISÉE AVEC DE LA GELÉE DÉSHYDRATÉE)
1 C. À S. LÉGÈREMENT BOMBÉE DE SEL
1 C. À S. RASE DE POIVRE MOULU

1 – La veille, coupez la viande de cerf, la poitrine, la gorge et le foie en petits morceaux, mettez-les dans un récipient. Arrosez-les de cognac, ajoutez les brins de thym et de romarin. Couvrez avec un film alimentaire et mettez la préparation à mariner 12 heures au réfrigérateur.

2 – Le lendemain, sortez les viandes du réfrigérateur, hachez-les au hachoir avec une grosse grille.

3 – Épluchez et hachez l'oignon et l'échalote. Faites-les fondre 5 minutes dans une poêle dans le beurre sur feu moyen. Ajoutez le fond de veau, laissez réduire de moitié puis laissez refroidir.

4 – Préchauffez le four à 160 °C (th. 5-6). Coupez les pruneaux en petits morceaux. Mélangez les viandes hachées avec les morceaux de pruneau, les noisettes entières, l'oignon et l'échalote avec le fond de veau réduit, la crème fraîche, le sel et le poivre.

5 – Chemisez une terrine de 20 x 12 cm environ avec la barde en la laissant dépasser légèrement sur les côtés. Mettez la farce dans la terrine et tassez bien, rabattez la barde sur le dessus, couvrez la terrine. Placez la terrine dans un bain-marie et enfournez pour 2 heures. Au bout de ce temps, augmentez la température à 190 °C (th. 6-7), retirez le couvercle et prolongez la cuisson de 30 minutes.

6 – Sortez la terrine, laissez-la refroidir, versez la gelée, posez son couvercle dessus. Placez-la 48 heures au réfrigérateur avant de la déguster.

À DÉGUSTER

avec un madiran

LE CHEVREUIL

CIVET DE CHEVREUIL AU CHOCOLAT

Pour **4 personnes** / Préparation **30 min** / Marinade **12 h** / Cuisson **2 h**

POUR LA MARINADE :

1 OIGNON JAUNE
2 ÉCHALOTES
1 CAROTTE
1 BRANCHE DE THYM
60 CL DE VIN ROUGE
1 EXPRESSO TRÈS FORT

1,2 KG D'ÉPAULE DE CHEVREUIL COUPÉE EN MORCEAUX
3 C. À S. D'HUILE DE TOURNESOL
1 C. À S. BOMBÉE DE FARINE
1 C. À S. DE SUCRE
40 CL DE FOND DE VEAU OU DE GIBIER
30 G DE CHOCOLAT NOIR À 70 % DE CACAO MINIMUM
SEL ET POIVRE DU MOULIN

À DÉGUSTER

avec un madiran

1 La veille, épluchez l'oignon et les échalotes et émincez-les. Pelez et coupez la carotte en dés.

2 Dans un grand récipient, mettez les morceaux de chevreuil avec l'oignon, les échalotes, la carotte et le thym. Ajoutez le vin rouge et le café, mélangez, couvrez la viande et placez le tout 12 heures au frais.

3 Le jour même, égouttez la viande. Retirez bien l'excédent de marinade avec de l'essuie-tout.

4 Dans une cocotte, faites saisir la viande avec l'huile 6 à 8 minutes sur feu vif. Saupoudrez de la farine, puis faites roussir 2 minutes de plus en mélangeant.

5 Versez la marinade et sa garniture dans la cocotte. Ajoutez le sucre, salez et poivrez. Portez le tout à ébullition, puis laissez ainsi cuire 5 minutes sur feu vif.

6 Ajoutez le fond de veau ou de gibier et couvrez la cocotte. Laissez cuire 1 h 45 sur feu moyen en écumant et en remuant régulièrement.

7 Après avoir vérifié que la viande est moelleuse, retirez-la de la cocotte et réservez. Faites réduire la sauce jusqu'à ce qu'elle devienne onctueuse. Filtrez-la, puis nettoyez la cocotte.

8 Remettez la sauce dans la cocotte. Faites chauffer sur feu doux et ajoutez le chocolat en fouettant jusqu'à ce qu'il ait complètement fondu. Ajoutez alors la viande, réchauffez le tout sur feu très doux. Servez avec des tagliatelles.

TAJINE DE CHEVREUIL AU POTIMARRON ET AUX RAISINS SECS

Pour **4 personnes** / Préparation **30 min** / Cuisson **2 h 30**

1,3 KG D'ÉPAULE DE CHEVREUIL COUPÉE EN GROS MORCEAUX
3 CM DE RACINE DE GINGEMBRE
2 OIGNONS ROUGES MOYENS
3 GOUSSES D'AIL
1 C. À S. RASE DE CORIANDRE EN POUDRE
1 C. À C. BOMBÉE DE CURCUMA EN POUDRE
1 C. À S. BOMBÉE DE GRAINES DE CUMIN
1 C. À S. RASE DE GINGEMBRE EN POUDRE
8 CL D'HUILE D'OLIVE
3 C. À S. DE MIEL LIQUIDE
120 G DE GROS RAISINS SECS
600 G DE POTIMARRON
4 BRINS DE CORIANDRE FRAÎCHEMENT CISELÉE
SEL ET POIVRE DU MOULIN

1 Préchauffez le four à 150 °C (th. 5). Épluchez et râpez la racine de gingembre. Pelez et émincez grossièrement les oignons et l'ail. Dans un bol, mélangez la coriandre en poudre avec le curcuma, le cumin, le gingembre en poudre et le gingembre râpé.

2 Dans une grande cocotte, faites saisir la viande sur toutes ses faces avec la moitié de l'huile d'olive 6 à 8 minutes. Salez et poivrez. Baissez le feu, ajoutez les oignons et l'ail, et faites-les rissoler 6 à 8 minutes en remuant régulièrement. Ajoutez le mélange d'herbes et d'épices et laissez roussir 2 minutes. Ajoutez 2 cuillerées à soupe de miel, laissez légèrement caraméliser 1 minute.

3 Couvrez d'eau froide et portez à ébullition. Couvrez la cocotte, puis placez-la au four 1 h 30 sans soulever le couvercle.

4 Au bout de ce temps, ajoutez les raisins secs dans la cocotte. Mélangez et remettez à cuire dans le four 30 minutes.

5 Pendant ce temps, nettoyez le potimarron, puis coupez-le en cubes. Dans une poêle, faites-le saisir avec le reste de l'huile d'olive 3 minutes sur feu vif. Ajoutez 1 cuillerée de miel et laissez caraméliser 2 minutes.

6 Sortez la cocotte du four et ajoutez le potimarron. Enfournez à nouveau et laissez cuire 15 minutes à découvert. Parsemez de coriandre et servez.

À DÉGUSTER

avec un pic-saint-loup

Goulasch de chevreuil aux airelles

Pour **4 personnes** / Préparation **20 min** / Cuisson **2 h 30**

1,2 KG D'ÉPAULE DE CHEVREUIL COUPÉE EN MORCEAUX
4 BAIES DE GENIÈVRE
1 C. À C. DE GINGEMBRE
1 C. À C. DE CANNELLE
1 C. À C. DE PIMENT DOUX
2 CAROTTES
1 POIREAU
4 GROSSES ÉCHALOTES
20 G DE BEURRE
5 CL D'HUILE DE TOURNESOL
1 BRANCHE DE THYM SÉCHÉ
1 FEUILLE DE LAURIER SÉCHÉE
40 CL DE VIN ROUGE
3 GROSSES C. À S. DE CRÈME FRAÎCHE
150 G D'AIRELLES EN BOCAL PRÉALABLEMENT ÉGOUTTÉES
SEL ET POIVRE DU MOULIN

1 À l'aide d'un couteau, hachez les baies de genièvre. Placez-les dans un grand saladier et ajoutez le gingembre, la cannelle et le piment. Placez-y les morceaux de chevreuil, salez, poivrez, puis mélangez le tout à la main, afin de bien imprégner la chair des épices.

2 Épluchez, lavez et émincez finement les carottes et le poireau. Épluchez et hachez les échalotes.

3 Dans une cocotte, faites fondre le beurre avec l'huile sur feu moyen, puis faites revenir la viande 6 à 8 minutes sur feu vif en remuant. Ajoutez les échalotes, le poireau et les carottes, et laissez cuire 6 à 8 minutes de plus en mélangeant régulièrement. Les légumes doivent être fondants. Ajoutez le thym et le laurier, et versez le vin ainsi que 30 cl d'eau.

4 Couvrez et laissez cuire sur feu doux pendant 2 heures jusqu'à ce que la viande soit bien fondante. Si nécessaire, ajoutez de l'eau pendant la cuisson.

5 Mettez la crème et les airelles dans la cocotte. Faites mijoter 10 minutes sur feu doux, puis servez sans attendre avec des pommes de terre vapeur persillées.

À DÉGUSTER

avec un terrasses-du-Larzac

Civet de chevreuil aux poires et aux pleurotes

Pour **4 personnes** / Préparation **30 min** / Marinade **12 h** / Cuisson **2 h**

POUR LA MARINADE :

1 GROS OIGNON JAUNE
1 GOUSSE D'AIL
2 CAROTTES
1 PETITE BRANCHE DE ROMARIN FRAIS
1 FEUILLE DE LAURIER SÉCHÉE
3 BAIES DE GENIÈVRE
5 CL DE VINAIGRE BALSAMIQUE
75 CL DE VIN BLANC

1,2 KG D'ÉPAULE DE CHEVREUIL COUPÉE EN MORCEAUX
5 CL D'HUILE D'OLIVE
15 CL DE FOND DE VEAU OU DE GIBIER
1 C. À S. BOMBÉE DE FARINE
2 POIRES
50 G DE BEURRE
1 C. À S. DE MIEL
400 G DE PLEUROTES
SEL ET POIVRE DU MOULIN

À DÉGUSTER

avec un pauillac

1 La veille, épluchez et émincez l'oignon et l'ail. Épluchez, lavez et coupez les carottes en cubes. Dans un grand saladier, mélangez la viande avec l'oignon, l'ail, et les carottes, puis ajoutez le romarin, le laurier, les baies de genièvre, le vinaigre balsamique et le vin blanc. Poivrez, puis couvrez avec un film alimentaire. Placez le tout 12 heures au réfrigérateur.

2 Le jour même, égouttez la viande. Retirez bien l'excédent de marinade avec de l'essuie-tout.

3 Dans une cocotte, faites saisir la viande avec l'huile d'olive 6 à 8 minutes sur feu vif. Saupoudrez de la farine, laissez roussir 2 minutes sur feu vif, puis versez la marinade et sa garniture dans la cocotte. Faites bouillir 5 minutes, ajoutez le fond de veau ou de gibier et salez. Portez à ébullition, couvrez la cocotte, puis laissez cuire 1 h 30 sur feu doux.

4 Pendant ce temps, épluchez les poires et coupez-les en quartiers. Dans une poêle, faites-les saisir avec la moitié du beurre 5 minutes. Ajoutez le miel et laissez caraméliser 3 minutes. Réservez.

5 Nettoyez les pleurotes et coupez-les en morceaux. Dans une autre poêle, faites-les cuire avec le reste du beurre 6 à 8 minutes sur feu moyen. Salez, poivrez et réservez.

6 Lorsque la viande est cuite (elle doit être fondante), ajoutez les pleurotes et les poires. Faites cuire encore 10 minutes sur feu moyen, puis servez.

PARMENTIER DE CHEVREUIL AU CÉLERI

Pour **4 personnes** / Préparation **45 min** / Cuisson **2 h 25**

800 G D'ÉPAULE DE CHEVREUIL COUPÉE EN PETITS MORCEAUX
1 GROS OIGNON
2 GOUSSES D'AIL
3 CM DE RACINE DE GINGEMBRE
1 CAROTTE
5 CL D'HUILE D'OLIVE
½ C. À C. DE CANNELLE EN POUDRE
2 PINCÉES DE CUMIN EN POUDRE
2 C. À S. DE SIROP D'ÉRABLE
2 C. À S. DE CRÈME FRAÎCHE ÉPAISSE
2 GROSSES C. À S. DE CHAPELURE
20 G DE BEURRE COUPÉ EN PETIT MORCEAUX
SEL ET POIVRE DU MOULIN

POUR LA PURÉE :

1 KG DE CÉLERI-RAVE
120 G DE BEURRE

À DÉGUSTER

avec un saint-julien

1 Épluchez et hachez l'oignon et l'ail. Pelez et râpez le gingembre. Épluchez, lavez et coupez la carotte en petits morceaux.

2 Dans une cocotte, faites saisir la viande avec l'huile d'olive 5 minutes sur feu vif. Baissez le feu et ajoutez l'oignon, la carotte, l'ail et le gingembre. Laissez rissoler 5 minutes. Ajoutez ensuite la cannelle, le cumin et le sirop d'érable. Salez, poivrez et faites légèrement caraméliser 5 minutes en mélangeant. Ajoutez 40 cl d'eau et couvrez. Laissez ainsi cuire 1 h 30 sur feu doux en mélangeant régulièrement.

3 Pendant ce temps, épluchez, lavez et coupez le céleri en morceaux. Faites-le cuire 30 minutes dans un grand volume d'eau bouillante salée, départ eau froide. Égouttez-le et laissez-le 5 minutes dans la passoire. Mettez-le ensuite dans un récipient haut, ajoutez le beurre et la crème. Salez et poivrez. Réduisez le tout en une purée bien lisse à l'aide d'un mixeur plongeant.

4 Préchauffez le gril du four à 180 °C (th. 6). Lorsque la viande est cuite (elle doit être fondante), laissez-la tiédir dans la cocotte, puis effilochez-la grossièrement à l'aide d'une fourchette. Sortez la viande de la cocotte à l'aide d'une écumoire et faites réduire le jus de cuisson et la garniture. Hors du feu, remettez la viande et mélangez bien.

5 Dans un grand plat à gratin, mettez la viande et sa garniture. Étalez la purée par-dessus, saupoudrez de chapelure et ajoutez le beurre. Enfournez à mi-hauteur et faites gratiner 20 minutes. Servez bien chaud.

EFFILOCHÉE DE CHEVREUIL CONFIT AUX OIGNONS ET À LA MOUTARDE

Pour **4 personnes** / Préparation **45 min** / Cuisson **4 h 45**

700 G D'ÉPAULE DE CHEVREUIL COUPÉE EN 2 MORCEAUX
1 C. À S. DE CUMIN EN POUDRE
2 GROSSES C. À S. DE KETCHUP
3 C. À S. DE MOUTARDE FORTE
8 CL DE VINAIGRE DE VIN ROUGE
50 G DE SUCRE CASSONADE
3 OIGNONS MOYENS
5 CL D'HUILE D'OLIVE
30 G DE BEURRE
SEL ET POIVRE DU MOULIN

À DÉGUSTER

avec un saumur-champigny

1 Préchauffez le four à 130 °C (th. 4-5). Dans un bol, mélangez le cumin, le ketchup, la moutarde, le vinaigre et la cassonade, puis salez et poivrez. Épluchez et émincez les oignons.

2 Dans une cocotte, faites saisir les 2 morceaux d'épaule avec l'huile d'olive 5 minutes de chaque côté sur feu vif. Une fois dorée, retirez et réservez la viande et dégraissez la cocotte.

3 Faites fondre le beurre dans la cocotte sur feu doux, ajoutez les oignons, laissez légèrement dorer 15 minutes sur feu moyen en remuant régulièrement. Ajoutez la viande et la sauce épicée, puis ajoutez 25 cl d'eau. Couvrez, puis enfournez 4 h 30, en tournant la viande toutes les heures.

4 Lorsque la viande est cuite (elle doit être très fondante) et le jus réduit, sortez la cocotte. Laissez reposer la viande 15 minutes sans retirer le couvercle, puis effilochez-la à l'aide d'une fourchette. Mélangez avec les oignons, servez accompagné de salsifis rôtis au beurre persillé (voir p. 94).

Côtelettes de chevreuil, sauce poivrade

Pour **4 personnes** / Préparation **30 min** / Marinade **6 h** / Cuisson **30 min**

16 CÔTELETTES DE CHEVREUIL
1 OIGNON
1 CAROTTE
4 GOUSSES D'AIL
8 CL D'HUILE D'OLIVE
40 CL DE VIN ROUGE
40 CL DE VIN BLANC
8 CL DE VINAIGRE DE VIN
2 BRANCHES DE THYM
1 FEUILLE DE LAURIER
80 G DE GELÉE DE GROSEILLES
100 G D'AIRELLES EN BOCAL OU SURGELÉES
20 CL DE FOND DE GIBIER
SEL, POIVRE DU MOULIN

—

À DÉGUSTER

avec un châteauneuf-du-pape

1 Épluchez, lavez et émincez la carotte. Épluchez et émincez l'oignon. Épluchez les gousses d'ail. Faites revenir l'ensemble 3 minutes dans une casserole sur feu moyen avec la moitié de l'huile d'olive. Ajoutez le vin rouge, le vin blanc, le vinaigre, le thym, le laurier et du sel. Faites bouillir 5 minutes, puis éteignez le feu et laissez tiédir la marinade.

2 Déposez les côtelettes dans un plat creux, puis versez la marinade tiède dessus. Couvrez avec un film alimentaire et mettez la préparation à mariner 6 heures.

3 Égouttez les côtelettes de la marinade. Filtrez 50 cl de marinade à l'aide d'une passoire fine. Saisissez les côtelettes 2 minutes de chaque côté dans un sautoir sur feu vif avec le reste de l'huile d'olive. Déposez les côtelettes dans une assiette, dégraissez le sautoir puis déglacez-le avec la marinade filtrée ; faites-la réduire pour qu'il en reste 15 cl environ. Ajoutez ensuite le fond de gibier, du sel et du poivre et faites réduire de moitié sur feu vif. Ajoutez la gelée de groseilles en fouettant, laissez cuire 3 minutes sur feu vif puis ajoutez les airelles. Mettez les côtelettes dans la sauce, faites cuire le tout 5 minutes sur feu moyen et servez.

4 Accompagnez avec une purée de céleri (voir p. 90) parfumée à la sauge.

Daube de chevreuil aux carottes

Pour **4 personnes** / Préparation **30 min** / Marinade **12 h** / Cuisson **2 h**

POUR LA MARINADE :

1 GROS OIGNON
1 ORANGE BIO
2 BÂTONS DE CANNELLE
10 GRAINS DE POIVRE NOIR
1 C. À C. DE GINGEMBRE EN POUDRE
1 C. À C. DE SUCRE CASSONADE
75 CL DE VIN BLANC

1,2 KG D'ÉPAULE DE CHEVREUIL COUPÉE EN MORCEAUX
700 G DE CAROTTES
5 CL D'HUILE D'OLIVE
1 C. À S. DE FARINE
25 CL DE FOND DE VEAU OU DE GIBIER
SEL ET POIVRE DU MOULIN

1 La veille, épluchez et émincez l'oignon. Pressez l'orange et râpez le zeste. Dans un grand récipient, placez l'oignon, la cannelle, les grains de poivre, le gingembre, la cassonade, le jus et le zeste de l'orange, et la viande. Mélangez, versez le vin blanc, puis couvrez de film alimentaire. Laissez reposer 12 heures au réfrigérateur.

2 Le jour même, épluchez, lavez et coupez les carottes en rondelles épaisses. Égouttez les morceaux de viande et l'oignon.

3 Dans une grande cocotte, saisissez la viande et l'oignon avec l'huile d'olive 5 minutes sur feu vif. Une fois dorés, saupoudrez-les de farine et laissez roussir 2 minutes. Ajoutez la marinade, puis portez à ébullition pendant 5 minutes. Ajoutez les carottes, le fond de veau ou de gibier et, si nécessaire, un peu d'eau afin de couvrir. Salez et poivrez. Couvrez et faites cuire 1 h 45 sur feu moyen en mélangeant régulièrement.

À DÉGUSTER

avec un bourgueil

CHEVREUIL À LA MOUTARDE FAÇON *PULLED PORK*

Pour **4 personnes** / Préparation **30 min** / Cuisson **4 h 40**

800 G D'ÉPAULE DE CHEVREUIL COUPÉE EN MORCEAUX
2 GOUSSES D'AIL
1 GROS OIGNON
2 GROSSES C. À S. DE MOUTARDE FORTE
1 C. À C. BOMBÉE DE PAPRIKA
1 C. À C. BOMBÉE DE CUMIN EN POUDRE
15 CL DE KETCHUP
8 CL DE SAUCE WORCESTERSHIRE
5 CL DE VINAIGRE DE VIN ROUGE
40 G DE SUCRE CASSONADE
5 CL D'HUILE D'OLIVE
SEL ET POIVRE DU MOULIN

1 Préchauffez le four à 140 °C (th. 4-5). Épluchez et émincez l'ail et l'oignon. Dans un bol, mélangez la moutarde, le paprika, le cumin, le ketchup, la sauce Worcestershire, le vinaigre et la cassonade. Salez et poivrez.

2 Dans une cocotte, faites saisir la viande avec l'huile d'olive 8 à 10 minutes sur feu vif. Une fois dorée, ajoutez l'ail et l'oignon. Laissez cuire 5 minutes sur feu moyen, puis ajoutez la sauce épicée ainsi que 25 cl d'eau. Couvrez et enfournez pour 4 h 30 en tournant la viande toutes les heures environ. Si nécessaire, ajoutez un peu d'eau pendant la cuisson.

3 Au sortir du four, laissez reposer la viande 20 minutes, puis effilochez-la avec une fourchette. Servez avec un bon pain frais ou grillé.

À DÉGUSTER

avec un chinon

STAUB

CHEVREUIL CONFIT AU FOUR À LA BIÈRE BRUNE

Pour **4 personnes** / Préparation **20 min** / Cuisson **4 h 30**

1,2 KG D'ÉPAULE DE CHEVREUIL COUPÉE EN MORCEAUX
2 GROS OIGNONS
5 CL D'HUILE DE TOURNESOL
30 G DE BEURRE
60 G DE SUCRE CASSONADE
1 C. À S. RASE DE FARINE
2 PINCÉES DE CANNELLE
2 PINCÉES DE QUATRE-ÉPICES
40 CL DE BIÈRE BRUNE
25 CL DE FOND DE VEAU OU DE GIBIER
1 TRANCHE DE PAIN D'ÉPICE
SEL ET POIVRE DU MOULIN

À DÉGUSTER

avec un bière brune
ou un crozes-hermitage

1 Préchauffez le four à 130 °C (th. 4-5). Épluchez et émincez les oignons.

2 Dans une cocotte, faites saisir les morceaux de chevreuil avec l'huile 5 minutes sur feu vif. Retirez et réservez la viande, puis dégraissez la cocotte.

3 Dans la cocotte, faites fondre le beurre. Ajoutez les oignons, salez, poivrez et faites cuire 10 minutes sur feu moyen. Ajoutez la cassonade et laissez caraméliser 8 à 10 minutes.

4 Remettez les morceaux de viande dans la cocotte. Ajoutez également la farine, la cannelle et le quatre-épices. Salez, poivrez et mélangez le tout 3 minutes sur feu vif. Versez la bière, puis portez à ébullition pendant 3 minutes. Ajoutez le fond de veau ou de gibier et la tranche de pain d'épice émiettée. Couvrez, portez à ébullition et enfournez pour 4 heures, en remuant délicatement la viande toutes les heures.

5 Au sortir du four, laissez reposer 15 minutes avant de servir avec des pommes paille ou des frites fraîches.

Chevreuil à l'orange façon osso-buco

Pour **4 personnes** / Préparation **30 min** / Cuisson **2 h**

4 TRANCHES DE 250 G ENVIRON DE GIGUE DE CHEVREUIL
1 CAROTTE
2 BRANCHES DE CÉLERI
1 GROS OIGNON
2 ORANGES
4 BRANCHES DE PERSIL
60 G DE FARINE
5 CL D'HUILE D'OLIVE
4 GOUSSES D'AIL ENTIÈRES
40 CL DE VIN BLANC
40 CL DE FOND DE VEAU
SEL ET POIVRE DU MOULIN

À DÉGUSTER

avec un coteaux-du-languedoc blanc ou un fiefs-vendéens rouge

1 Préchauffez le four à 160 °C (th. 5-6). Épluchez, lavez et taillez la carotte et le céleri-branche en petits cubes. Épluchez et hachez l'oignon. Lavez, zestez et pressez les 2 oranges. Lavez et hachez le persil. Farinez les tranches de gigue.

2 Dans une grande cocotte, faites chauffer l'huile et saisissez les tranches de gigue 5 minutes de chaque côté sur feu vif. Retirez-les et réservez.

3 Dans la cocotte, ajoutez les cubes de carotte et de céleri, l'oignon et les gousses d'ail non épluchées. Laissez rissoler 5 minutes sur feu vif en mélangeant.

4 Déposez la viande sur les légumes. Déglacez avec le vin blanc, ajoutez le jus des oranges et 1/3 des zestes. Faites bouillir 5 minutes sur feu vif.

5 Ajoutez le fond de veau, salez et poivrez. Couvrez la cocotte et faites cuire 2 heures au four en retournant les tranches après 1 heure de cuisson.

6 Au sortir du four, parsemez la viande avec le reste des zestes d'oranges mélangés au persil. Servez avec des tagliatelles.

Cocotte de chevreuil au vin cuit et au vinaigre

Pour **4 personnes** / Préparation **30 min** / Marinade **12 h** / Cuisson **2 h 15**

POUR LA MARINADE :

1 OIGNON JAUNE
2 ÉCHALOTES
2 GOUSSES D'AIL
2 CAROTTES
1 BRANCHE DE THYM FRAIS
1 FEUILLE DE LAURIER SÉCHÉE
50 CL DE VIN ROUGE
5 CL DE VINAIGRE BALSAMIQUE
5 CL DE VINAIGRE DE VIN
15 CL DE PORTO OU DE MADÈRE

1,2 KG D'ÉPAULE DE CHEVREUIL COUPÉE EN MORCEAUX
5 CL D'HUILE DE TOURNESOL
1 C. À S. BOMBÉE DE FARINE
40 CL DE FOND DE VEAU OU DE GIBIER
1 C. À S. DE SUCRE
600 G DE POMMES DE TERRE GRENAILLE
25 G DE BEURRE
1 BOTTE DE CIBOULETTE FINEMENT CISELÉE
SEL ET POIVRE DU MOULIN

1 La veille, épluchez l'oignon, les échalotes et l'ail, puis émincez-les. Pelez et coupez les carottes en dés. Dans un grand récipient, mettez les morceaux de chevreuil avec l'oignon, l'ail, les échalotes, les carottes, le thym et le laurier. Ajoutez le vin rouge, les 2 vinaigres et le porto ou le madère, et mélangez bien. Couvrez de film alimentaire et placez 12 heures au réfrigérateur.

2 Le jour même, égouttez la viande. Retirez bien l'excédent de marinade avec de l'essuie-tout.

3 Dans une cocotte, faites saisir la viande avec la moitié de l'huile 6 à 8 minutes sur feu vif. Saupoudrez de farine et faites roussir 2 minutes en mélangeant. Ajoutez la marinade et sa garniture, le sucre, salez et poivrez. Portez à ébullition pendant 5 minutes, puis ajoutez le fond de veau ou de gibier. Couvrez et laissez cuire 1 h 30 sur feu moyen en écumant et en remuant régulièrement.

4 Pendant ce temps, lavez les pommes de terre. Dans une poêle, faites-les rissoler avec le beurre et le reste de l'huile 15 minutes sur feu moyen. Réservez.

5 Après 1 h 30 de cuisson, ajoutez les pommes de terre dans la cocotte. Baissez le feu et prolongez la cuisson de 30 minutes.

6 Lorsque la viande est cuite (elle doit être moelleuse), parsemez de ciboulette juste au moment de servir et dégustez.

À DÉGUSTER

avec un madiran

CURRY ROUGE DE CHEVREUIL

Pour **4 personnes** / Préparation **30 min** / Marinade **4 h** / Cuisson **1 h 30**

POUR LA MARINADE :

50 G DE RACINE DE GINGEMBRE FRAIS
2 PIMENTS ROUGES
SEL

800 G D'ÉPAULE DE CHEVREUIL COUPÉE EN MORCEAUX
2 OIGNONS ROUGES
4 GOUSSES D'AIL
5 CL D'HUILE DE TOURNESOL
2 GROSSES C. À S. DE PÂTE DE CURRY ROUGE
30 CL DE LAIT DE COCO
1 PETIT BOUQUET DE CORIANDRE FRAÎCHE
SEL ET POIVRE DU MOULIN

À DÉGUSTER

avec un alsace pinot noir ou un bandol rouge

1 Épluchez le gingembre et râpez-le dans un grand récipient. Nettoyez et hachez finement les piments, puis mélangez-les avec le gingembre. Ajoutez les morceaux de chevreuil et salez. Mélangez afin de bien enrober la viande. Couvrez de film alimentaire et placez 4 heures au réfrigérateur.

2 Épluchez et hachez les oignons et l'ail.

3 Dans une grande cocotte, faites saisir les morceaux de viande, le gingembre et le piment avec l'huile 6 à 8 minutes sur feu vif. Retirez la viande, baissez le feu et mettez les oignons et l'ail. Laissez fondre 5 à 7 minutes sur feu moyen.

4 Remettez la viande dans la cocotte. Ajoutez la pâte de curry rouge, enrobez-en bien les morceaux et laissez roussir 5 minutes sur feu moyen. Versez le lait de coco et couvrez d'eau. Salez légèrement. Portez à ébullition, puis couvrez. Laissez cuire 1 h 30 environ sur feu moyen en remuant régulièrement. Si nécessaire, ajoutez un peu d'eau pendant la cuisson.

5 Effeuillez et ciselez la coriandre, et ajoutez-la dans la sauce juste au moment de servir. Dégustez avec un chou rouge confit à l'orange (voir p. 92) ou un riz grillé.

Rôti de chevreuil aux épices, échalotes et oranges

Pour **6 à 8 personnes** / Préparation **30 min** / Marinade **12 h** / Cuisson **45 min**

POUR LA MARINADE :

2 ORANGES
5 CL D'HUILE D'OLIVE
1 C. À C. RASE DE CANNELLE
1 C. À S. RASE DE QUATRE-ÉPICES
1 C. À C. BOMBÉE DE GINGEMBRE EN POUDRE

1,2 KG ENVIRON DE RÔTI DANS LA GIGUE
12 GROSSES ÉCHALOTES
50 CL D'HUILE D'ARACHIDE
2 C. À S. D'HUILE D'OLIVE
15 CL DE FOND DE VEAU OU DE GIBIER
20 G DE BEURRE
SEL ET POIVRE DU MOULIN

À DÉGUSTER

avec un cahors

1 La veille, lavez, zestez et pressez les oranges. Dans un récipient, mélangez le jus et les zestes avec l'huile d'olive, la cannelle, le quatre-épices, le gingembre et du poivre.

2 Mettez le rôti de chevreuil dans un plat pas trop large à bords hauts. Versez la marinade sur le rôti et enrobez-le bien, puis couvrez de film alimentaire. Placez le plat au réfrigérateur 12 heures en retournant le rôti après 6 heures pour qu'il s'imprègne bien de la marinade sur tous les côtés.

3 Le jour même, épluchez les échalotes en les gardant entières. Mettez-les dans une casserole, couvrez-les d'huile d'arachide et faites chauffer sur feu doux. Laissez les échalotes confire 15 minutes, éteignez le feu et laissez refroidir les échalotes dans l'huile avant de les égoutter.

4 Préchauffez le four à 210 °C (th. 7). Égouttez le rôti en l'essuyant légèrement. Dans une plaque à rôtir, faites-le saisir avec l'huile d'olive 5 minutes sur feu vif sur toutes ses faces.

5 Placez la plaque dans le four et faites cuire le rôti 20 minutes pour une cuisson rosée. Sortez-le du four, couvrez-le de papier aluminium et laissez reposer 10 minutes.

6 Dégraissez la plaque de cuisson, posez-la sur le feu et déglacez avec la marinade. Laissez réduire de moitié. Ajoutez le fond de veau ou de gibier, le beurre, du sel et du poivre. Faites bouillir 3 minutes en fouettant. Ajoutez les échalotes confites et laissez chauffer 5 minutes sur feu doux. Réservez.

7 Coupez le rôti en tranches, servez avec la sauce et les échalotes. Accompagnez avec des légumes rôtis, des endives caramélisées ou une purée de pommes de terre (voir p. 90).

CIVET DE CHEVREUIL AU GENIÈVRE ET AUX FRUITS ROUGES

Pour **4 personnes** / Préparation **30 min** / Marinade **12 h** / Cuisson **2 h**

POUR LA MARINADE :

1 OIGNON JAUNE
2 ÉCHALOTES
1 CAROTTE
1 BRANCHE DE THYM
1 FEUILLE DE LAURIER
2 BAIES DE GENIÈVRE
60 CL DE VIN ROUGE
8 CL DE CRÈME DE CASSIS
5 CL DE SIROP DE FRAISE OU DE CASSIS

1,2 KG DE VIANDE DE CHEVREUIL COUPÉE EN MORCEAUX
3 C. À S. D'HUILE DE TOURNESOL
1 C. À S. BOMBÉE DE FARINE
40 CL DE FOND DE VEAU OU DE GIBIER
1 C. À S. DE SUCRE
2 C. À S. DE CONFITURE DE CERISES NOIRES
125 G DE MYRTILLES FRAÎCHES
125 G DE GROSEILLES FRAÎCHES
SEL ET POIVRE DU MOULIN

À DÉGUSTER

avec un côte-du-marmandais

1 La veille, épluchez l'oignon et les échalotes, et émincez-les. Épluchez, lavez et coupez la carotte en dés. Dans un grand récipient, mettez les morceaux de chevreuil avec l'oignon, les échalotes, la carotte, le thym, le laurier et les baies de genièvre. Ajoutez le vin rouge, la crème de cassis et le sirop de fraise. Mélangez, couvrez de film alimentaire et placez 12 heures au réfrigérateur.

2 Le jour même, égouttez la viande. Retirez bien l'excédent de marinade avec de l'essuie-tout.

3 Dans une cocotte, faites saisir la viande avec l'huile 6 à 8 minutes sur feu vif. Saupoudrez de farine et faites roussir 2 minutes en mélangeant. Versez la marinade et sa garniture, le sucre, salez et poivrez. Portez à ébullition pendant 5 minutes, puis ajoutez le fond de veau ou de gibier. Couvrez et laissez cuire 1 h 45 sur feu moyen en écumant et en remuant régulièrement.

4 Lorsque la viande est cuite (elle doit être moelleuse), retirez-la de la cocotte, puis faites réduire la sauce jusqu'à ce qu'elle devienne onctueuse. Filtrez la sauce à l'aide d'un chinois ou d'une passoire fine et nettoyez la cocotte.

5 Remettez la sauce dans la cocotte. Faites chauffer sur feu doux, ajoutez la viande et la confiture. Laissez mijoter 10 minutes sur feu très doux. Ajoutez les myrtilles et les groseilles, et laissez encore cuire 5 minutes sans faire bouillir.

6 Servez ce civet accompagné de pommes paille.

Daube de chevreuil au vin rouge et à l'ail

Pour **4 personnes** / Préparation **30 min** / Cuisson **2 h 30**

800-900 G DE VIANDE DE CHEVREUIL
2 OIGNONS JAUNES MOYENS
4 GOUSSES D'AIL
1 BRANCHE DE CÉLERI
1 CAROTTE MOYENNE
5 CL D'HUILE D'OLIVE
1 C. À S. BOMBÉE DE FARINE
60 CL DE VIN ROUGE
40 CL DE FOND DE GIBIER À POIL OU DE FOND DE VEAU
1 PETIT BOUQUET DE THYM
SEL, POIVRE DU MOULIN

—

À DÉGUSTER

avec un anjou rouge ou un coteaux-du-languedoc rouge

1 Coupez la viande en cubes de 2 cm environ. Épluchez les oignons, les gousses d'ail, le céleri et la carotte et coupez-les en petits morceaux. Saisissez 5 minutes les cubes de viande dans une grande cocotte avec l'huile. Retirez ensuite les morceaux de chevreuil, mettez les légumes dans la cocotte et faites-les cuire 5 minutes sur feu moyen. Remettez ensuite la viande, saupoudrez de farine et mélangez le tout 3 minutes sur feu vif.

2 Versez ensuite le vin dans la cocotte et portez à ébullition. Versez le fond de veau, salez, poivrez. Couvrez la cocotte et laissez mijoter 1 h 45 sur feu doux en mélangeant les morceaux régulièrement et en écumant la surface.

3 Sortez la viande et la garniture de la cocotte. Dans un plat, conservez uniquement la viande et couvrez-la avec du film alimentaire. Faites réduire le fond de cuisson jusqu'à ce qu'il ait une consistance sirupeuse puis filtrez-le dans une passoire fine. Remettez la sauce filtrée dans la cocotte propre et ajoutez-y les morceaux de viande.

4 Faites légèrement brûler les branches de thym, ajoutez-les dans la cocotte et laissez mijoter 10 minutes.

5 Servez la daube avec une purée de panais au wasabi (voir p. 90) ou de potiron, ou de la polenta.

Filets de chevreuil au poivre et chicons

Pour **4 personnes** / Préparation **20 min** / Réfrigération **24 h** / Cuisson **35 min**

800 G DE FILETS DE CHEVREUIL
15 G DE POIVRE DE SICHUAN CONCASSÉ
8 PETITS CHICONS
30 G DE BEURRE
1 C. À S. DE MIEL LIQUIDE
2 C. À S. D'HUILE DE TOURNESOL
5 CL D'ARMAGNAC OU DE COGNAC
20 CL DE FOND DE VEAU OU DE GIBIER
1 C. À S. DE CRÈME FRAÎCHE ÉPAISSE
SEL ET POIVRE DU MOULIN

À DÉGUSTER

avec un anjou rouge

1 La veille, roulez les filets de chevreuil dans le poivre en appuyant bien dessus pour le faire pénétrer. Enveloppez-les de 2 ou 3 épaisseurs de film alimentaire et placez-les 24 heures au réfrigérateur.

2 Le jour même, nettoyez les chicons, puis faites-les dorer avec le beurre dans une poêle 6 à 8 minutes sur feu moyen. Versez le miel, salez, poivrez et laissez légèrement caraméliser pendant 5 minutes sur feu moyen. Ajoutez 15 cl d'eau et laissez cuire les chicons 15 minutes sur feu doux en les tournant régulièrement. Réservez.

3 Dans une autre poêle, faites saisir les filets de chevreuil avec l'huile 3 à 5 minutes (selon la cuisson désirée) de chaque côté sur feu vif. Salez, puis déposez-les sur une grille ou une assiette. Couvrez de papier aluminium et réservez.

4 Dégraissez la poêle, remettez-la sur le feu et déglacez-la avec l'armagnac. Ajoutez le fond de veau ou de gibier et faites réduire jusqu'à obtenir une sauce légèrement épaisse. Ajoutez la crème fraîche, salez, et faites encore réduire 3 minutes sur feu vif en fouettant. Remettez les filets dans la poêle et faites chauffer 2 minutes. Coupez-les en morceaux, arrosez-les de sauce et servez avec les chicons.

NOISETTE DE CHEVREUIL, SAUCE LIE DE VIN, MOUSSELINE DE CÉLERI

Pour **4 personnes** / Préparation **30 min** / Cuisson **55 min**

700 G DE FILETS DE CHEVREUIL
1 CAROTTE
1 OIGNON MOYEN
1 PETITE BRANCHE DE CÉLERI
75 CL DE VIN ROUGE
1 C. À S. BOMBÉE DE SUCRE CASSONADE
10 CL DE FOND DE VEAU OU DE GIBIER
2 C. À S. D'HUILE D'OLIVE
SEL ET POIVRE DU MOULIN

POUR LA MOUSSELINE :

600 G DE CÉLERI-RAVE
90 G DE BEURRE
6 FEUILLES DE SAUGE

—

À DÉGUSTER

avec un bourgueil

1. Épluchez, lavez et coupez la carotte et le céleri-branche en petits cubes. Épluchez et hachez l'oignon. Mettez les légumes dans une casserole avec le vin et le sucre cassonade. Faites réduire une vingtaine de minutes sur feu moyen jusqu'à ce qu'il reste ¼ du vin environ.

2. Ajoutez le fond de veau ou de gibier. Salez et poivrez. Faites cuire encore 8 à 10 minutes sur feu moyen jusqu'à obtenir une sauce bien brillante. Filtrez la sauce dans une casserole propre et gardez-la au chaud, au bain-marie.

3. Préparez la mousseline. Épluchez et coupez le céleri-rave en petits cubes. Dans une casserole, couvrez-le entièrement d'eau froide. Salez, poivrez et portez à ébullition. Faites cuire 20 minutes sur feu moyen.

4. Égouttez le céleri dans une passoire, puis mettez-le dans un récipient à bords hauts. Ajoutez le beurre en petits morceaux, du sel et du poivre et réduisez le tout en une mousseline bien lisse à l'aide d'un mixeur plongeant (environ 3 minutes). Plus vous mettrez de beurre, meilleure sera la mousseline !

5. Lavez et ciselez les feuilles de sauge. Ajoutez-les dans la mousseline et mélangez. Transvasez la mousseline dans un récipient et gardez-la au chaud, au bain-marie.

6. Coupez les filets de chevreuil en tronçons de 3 centimètres environ. Assaisonnez de sel et de poivre. Au dernier moment, faites saisir la viande 2 minutes de chaque côté sur feu vif. Servez aussitôt avec la mousseline de céleri et la sauce lie de vin.

Noisette de chevreuil aux cèpes et aux amandes en persillade

Pour **4 personnes** / Préparation **30 min** / Cuisson **30 min**

700 G DE FILET DE CHEVREUIL
20 CL DE FOND DE VEAU OU DE GIBIER
4 BRANCHES DE PERSIL FRISÉ
30 G D'AMANDES ENTIÈRES NON MONDÉES
1 ÉCHALOTE
1 C. À S. RASE DE POUDRE D'AMANDES
300 G DE CÈPES
20 G + **10** G DE BEURRE
12 TRANCHES DE LARD FUMÉ
2 C. À S. D'HUILE DE NOIX OU DE NOISETTE
SEL ET POIVRE DU MOULIN

—

À DÉGUSTER
avec un côte-rôtie

1. Dans une casserole, faites réduire de moitié le fond de veau ou de gibier sur feu doux. Réservez.
2. Lavez et hachez le persil. Dans une poêle chaude, faites torréfier les amandes 5 minutes à sec. Hachez-les grossièrement avec un couteau, puis mélangez-les avec la poudre d'amandes et le persil.
3. Nettoyez les cèpes et hachez-les au couteau. Dans une poêle, faites-les cuire avec 20 grammes de beurre 5 à 6 minutes sur feu moyen. Salez et poivrez. Ajoutez le mélange aux amandes et la moitié du fond réduit. Faites cuire 5 minutes jusqu'à ce que les cèpes soient compotés. Laissez refroidir.
4. Ouvrez les morceaux de filet en portefeuille. Salez et poivrez. Garnissez-les avec la compotée de cèpes. Entourez-les ensuite avec les tranches de lard en serrant bien et ficelez pour former un rôti. Placez-le au réfrigérateur jusqu'au moment de servir.
5. Dans une casserole, chauffez le reste du fond de veau sur feu moyen. Salez, poivrez, ajoutez le beurre restant et fouettez.
6. Au dernier moment, coupez le filet en morceaux de 3 centimètres d'épaisseur environ. Dans une poêle, faites-les saisir avec l'huile de noix ou de noisette 1 à 3 minutes sur feu vif de chaque côté selon la cuisson désirée.
7. Servez avec le fond monté au beurre, accompagné de légumes-racines rôtis ou de topinambours confits (voir p. 94).

Filets de chevreuil à l'orange, chicorées rouges grillées

Pour **4 personnes** / Préparation **15 min** / Marinade **6 h** / Cuisson **20 min**

POUR LA MARINADE :

1 ORANGE BIO À JUS
3 CL D'HUILE D'OLIVE

700 G DE FILETS DE CHEVREUIL
1 ORANGE BIO À JUS
1 GROSSE C. À S. DE MIEL LIQUIDE
2 C. À S. DE VINAIGRE DE VIN
10 CL DE FOND DE VEAU OU DE GIBIER
8 PETITES CHICORÉES ROUGES
25 G DE BEURRE
SEL ET POIVRE DU MOULIN

À DÉGUSTER

avec un crozes-hermitage

1. Lavez et zestez l'orange (conservez le jus pour le reste de la recette). Dans un bol, mélangez les zestes avec l'huile d'olive.
2. Mettez les filets dans un plat à bords hauts, badigeonnez-les avec l'huile d'olive à l'orange et couvrez de film alimentaire. Placez 6 heures au réfrigérateur.
3. Zestez la deuxième orange, réservez. Pressez les 2 oranges. Dans une casserole, faites chauffer le miel avec le vinaigre 5 minutes sur feu doux. Ajoutez le jus des oranges, laissez réduire de moitié sur feu moyen. Ajoutez le fond de veau ou de gibier et faites réduire 5 minutes. Salez et poivrez. Gardez la sauce au chaud, au bain-marie.
4. Retirez le pied des chicorées en les gardant entières. Si elles sont grosses, coupez-les en 2 ou en 4.
5. Dans une poêle, faites chauffer le beurre. Quand il devient mousseux, ajoutez les chicorées et faites-les dorer 5 minutes sur feu vif en les retournant à mi-cuisson. Salez et poivrez. Réservez.
6. Dans une poêle, saisissez les filets 6 à 8 minutes sur feu vif avec l'huile de la marinade. Salez et poivrez.
7. Coupez les filets en tranches épaisses, servez avec la chicorée et la sauce. Vous pouvez parsemer les filets des zestes d'orange mis de côté au moment de servir.

FILETS DE CHEVREUIL PANÉS AUX HERBES ET À LA MOUTARDE, PANAIS RÔTIS

Pour **4 personnes** / Préparation **20 min** / Cuisson **50 min**

700 G DE FILETS DE CHEVREUIL
600 G DE PANAIS
8 CL + **2** C. À S. D'HUILE D'OLIVE
5 CL DE SIROP D'ÉRABLE
3 PINCÉES DE PIMENT D'ESPELETTE
3 PINCÉES DE CUMIN EN POUDRE

POUR LA PANURE :

4 BRANCHES D'ESTRAGON
4 BRANCHES DE CERFEUIL
½ BOTTE DE CIBOULETTE
3 BRANCHES DE PERSIL
2 C. À S. DE MOUTARDE
2 C. À S. DE GRAINES DE MOUTARDE
SEL

—

À DÉGUSTER

avec un gaillac rouge

1 Préchauffez le four à 180 °C (th. 6). Épluchez et lavez les panais, coupez-les en deux dans le sens de la longueur. Déposez-les dans une plaque à rôtir. Arrosez-les avec les 8 centilitres d'huile d'olive et le sirop d'érable. Saupoudrez de piment d'Espelette et de cumin. Salez.

2 Placez la plaque dans le four et faites rôtir 40 minutes.

3 Pendant ce temps, préparez la panure. Lavez et hachez les herbes. Dans un bol, mélangez-les avec la moutarde et les graines de moutarde.

4 Dans une poêle, faites saisir les filets de chevreuil entiers avec les 2 cuillerées à soupe d'huile d'olive 1 minute sur feu vif. Salez, poivrez.

5 Badigeonnez les filets avec le mélange aux herbes et à la moutarde. Déposez-les dans un plat à four.

6 Une fois les panais cuits, sortez-les et couvrez-les avec du papier aluminium. Augmentez la température du four à 240 °C (th. 8). Mettez les filets de chevreuil au four et faites cuire 5 à 10 min selon la cuisson désirée.

7 Sortez les filets du four. Découpez-les en tronçons de 3 centimètres et servez-les avec les panais et leur jus de cuisson.

FILETS DE CHEVREUIL RÔTIS AUX FRUITS SECS ET À LA CANNELLE

Pour **4 personnes** / Préparation **30 min** / Cuisson **20 min**

800 G DE FILETS DE CHEVREUIL
20 G DE NOISETTES ENTIÈRES
20 G D'AMANDES ENTIÈRES
10 G DE PIGNONS DE PIN
1 FIGUE SÉCHÉE MOELLEUSE
2 ABRICOTS SECS MOELLEUX
1 C. À S. DE MIEL LIQUIDE
2 PINCÉES DE CANNELLE
15 G DE CRANBERRIES SÉCHÉES
400 G DE POTIMARRON
8 CL D'HUILE D'OLIVE
SEL ET POIVRE DU MOULIN

À DÉGUSTER

avec un bandol rosé

1. Hachez grossièrement les noisettes, les amandes et les pignons de pin avec un couteau. Coupez la figue et les abricots en petits morceaux.

2. Dans une poêle chaude, faites torréfier les fruits secs à sec 3 minutes. Ajoutez la figue, les abricots, le miel et la cannelle. Faites légèrement caraméliser 2 minutes sur feu moyen, puis laissez refroidir.

3. Préchauffez le four à 210 °C (th. 7). Pour chaque filet, procédez ainsi : coupez les filets en 2 morceaux de longueur égale et entaillez ceux-ci sur toute leur longueur. Garnissez un des morceaux avec les fruits secs caramélisés et le miel, puis posez le second par-dessus. Ficelez-le tout pour former un rôti. Réservez.

4. Lavez et coupez le potimarron en cubes. Dans une poêle, faites-le dorer avec la moitié de l'huile d'olive 5 minutes sur feu vif. Déposez-le ensuite dans un grand plat à four.

5. Versez le reste de l'huile dans la poêle et faites saisir les rôtis 2 minutes de chaque côté sur feu vif. Déposez les rôtis dans le plat contenant le potimarron, salez et poivrez. Enfournez pour 10 à 15 minutes, selon la cuisson désirée.

6. Au sortir du four, laissez reposer 5 minutes avant de découper les rôtis et de les servir accompagnés des cubes de potimarron.

Rôti de chevreuil mariné aux aromates, topinambours sautés aux noix

Pour **6 à 8 personnes** / Préparation **40 min** / Marinade **24 h** / Cuisson **1 h**

POUR LA MARINADE :

4 BAIES DE GENIÈVRE
4 FEUILLES DE LAURIER
10 GRAINS DE POIVRE NOIR
1 CLOU DE GIROFLE
2 BRANCHES DE THYM
1 C. À C. DE FEUILLES DE ROMARIN
8 CL D'HUILE D'OLIVE
10 CL DE VIN BLANC

1,4 KG DE RÔTI DE CHEVREUIL DANS LA GIGUE
700 G DE TOPINAMBOURS
2 C. À S. D'HUILE D'OLIVE
80 G DE CERNEAUX DE NOIX
30 G DE BEURRE
SEL ET POIVRE DU MOULIN

—

À DÉGUSTER

avec un côte-de-bourg blanc

1 La veille, hachez les baies de genièvre, les feuilles de laurier, les grains de poivre, le clou de girofle, les branches de thym effeuillées et le romarin avec un couteau. Mélangez le tout dans un récipient avec l'huile d'olive et le vin blanc.

2 Déposez le rôti dans un plat. Badigeonnez-le avec la marinade et couvrez de film alimentaire. Placez 24 heures au réfrigérateur en retournant la viande au bout de 12 heures.

3 Le jour même, épluchez et lavez les topinambours. Dans une casserole, faites-les cuire 15 minutes dans de l'eau bouillante salée. Égouttez-les et rafraîchissez-les dans l'eau froide. Réservez.

4 Préchauffez le four à 200 °C (th. 6-7). Égouttez le rôti et retirez l'excédent de marinade en l'essuyant avec un essuie-tout. Dans une plaque à rôtir, faites-le saisir avec 2 cuillerées à soupe d'huile d'olive 5 minutes sur toutes ses faces.

5 Placez la plaque dans le four et faites cuire le rôti 25 minutes pour une cuisson rosée. Prolongez de 15 minutes pour un rôti bien cuit.

6 Hachez grossièrement les cerneaux de noix avec un couteau.

7 Dans une poêle, faites dorer les topinambours avec le beurre 6 à 8 minutes sur feu moyen. Ajoutez les noix. Salez et poivrez.

8 Sortez le rôti du four, enveloppez-le dans du papier aluminium et laissez-le reposer 10 minutes avant de le trancher et de le servir accompagné des topinambours.

Gigue de chevreuil marinée au laurier et rôtie, crème d'ail

Pour **6 à 8 personnes** / Préparation **30 min** / Marinade **24 h** / Cuisson **1 h**

POUR LA MARINADE :

1 GROS OIGNON
2 TÊTES D'AIL
1 BRANCHE DE CÉLERI
4 BAIES DE GENIÈVRE
1 BELLE BRANCHE DE LAURIER SÉCHÉE
10 GRAINS DE POIVRE NOIR
75 CL DE VIN BLANC

1 GIGUE DE CHEVREUIL
1 TÊTE D'AIL
40 CL DE CRÈME LIQUIDE
5 CL D'HUILE D'OLIVE
SEL ET POIVRE DU MOULIN

À DÉGUSTER

avec un châteauneuf-du-pape rouge

1. La veille, désossez la gigue en grattant l'os par l'intérieur, ceci qui permettra de la conserver entière sans avoir à la ficeler. Épluchez et coupez l'oignon en rondelles. Coupez les têtes d'ail en deux dans le sens de l'épaisseur. Lavez et épluchez le céleri, puis coupez-le en tronçons. Concassez les baies de genièvre à l'aide d'un pilon ou d'un couteau.

2. Garnissez la gigue avec la branche de laurier, puis déposez le tout dans un grand plat à four à bords hauts. Répartissez autour les 2 têtes d'ail, les baies de genièvre, le céleri et les grains de poivre. Versez le vin blanc par-dessus. Couvrez de film alimentaire et placez 24 heures au réfrigérateur en tournant la gigue à mi-temps.

3. Le jour même, épluchez la tête d'ail, puis faites blanchir ses gousses 3 minutes dans une casserole d'eau, départ eau froide. Renouvelez deux fois l'opération.

4. Dans une casserole, versez la crème liquide et 5 cl d'eau, puis déposez les gousses d'ail. Salez, poivrez et faites cuire cette sauce 20 minutes sur feu doux. Mixez-la ensuite à l'aide d'un mixeur plongeant. Réservez la sauce au chaud au bain-marie.

5. Préchauffez le four à 210 °C (th. 7). Égouttez la viande en retirant bien l'excédent de marinade avec de l'essuie-tout. Arrosez-la d'huile d'olive, salez, poivrez, et déposez les têtes d'ail de la marinade autour.

6. Faites cuire la gigue 35 à 50 minutes selon la cuisson désirée, en l'arrosant régulièrement.

7. Au sortir du four, couvrez la gigue de papier aluminium et laissez reposer 10 minutes avant de la découper et de la déguster avec la crème d'ail. Accompagnez de potirons rôtis aux graines (voir p. 94).

GIGUE DE CHEVREUIL EN COCOTTE À LA CRÈME POIVRÉE

Pour **8 personnes** / Préparation **30 min** / Cuisson **40 min**

1 GIGUE DE CHEVREUIL DÉSOSSÉE ET FICELÉE
2 ÉCHALOTES
1 OIGNON
1 CAROTTE
1 C. À S. BOMBÉE DE POIVRE MOULU
5 CL D'HUILE D'OLIVE
5 CL DE COGNAC
10 CL DE VIN BLANC
30 CL DE CRÈME LIQUIDE
2 BRANCHES DE THYM
2 FEUILLES DE LAURIER
SEL

À DÉGUSTER

avec un côte-rôtie

1. Épluchez et émincez les échalotes et l'oignon. Épluchez et taillez la carotte en cubes.
2. Badigeonnez la gigue de poivre moulu en appuyant bien dessus avec vos mains pour le faire pénétrer.
3. Préchauffez le four à 210 °C (th. 7). Dans une grande cocotte, faites saisir la gigue avec l'huile d'olive 5 minutes de chaque côté sur feu vif. Salez. Ajoutez les échalotes, l'oignon et la carotte et faites rissoler 3 minutes.
4. Arrosez la gigue de cognac et faites flamber.
5. Versez le vin blanc, le thym et le laurier dans le fond de la cocotte et enfournez sans couvrir. Faites cuire la gigue 25 minutes pour une cuisson rosée, prolongez de 15 minutes pour une viande bien cuite.
6. Sortez la cocotte du four et enveloppez la gigue dans du papier aluminium. Laissez reposer 10 minutes.
7. Pendant ce temps, placez la cocotte sur le feu et versez-y la crème avec 10 cl d'eau et du sel. Faites réduire jusqu'à ce que la sauce soit légèrement épaisse. Puis filtrez avec une passoire fine et réservez dans un bol de service.
8. Coupez la gigue en tranches et servez avec la crème au poivre. Accompagnez ce plat d'un gratin dauphinois ou d'une purée de carottes et céleri aux noisettes.

CÔTELETTES DE CHEVREUIL AUX GRAINES ET AUX NOISETTES, MOUSSELINE DE PATATES DOUCES

Pour **4 personnes** / Préparation **30 min** / Cuisson **55 min**

POUR LE CRUMBLE :

25 G DE BEURRE MOU
40 G DE FARINE
30 G DE PARMESAN RÂPÉ
1 C. À S. DE GRAINES DE SÉSAME
1 C. À S. DE GRAINES DE COURGE
2 C. À S. DE GRAINES DE LIN
1 C. À S. DE NOISETTES
SEL ET POIVRE DU MOULIN

12 CÔTELETTES DE CHEVREUIL
600 G DE PATATES DOUCES
30 CL DE FOND DE VEAU OU DE GIBIER
75 G DE BEURRE
1 PINCÉE DE CANNELLE EN POUDRE
2 C. À S. D'HUILE D'OLIVE

À DÉGUSTER

avec un côte-de-beaune rouge

1 Préchauffez le four à 180 °C (th. 6). Préparez le crumble : concassez les noisettes avec un couteau. Dans un récipient, mélangez le beurre avec la farine, le parmesan, les graines, les noisettes du sel et du poivre jusqu'à obtenir une pâte friable. Émiettez cette pâte sur une plaque à four, puis enfournez pour 18 à 20 minutes. Au sortir du four, laissez refroidir sur la plaque.

2 Épluchez, lavez et coupez les patates douces en gros morceaux. Faites-les cuire 20 minutes dans un grand volume d'eau bouillante salée.

3 Pendant ce temps, dans une casserole, faites réduire de moitié le fond de veau ou de gibier avec du sel et du poivre.

4 Égouttez les patates douces, mettez-les dans un récipient haut, ajoutez le beurre et la cannelle, salez et poivrez. Réduisez le tout en mousseline à l'aide d'un mixeur plongeant. Réservez au chaud, au bain-marie.

5 Dans une poêle, faites saisir les côtelettes avec l'huile d'olive 2 à 3 minutes de chaque côté, selon la cuisson désirée. Salez et poivrez.

6 Servez les côtelettes avec la purée de patates douces et le jus réduit, parsemez de crumble aux graines et dégustez.

Côtelettes de chevreuil à la moutarde douce et aux herbes

Pour **4 personnes** / Préparation **15 min** / Cuisson **8 min**

16 CÔTELETTES DE CHEVREUIL ÉPAISSES
1 BOUQUET DE CERFEUIL
4 BRANCHES DE PERSIL
2 GROSSES C. À S. DE MOUTARDE SAVORA
8 CL D'HUILE D'OLIVE
2 C. À S. DE CHAPELURE
SEL ET POIVRE DU MOULIN

1. Préchauffez le gril du four à 240 °C (th. 8). Hachez le cerfeuil et le persil. Dans un bol, mélangez-les avec la moutarde, 2 cuillerées à soupe d'huile d'olive et 2 cuillerées à soupe d'eau. Salez et poivrez.
2. Dans une poêle, faites saisir les côtelettes avec le reste de l'huile d'olive 2 minutes de chaque côté. Salez et poivrez.
3. Déposez les côtelettes sur une plaque à four. Versez la sauce aux herbes par-dessus et parsemez de chapelure. Enfournez pour 3 à 4 minutes. Servez aussitôt accompagnés de poireaux grillés (voir p. 92).

À DÉGUSTER

avec un bourgueil

Carrés de côtelettes de chevreuil aux noix et au cidre

Pour **4 personnes** / Préparation **30 min** / Cuisson **35 min**

4 CARRÉS DE 3 CÔTELETTES DE CHEVREUIL
1 ÉCHALOTE
30 CL DE CIDRE
10 CL DE FOND DE VEAU OU DE GIBIER
1 C. À S. DE CRÈME FRAÎCHE ÉPAISSE
2 C. À S. D'HUILE D'OLIVE
SEL ET POIVRE DU MOULIN

POUR LA PÂTE :

50 G DE CERNEAUX DE NOIX
20 G DE BEURRE MOU
20 G DE PARMESAN RÂPÉ
1 C. À S. RASE DE FARINE
2 GROSSES C. À S. DE CHAPELURE
2 BRANCHES D'ESTRAGON HACHÉES

1 Épluchez et hachez l'échalote.

2 Dans une casserole, faites réduire de ⅔ le cidre avec l'échalote sur feu moyen. Ajoutez le fond de veau ou de gibier, et faites réduire le tout de moitié sur feu moyen. Ajoutez la crème fraîche, salez et poivrez. Réservez au chaud, au bain-marie.

3 Dans une poêle, faites saisir les carrés de côtelettes avec l'huile d'olive sur toutes leurs faces. Salez et poivrez. Réservez.

4 Préchauffez le four à 180 °C (th. 6). Préparez la pâte : hachez les noix à l'aide d'un minirobot hachoir. Dans un récipient, mélangez-les avec le beurre, le parmesan, la farine, la chapelure, l'estragon, du sel et du poivre.

5 Déposez les carrés dans un plat à four et badigeonnez la chair de cette pâte. Enfournez pour 10 à 15 minutes selon la cuisson désirée.

6 Servez avec la sauce au cidre et des topinambours confits (voir p. 94).

À DÉGUSTER

avec un cornas ou du cidre

ÉPAULES DE CHEVREUIL DE 7 HEURES AU FOIN

Pour **4 à 6 personnes** / Préparation **20 min** / Cuisson **7 h**

2 ÉPAULES DE CHEVREUIL
3 CAROTTES
2 OIGNONS JAUNES
2 GOUSSES D'AIL
3 C. À S. D'HUILE D'OLIVE
50 CL DE VIN BLANC
1 GROSSE POIGNÉE DE FOIN
3 FEUILLES DE LAURIER SÉCHÉES
4 BAIES DE GENIÈVRE ENTIÈRES
SEL ET POIVRE DU MOULIN

À DÉGUSTER

avec un chinon rouge

1 Désossez les épaules en suivant bien l'os avec le couteau afin d'obtenir un minimum de morceaux possible. Ficelez ces derniers pour former un rôti.

2 Épluchez, lavez et taillez les carottes en dés. Pelez et hachez les oignons et les gousses d'ail.

3 Préchauffez le four à 120 °C (th. 4). Dans une grande cocotte, faites saisir le rôti d'épaule avec l'huile d'olive sur toutes ses faces 6 à 8 minutes. Baissez le feu et ajoutez l'oignon, les carottes et l'ail. Laissez cuire 5 minutes sur feu moyen.

4 Versez le vin blanc et 15 cl d'eau, ajoutez le laurier et les baies de genièvre, salez et poivrez. Répartissez le foin autour du rôti en le tassant de sorte qu'il soit légèrement immergé. Couvrez la cocotte et enfournez pendant 7 heures, en tournant délicatement le rôti deux fois pendant la cuisson.

5 Servez avec une purée de pommes de terre (voir p. 90) ou de céleri (voir p. 90).

CREUSET

Poêlée de foie de chevreuil aux champignons et croûtons à l'ail

Pour **4 personnes** / Préparation **30 min** / Cuisson **20 min**

1 FOIE DE CHEVREUIL DE 600-700 G COUPÉ EN MORCEAUX
1 BOUQUET DE PERSIL
3 GOUSSES D'AIL
400 G DE CÈPES
50 G DE NOISETTES
2 TRANCHES ÉPAISSES DE PAIN
2 C. À S. DE FARINE
5 CL D'HUILE DE NOISETTE
30 G DE BEURRE
SEL, POIVRE DU MOULIN

—

À DÉGUSTER

avec un saint-véran

1. Lavez et hachez le persil. Épluchez les gousses d'ail, puis hachez-en deux et gardez la troisième entière. Nettoyez les cèpes, coupez-les en quartiers. Concassez grossièrement les noisettes.

2. Préchauffez le gril du four. Frottez les tranches de pain avec la gousse d'ail entière, puis coupez le pain en croûtons et déposez-les sur une plaque de four. Faites-les dorer quelques minutes sous le gril.

3. Assaisonnez les morceaux de foie et passez-les dans la farine, puis réservez.

4. Faites cuire les cèpes 5 minutes dans une poêle sur feu vif avec la moitié de l'huile de noisette. Ajoutez les noisettes, salez, poivrez, faites cuire encore 1 minute puis débarrassez le tout sur une assiette. Réservez.

5. Mettez le reste de l'huile dans la poêle et faites cuire les morceaux de foie 8 à 10 minutes sur feu moyen. Ajoutez ensuite les cèpes et les noisettes dans la poêle, l'ail et le persil haché, le beurre, du sel et du poivre. Faites cuire le tout pendant 3 minutes sur feu moyen en mélangeant. Servez aussitôt avec les croûtons de pain dorés à l'ail.

Rognons de chevreuil à la harissa et à l'oignon frit

Pour **4 personnes** / Préparation **30 min** / Cuisson **50 min**

800 G DE ROGNONS DE CHEVREUIL
600 G DE PETITES POMMES DE TERRE GRENAILLE
1 C. À S. DE GRAINES DE CARVI
40 G DE BEURRE
5 CL D'HUILE DE TOURNESOL
1 OIGNON JAUNE MOYEN
1 C. À S. BOMBÉE DE HARISSA
25 CL DE VIN BLANC
3 BRINS DE CORIANDRE
SEL, POIVRE DU MOULIN

À DÉGUSTER

avec un collioure rouge

1 Lavez les pommes de terre avec leur peau, faites-les cuire 15 minutes dans l'eau salée, froide au départ. Égouttez-les et mettez-les dans une poêle avec les graines de carvi, le beurre et une cuillère à soupe d'huile. Salez, poivrez et laissez cuire 10 minutes sur feu moyen.

2 Épluchez et hachez l'oignon. Préparez et coupez les rognons en morceaux, puis saisissez-les 6 à 8 minutes dans une grande poêle sur feu vif avec le reste de l'huile. Salez, poivrez, puis retirez les morceaux de rognons. Dans la poêle, faites rissoler l'oignon 5 minutes sur feu vif en remuant. Ajoutez la harissa et laissez roussir 2 minutes en remuant, puis versez le vin blanc. Mélangez avec un fouet, salez et faites cuire 5 minutes sur feu moyen.

3 Mettez les morceaux de rognons et les pommes de terre dans la poêle et faites chauffer le tout 5 minutes en mélangeant. Parsemez de coriandre ciselée et servez aussitôt.

ROGNONS DE CHEVREUIL AUX CHAMPIGNONS ET AUX NOISETTES EN PERSILLADE

Pour **4 personnes** / Préparation **30 min** / Cuisson **25 min**

700 G DE ROGNONS DE CHEVREUIL NETTOYÉS ET COUPÉS EN MORCEAUX
400 G DE CHAMPIGNONS DE PARIS
1 PETIT BOUQUET DE PERSIL FRISÉ
2 ÉCHALOTES
60 G DE NOISETTES ENTIÈRES
40 G DE BEURRE
5 CL D'HUILE DE TOURNESOL
10 CL DE PORTO
20 CL DE FOND DE VEAU OU DE GIBIER
SEL ET POIVRE DU MOULIN

—

À DÉGUSTER

avec un gaillac rouge

1. Lavez et coupez les champignons en quartiers. Lavez et hachez le persil. Pelez et émincez les échalotes.
2. Dans une poêle, faites torréfier les noisettes 5 minutes à sec. Laissez-les refroidir, puis hachez-les grossièrement avec un couteau. Dans un récipient, mélangez-les au persil. Réservez.
3. Dans une poêle, faites sauter les champignons avec la moitié du beurre sur feu vif. Salez, poivrez et réservez.
4. Dans une grande poêle, faites saisir les rognons avec l'huile et le reste de beurre 5 minutes. Ajoutez les échalotes, salez, poivrez et laissez cuire encore 3 minutes.
5. Augmentez le feu et versez la moitié du porto pour faire flamber les rognons. Laissez réduire 3 minutes. Retirez les rognons de la poêle et déposez-les dans une passoire. Versez le reste de porto et le fond de veau ou de gibier dans la poêle. Salez, poivrez, puis faites réduire sur feu vif jusqu'à obtenir une sauce sirupeuse. Ajoutez le reste du beurre en fouettant.
6. Remettez les rognons dans la poêle. Ajoutez les champignons et faites cuire le tout 5 minutes sur feu moyen. Parsemez de noisettes persillées et servez aussitôt.

BARBECUE DE NOISETTES DE CHEVREUIL LARDÉES ET FUMÉES

Pour **4 personnes** / Préparation **20 min** / Fumage **30 min** / Cuisson **45 min**

800 G DE FILET DE CHEVREUIL
12 TRANCHES FINES DE POITRINE FUMÉE
8 MINIPOIREAUX
5 CL D'HUILE D'OLIVE
1 C. À S. DE MOUTARDE SAVORA
1 C. À S. DE MIEL LIQUIDE
1 C. À S. DE SAUCE BARBECUE
1 GROSSE POIGNÉE DE BRINDILLES DE PIN OU DE FEUILLES SÈCHES
1 C. À S. D'HUILE D'OLIVE
SEL, POIVRE DU MOULIN

—

À DÉGUSTER

avec un gigondas

1 Coupez le filet de chevreuil en douze tranches de 2 cm d'épaisseur environ, puis entourez chaque tranche d'une tranche de poitrine fumée. Disposez des brindilles de pin ou des feuilles sèches et des branchages dans le fond d'une grande cocotte. Posez une grande grille dessus et déposez les noisettes de chevreuil sur la grille. Allumez les brindilles avec un petit chalumeau sans les faire complètement brûler. Couvrez la cocotte en laissant un peu d'air passer, afin que les brindilles se consument doucement et dégagent de la fumée. Laissez fumer 30 minutes environ ; rallumez les brindilles si besoin pendant le fumage.

2 Nettoyez les poireaux. Faites-les griller entiers dans une poêle ou sur un gril à feu très doux pendant 30 à 40 minutes selon leur grosseur, en les badigeonnant d'huile d'olive et en les tournant régulièrement.

3 Mélangez la moutarde dans un bol avec le miel, la sauce barbecue, du sel et du poivre.

4 Une fois qu'elles sont fumées, faites griller dans une poêle les noisettes de chevreuil 3 à 5 minutes de chaque côté, salez, poivrez.

5 Servez avec les poireaux grillés et la sauce.

NOISETTES DE CHEVREUIL AUX CLÉMENTINES, CAROTTES VICHY À L'ANIS

Pour **4 personnes** / Préparation **30 min** / Cuisson **30 min**

700 G DE FILET DE CHEVREUIL
2 CLÉMENTINES
600 G DE CAROTTES
70 G DE BEURRE
40 G DE SUCRE
1 C. À S. DE GRAINES DE FENOUIL
2 ÉTOILES DE BADIANE
5 CL DE VINAIGRE DE VIN
LE JUS DE **4** CLÉMENTINES
2 C. À S. D'HUILE D'OLIVE
2 BRINS DE CERFEUIL
SEL, POIVRE DU MOULIN

À DÉGUSTER

avec un bandol rouge

1 Coupez le filet de chevreuil en morceaux, façon tournedos, de 3 cm d'épaisseur environ. Lavez et zestez finement une clémentine sur les noisettes de chevreuil, assaisonnez-les et placez-les 15 minutes au réfrigérateur. Épluchez et taillez les carottes en fines rondelles.

2 Faites fondre 50 g de beurre dans une sauteuse. Ajoutez les carottes, 20 g de sucre, les graines de fenouil, la badiane, du sel et du poivre. Enrobez les carottes de sucre et de beurre, puis mouillez d'eau à hauteur. Posez ensuite sur les carottes du papier sulfurisé découpé au bon diamètre et faites-les cuire 15 à 20 minutes sur feu moyen.

3 Faites cuire le reste du sucre avec le vinaigre dans une casserole pour obtenir un sirop épais. Ajoutez le jus des quatre clémentines, laissez mijoter 6 à 8 minutes sur feu vif, puis ajoutez le reste du beurre en fouettant pour obtenir une sauce légèrement épaisse.

4 Épluchez les deux clémentines et coupez-les en deux. Faites-les dorer 3 à 4 minutes dans une poêle avec l'huile d'olive, puis mettez-les dans la casserole avec la sauce.

5 Faites cuire les noisettes de chevreuil 3 à 4 minutes de chaque côté dans une poêle sur feu moyen ; elles doivent rester rosées (6 à 8 minutes de cuisson pour qu'elles soient bien cuites). Répartissez les noisettes de chevreuil dans les assiettes avec les carottes et les demi-clémentines et nappez de sauce à la clémentine. Parsemez de brins de cerfeuil ciselés et servez aussitôt.

Tourte de chevreuil aux champignons

Pour **4 à 6 personnes** / Préparation **45 min** / Repos **2 h** / Cuisson **3 h**

POUR LA PÂTE :

125 G DE BEURRE
+ **10** G POUR LE MOULE
20 G DE GRAINES DE PAVOT
15 G DE CURCUMA EN POUDRE
250 G DE FARINE
5 G DE SEL
1 JAUNE D'ŒUF
+ **1** POUR LA DORURE

600 G D'ÉPAULE DE CHEVREUIL COUPÉE EN PETITS MORCEAUX
2 OIGNONS JAUNES
2 TOMATES
5 CL D'HUILE D'OLIVE
1 C. À S. DE GRAINES DE CARVI
2 C. À S. DE MIEL LIQUIDE
350 G DE CHAMPIGNONS DE PARIS
30 G DE BEURRE
SEL ET POIVRE DU MOULIN

—

À DÉGUSTER

avec un saint-émilion

1 Préparez la pâte : dans un saladier, mélangez le beurre avec le pavot et le curcuma. Ajoutez la farine, le sel, 1 jaune d'œuf et 6 à 8 cl d'eau froide. Mélangez, puis formez une boule. Enveloppez celle-ci de film alimentaire et placez au réfrigérateur au moins 2 heures.

2 Épluchez et hachez les oignons, lavez et coupez les tomates en morceaux.

3 Dans une cocotte, faites saisir la viande avec l'huile d'olive 10 minutes sur feu vif. Ajoutez les oignons et les tomates et poursuivez la cuisson pendant 5 minutes sur feu moyen. Ajoutez les graines de carvi et le miel, salez et poivrez. Faites légèrement caraméliser en enrobant bien les morceaux de viande dans le miel, puis couvrez d'eau froide. Couvrez la cocotte et laissez cuire 2 heures sur feu moyen en remuant régulièrement. Si nécessaire, ajoutez un peu d'eau en cours de cuisson.

4 Pendant ce temps, lavez et émincez les champignons. Dans une poêle, faites-les cuire avec le beurre 8 à 10 minutes sur feu vif. Réservez.

5 Lorsque la viande est cuite (elle doit être filandreuse), retirez du feu et laissez refroidir dans la cocotte 45 minutes environ. Sortez la pâte du réfrigérateur et préchauffez le four à 180 °C (th. 6).

6 Effilochez la viande à la main, puis mélangez-la dans un saladier avec l'oignon, les champignons et un peu de sauce de cuisson.

7 Beurrez un moule à manqué de 22 cm de diamètre environ. Sur un plan de travail fariné, abaissez les ⅔ de la pâte sur 3 mm d'épaisseur environ et chemisez-en le moule. Piquez le fond avec les dents d'une fourchette, puis ajoutez la garniture en la répartissant bien. Abaissez le reste de la pâte sur 3 mm d'épaisseur et découpez un cercle de la taille du moule. Déposez celui-ci par-dessus la viande et soudez les bords en pinçant bien la pâte avec vos doigts. Faites un trou au milieu avec la pointe d'un couteau. Délayez le jaune d'œuf restant dans un peu d'eau, puis badigeonnez-en la surface de la tourte. Enfournez pour 50 minutes.

8 Au sortir du four, laissez reposer 10 minutes avant de déguster.

Terrine de chevreuil au genièvre

Pour **8 personnes** / Préparation **30 min** / Marinade **12 h** / Cuisson **1 h 30** / Réfrigération **48 h**

POUR LA MARINADE :

8 BAIES DE GENIÈVRE
10 CL DE VIN BLANC
5 CL DE GIN

500 G DE VIANDE DE CHEVREUIL DÉNERVÉE
350 G DE POITRINE DE PORC OU DE LARD GRAS
1 OIGNON MOYEN
20 G DE BEURRE
10 CL DE FOND DE VEAU
100 G DE FOIE DE CHEVREUIL OU DE PORC
1 ŒUF
15 G DE SEL
8 G DE POIVRE
1 BARDE DE 15 X 12 CM ENVIRON
15 CL DE GELÉE

À DÉGUSTER

avec un cornas

1. La veille, écrasez les baies de genièvre. Coupez la viande de chevreuil et la poitrine ou le lard en petits morceaux. Placez-les dans un plat et ajoutez le vin blanc, le gin et les baies de genièvre. Couvrez de film alimentaire et placez 12 heures au réfrigérateur.
2. Le jour même, épluchez et hachez l'oignon. Dans une poêle, faites-le fondre avec le beurre 5 minutes sur feu moyen. Déglacez la poêle avec le fond de veau, faites réduire de moitié, et laissez refroidir.
3. Préchauffez le four à 170 °C (th. 5-6). Hachez la viande de chevreuil, le lard ou la poitrine, le foie et les baies de genièvre à l'aide d'un hachoir (grosse grille). Dans un récipient, mélangez les viandes avec l'oignon confit, l'œuf, le sel et le poivre.
4. Chemisez une terrine de 15 x 12 cm environ avec la barde. Remplissez-la de la farce en tassant bien. Couvrez la terrine et faites cuire le tout 1 h 30 dans le four au bain-marie.
5. Au sortir du four, laissez refroidir. Retirez le jus rendu si nécessaire, puis coulez la gelée dans la terrine pour recouvrir les bords. Placez au moins 48 heures au réfrigérateur avant de déguster.

PÂTÉ DE CHEVREUIL EN CROÛTE

Pour **8 à 10 personnes** / Préparation **1 h** / Marinade **12 h** / Cuisson **1 h 30** / Repos **48 h**

400 G DE VIANDE DE CHEVREUIL DÉNERVÉE
350 G DE POITRINE DE PORC

POUR LA MARINADE :

10 CL DE VIN BLANC
5 CL DE COGNAC
5 G DE PIMENT D'ESPELETTE

POUR LA PÂTE :

200 G DE BEURRE MOU
1 ŒUF
1 C. À C. DE VINAIGRE D'ALCOOL BLANC
300 G DE FARINE
125 G DE MAÏZENA
10 G DE SEL
1 C. À C. BOMBÉE DE SUCRE

4 ÉCHALOTES
20 G DE BEURRE + **10** G POUR LE MOULE OU LA TERRINE + **20** G POUR LA DORURE PENDANT LA CUISSON
10 CL DE FOND DE VEAU OU DE GIBIER
400 G DE FILETS DE CHEVREUIL
1 C. À S. D'HUILE D'OLIVE
150 G DE FOIE DE CHEVREUIL OU À DÉFAUT DE PORC
100 G DE PISTACHES ENTIÈRES ET DÉCORTIQUÉES
1 ŒUF
15 G DE SEL
1 SACHET DE GELÉE AU MADÈRE

À DÉGUSTER

avec un saint-joseph

1 La veille, coupez la viande de chevreuil et la poitrine en petits morceaux. Mettez-les dans un récipient avec le vin blanc, le cognac et le piment d'Espelette. Couvrez de film alimentaire et placez 12 heures au réfrigérateur.

2 Préparez également la pâte : à l'aide d'un batteur équipé de sa feuille, mélangez à vitesse lente le beurre avec l'œuf, le vinaigre et 80 cl d'eau tiède. Ajoutez la farine, la Maïzena, le sel et le sucre. Augmentez la vitesse et mélangez 4 à 5 minutes jusqu'à obtenir une pâte homogène. Formez une boule, enveloppez-la de film alimentaire et placez-la 12 heures au réfrigérateur.

3 Le jour même, faites fondre les échalotes dans le beurre 5 minutes sur feu moyen. Ajoutez le fond de veau ou de gibier, faites réduire de moitié et laissez refroidir. Dans une poêle, faites saisir les filets de chevreuil avec l'huile d'olive 2 minutes de chaque côté. Salez et poivrez. Réservez.

4 Hachez la viande de chevreuil, le lard ou la poitrine et le foie à l'aide d'un hachoir (grosse grille). Mélangez les viandes hachées dans un récipient avec les échalotes fondues, les pistaches, l'œuf et le sel. Beurrez un moule à charnière de 22 x 8 cm environ. Étalez la pâte sur 5 mm d'épaisseur, puis coupez-la en 4 morceaux : 1 pour chemiser le fond de la terrine et ses côtés, 2 pour les extrémités et 1 pour le dessus. Soudez les bords à la main après avoir trempé vos doigts dans l'eau.

5 Garnissez la terrine avec la moitié de la farce, déposez les filets de chevreuil entiers et recouvrez avec le reste de la farce en tassant bien. Déposez le morceau de pâte supérieur, réalisez 3 trous de 1,5 cm de diamètre et placez 2 heures au réfrigérateur.

6 Préchauffez le four à 200 °C (th. 6-7). Dans une casserole, faites fondre les 20 grammes de beurre restant.

7 Placez 3 douilles métalliques de pâtisserie (ou 3 morceaux d'aluminium roulés) dans les trous de la pâte pour former des cheminées. Vous pouvez tracer des motifs en striant le dessus de la pâte avec la pointe d'un couteau.

8 Enfournez, puis baissez la température à 170 °C (th. 5-6) après 10 minutes de cuisson. Laissez cuire 1 h 20 en lustrant la surface de beurre fondu avec un pinceau toutes les 15 minutes.

9 Au sortir du four, laissez reposer 30 minutes, puis versez doucement la gelée par les trous de la pâte par petites quantités. Laissez complètement refroidir et placez 48 heures au réfrigérateur avant de démouler le pâté et le couper en tranches. **Conseil :** si vous le pouvez, utilisez un moule à charnière pour un démoulage parfait.

TERRINE DE CHEVREUIL À L'OIGNON CONFIT ET AU PIMENT D'ESPELETTE

Pour **8 personnes** / Préparation **30 min** / Marinade **12 h** / Cuisson **1 h 55** / Réfrigération **48 h**

POUR LA MARINADE :

10 CL DE VIN BLANC
5 CL D'ARMAGNAC
10 G DE PIMENT D'ESPELETTE

500 G DE VIANDE DE CHEVREUIL
350 G DE POITRINE DE PORC OU DE LARD GRAS
2 GROS OIGNONS
30 G DE BEURRE
25 G DE SUCRE CASSONADE
100 G DE FOIE DE CHEVREUIL OU DE PORC
2 C. À S. DE VINAIGRE DE VIN ROUGE
1 ŒUF
15 G DE SEL
1 MORCEAU DE CRÉPINE DE 30 X 20 CM ENVIRON
15 CL DE GELÉE

À DÉGUSTER

avec un mâcon blanc ou un irancy

1 La veille, coupez la viande de chevreuil et la poitrine ou le lard en petits morceaux. Mettez-les dans un récipient avec le vin blanc, l'armagnac et le piment d'Espelette. Couvrez de film alimentaire et placez 12 heures au réfrigérateur.

2 Le jour même, épluchez et hachez les oignons. Dans une poêle, faites-les fondre avec le beurre 10 minutes sur feu moyen. Ajoutez la cassonade et faites cuire encore 10 minutes jusqu'à ce que les oignons caramélisent légèrement. Versez le vinaigre, faites cuire 5 minutes, puis laissez refroidir.

3 Préchauffez le four à 170 °C (th. 5-6). Hachez la viande de chevreuil, le lard ou la poitrine et le foie à l'aide d'un hachoir (grosse grille). Dans un récipient, mélangez les viandes hachées avec l'oignon confit, l'œuf et le sel.

4 Chemisez une terrine de 15 x 12 cm environ avec la crépine, puis remplissez-la de la farce en tassant bien. Rabattez la crépine sur la farce. Couvrez la terrine et faites-la cuire 1 h 30 dans le four au bain-marie.

5 Au sortir du four, laissez la terrine refroidir. Retirez le jus rendu si nécessaire, puis coulez la gelée dans la terrine pour recouvrir les bords. Placez au moins 48 heures au réfrigérateur avant de déguster.

Mousse de foie de chevreuil à la crème de cassis

Pour **4 personnes** / Préparation **25 min** / Cuisson **25 min** / Réfrigération **6 h**

300 G DE FOIE DE CHEVREUIL COUPÉ EN CUBES DE 2 CM ENVIRON
1 OIGNON JAUNE MOYEN
130 G DE BEURRE
5 CL DE CALVADOS
10 CL DE CRÈME DE CASSIS
10 CL DE GELÉE DÉSHYDRATÉE
SEL ET POIVRE DU MOULIN

À DÉGUSTER

avec un lalande-de-pomerol

1. Épluchez et hachez l'oignon. Faites-le fondre 5 minutes avec 10 g de beurre dans une casserole. Ajoutez les morceaux de foie de chevreuil et faites-les dorer 5 minutes sur feu vif, puis ajoutez le calvados et la crème de cassis. Salez et poivrez. Laissez cuire 10 à 15 minutes sur feu moyen.
2. Laissez refroidir le tout puis mettez le contenu de la casserole dans le bol d'un robot. Ajoutez le reste du beurre légèrement mou coupé en morceaux, puis mixez pour obtenir une mousse de foie. Versez la préparation dans une terrine et laissez prendre au moins 6 heures au réfrigérateur.
3. Une fois la mousse prise, versez la gelée dessus et replacez la terrine au réfrigérateur pour 6 heures.
4. Dégustez avec du bon pain frais.

Terrine de chevreuil aux noisettes et aux figues moelleuses

Pour **8 personnes** / Préparation **30 min** / Marinade **12 h** / Cuisson **1 h 30** / Réfrigération **48 h**

POUR LA MARINADE :

10 CL DE VIN BLANC MOELLEUX
5 CL D'ARMAGNAC
2 FEUILLES DE LAURIER

500 G DE VIANDE DE CHEVREUIL
350 G DE POITRINE DE PORC
80 G D'ÉCHALOTES
100 G DE FOIE DE CHEVREUIL OU À DÉFAUT DE FOIE DE PORC
10 CL DE VIN BLANC MOELLEUX
1 ŒUF
10 CL DE FOND DE VEAU OU DE GIBIER
20 G DE BEURRE
8 FIGUES MOELLEUSES
120 G DE NOISETTES
2 FEUILLES DE LAURIER
15 G DE SEL
8 G DE POIVRE
15 CL DE GELÉE

1 La veille, coupez la viande de chevreuil et la poitrine en petits morceaux. Mettez-les dans un récipient avec la moitié du vin blanc, l'armagnac et le laurier. Couvrez de film alimentaire et placez 12 heures au réfrigérateur.

2 Le jour même, épluchez et hachez les échalotes. Dans une poêle, faites-les fondre avec le beurre 5 minutes sur feu moyen. Déglacez la poêle avec le vin, laissez-le réduire presque à sec, puis ajoutez le fond de veau. Faites réduire de moitié et laissez refroidir.

3 Dans une poêle chaude, faites torréfier les noisettes à sec 5 minutes, puis laissez refroidir.

4 Préchauffez le four à 170 °C (th. 5-6). Coupez les figues en petits morceaux. Hachez la viande de chevreuil, le lard et le foie avec la grosse grille du hachoir. Mélangez les viandes hachées dans un récipient avec les échalotes fondues, les noisettes torréfiées, les figues, l'œuf, le sel et le poivre.

5 Remplissez la terrine avec la farce en tassant bien, puis déposez les 2 feuilles de laurier dessus. Couvrez et faites cuire 1 h 30 au four, au bain-marie.

6 Au sortir du four, laissez refroidir. Retirez le jus rendu si nécessaire, puis coulez la gelée dans la terrine pour recouvrir les bords. Placez au moins 48 heures au réfrigérateur avant de déguster.

À DÉGUSTER

avec un syrah des côtes du Rhone

FONDS ET ACCOMPAGNEMENTS

FOND DE GIBIER

Pour environ **50 cl** / Préparation **30 min** / Cuisson **4 h 30** / Réfrigération **1 nuit**

2 KG D'OS DE GIBIER ET DE PARURES DE VIANDE COUPÉES EN MORCEAUX
2 OIGNONS
200 G DE CAROTTES
100 G DE CÉLERI-BRANCHE
1 C. À S. DE CONCENTRÉ DE TOMATE
4 TOMATES FRAÎCHES
1 BOUQUET GARNI

1 Préchauffez le four à 210 °C (th. 7). Mettez les os et les parures de viande sur une plaque de four avec les oignons épluchés et coupés en quatre. Faites-les rôtir 30 minutes dans le four pour qu'ils soient bien dorés.

2 Épluchez et coupez les carottes et le céleri en petits morceaux. Sortez les os, les parures et les oignons du four, mettez-les dans une grande casserole.

3 Dégraissez la plaque, déglacez-la avec un grand verre d'eau. Versez le déglaçage dans la casserole, ajoutez le concentré de tomate, les tomates lavées et coupées en quartiers, les carottes et le céleri. Faites cuire le tout 5 minutes sur feu vif puis couvrez largement d'eau froide, ajoutez le bouquet garni. Portez à ébullition, laissez cuire au moins 4 heures à petite ébullition sans couvrir, en écumant la surface régulièrement. Filtrez le fond de gibier, laissez-le refroidir et placez-le une nuit au réfrigérateur.

4 Le lendemain, retirez la couche de graisse qui s'est formée à la surface. Mettez le fond de gibier dans une casserole et faites-le réduire de moitié environ.

Purée de céleri

Pour **4 personnes** / Préparation **15 min** / Cuisson **35 min**

750 G DE CÉLERI-RAVE / **150** G DE BEURRE / **1** C. À C. DE SEL DE CÉLERI / SE ET POIVRE DU MOULIN

1 Épluchez, lavez et coupez le céleri en morceaux. Faites-le cuire 30 à 35 minutes dans une casserole d'eau bouillante avec le sel de céleri. Vérifiez la cuisson du céleri en enfonçant la pointe d'un couteau dedans : le céleri doit être tendre. Une fois cuit, utilisez une passoire et laissez-le s'égoutter 5 minutes.

2 Mettez ensuite le céleri dans la cuve d'un robot ou d'un blender avec le beurre en morceaux légèrement mous, salez et poivrez. Mixez le tout quelques minutes pour obtenir une purée lisse et onctueuse.

Purée de pommes de terre

Pour **4 personnes** / Préparation **20 min** / Cuisson **25 min**

1 KG DE POMMES DE TERRE / **20** CL DE LAIT / **120** G DE BEURRE / **3** C. À S. DE CRÈME FRAÎCHE ÉPAISSE / SEL ET POIVRE DU MOULIN

1 Épluchez, lavez et coupez les pommes de terre en morceaux. Faites-les cuire 20 à 25 minutes dans de l'eau salée froide. Une fois cuites, utilisez une passoire et laissez-les s'égoutter 5 minutes avant de les passer au presse-purée.

2 Faites chauffer le lait dans une casserole. Ajoutez le lait bouillant dans la purée avec le beurre en morceaux, la crème, salez et poivrez. Mélangez vivement à l'aide d'une spatule.

3 Gardez la purée au chaud au bain-marie jusqu'au moment de servir.

4 Pour une purée parfaite, après avoir passé les pommes de terre au presse-purée, passez-les dans un tamis fin avant d'ajouter les autres ingrédients.

Purée de panais au wasabi

Pour **4 personnes** / Préparation **15 min** / Cuisson **30 min**

750 G DE PANAIS / **1** CUBE DE BOUILLON DE LÉGUMES / **140** G DE BEURRE MOU / **1** C. À C. BOMBÉE DE WASABI / SEL

1 Épluchez, lavez et coupez les panais en petits morceaux. Faites-les cuire 30 minutes dans une casserole d'eau bouillante salée avec le cube de bouillon de légumes.

2 Une fois cuits, égouttez-les, mettez-les dans un récipient et mixez-les avec le beurre coupé en petits morceaux, le wasabi et du sel à l'aide d'un mixeur plongeant afin d'obtenir une purée onctueuse.

3 Gardez la purée au chaud au bain-marie ou servez aussitôt.

PURÉE DE CÉLERI
PURÉE DE POMMES DE TERRE
PURÉE DE PANAIS AU WASABI

Pommes de terre Hasselback rôties au piment

Pour **4 personnes** / Préparation **15 min** / Cuisson **45 min**

8 POMMES DE TERRE DE TAILLE MOYENNE / **40** G DE BEURRE MOU / **1** C. À C. RASE DE PIMENT D'ESPELETTE / **1** C. À C. RASE DE FLEUR DE SEL / **3** C. À S. D'HUILE D'OLIVE

1 Préchauffez le four à 200 °C (th. 6-7). Prenez soin de prendre des pommes de terre de la même taille pour que la cuisson soit uniforme.
2 Dans un bol, mélangez le beurre mou avec le piment d'Espelette et le sel. Lavez les pommes de terre, coupez-les en tranches de 3 mm environ mais sans aller jusqu'au bout pour pouvoir les ouvrir légèrement en éventail. Pour vous aider, posez la pomme de terre sur le plan de travail avec une baguette chinoise devant et derrière la pomme de terre. Coupez-la en vous arrêtant à la baguette qui servira de butoir.
3 Piquez chaque pomme de terre sur un pique à brochette en écartant légèrement la pomme de terre. Déposez-les sur une plaque à rôtir, badigeonnez-les de beurre au piment, arrosez-les d'huile d'olive. Placez la plaque dans le four, faites-les cuire 45 minutes jusqu'à ce qu'elles soient dorées.

Croquettes de pommes de terre à la mimolette

Pour **4 personnes** / Préparation **45 min** / Réfrigération **1 h** / Cuisson **35 min**

500 G DE POMMES DE TERRE CHARLOTTE OU BINTJE / **50** G DE BEURRE / **1** C. À S. DE CRÈME FRAÎCHE ÉPAISSE / **200** G DE MIMOLETTE RÂPÉE / **120** G DE FARINE / **3** ŒUFS / **250** G DE CHAPELURE / SEL ET POIVRE DU MOULIN / HUILE POUR FRITURE

1 Épluchez, lavez et coupez les pommes de terre en morceaux. Faites-les cuire 20 à 25 minutes dans l'eau salée. Égouttez-les 5 minutes dans une passoire puis passez-les au presse-purée. Mélangez la chair de pommes de terre avec le beurre en morceaux, la crème, du sel et du poivre. Ajoutez la mimolette. Mélangez puis laissez complètement refroidir la purée.
2 Dans un plat creux, versez la farine ; dans un deuxième plat, battez les œufs avec du sel et du poivre ; et dans un troisième plat, mettez la chapelure. Formez des boules de purée de la taille d'une noix et panez-les en les roulant dans la farine puis dans les œufs battus et enfin dans la chapelure. Placez les croquettes au moins une heure au frais.
3 Au dernier moment, faites chauffer une friteuse à 180 °C ou de l'huile dans une sauteuse. Plongez les croquettes 3 à 4 minutes dans l'huile chaude par petites quantités. Égouttez-les sur un papier absorbant, servez aussitôt.

Tian de pomme de terre, oignon, fenouil et courgette au romarin

Pour **4 personnes** / Préparation **30 min** / Cuisson **1 h 30**

700 G DE POMMES DE TERRE À CHAIR FERME / **2** OIGNONS ROUGES MOYENS / **1** GROS BULBE DE FENOUIL / **1** GROSSE COURGETTE / **1** BRANCHE DE ROMARIN / **20** CL DE VIN BLANC / **10** CL D'HUILE D'OLIVE / SEL ET POIVRE DU MOULIN

1. Épluchez les pommes de terre. Coupez-les en rondelles, lavez-les. Épluchez et émincez les oignons en tranches de 2 à 3 mm d'épaisseur. Nettoyez le fenouil et la courgette, coupez-les en tranches de 3 mm d'épaisseur. Récupérez les feuilles de romarin, hachez-les grossièrement au couteau.
2. Préchauffez le four à 160 °C (th. 5-6). Huilez un grand plat à gratin avec un pinceau. Répartissez la moitié du romarin dans le fond du plat. Disposez une rangée de tranches de pommes de terre en les chevauchant puis une rangée de tranches d'oignons, une rangée de courgette et une rangée de tranches de fenouil. Recommencez l'opération jusqu'à épuisement des ingrédients en serrant le tout légèrement. Salez et poivrez, parsemez la surface avec le reste du romarin. Arrosez le tout avec le vin blanc et l'huile d'olive. Couvrez le plat avec une feuille de papier aluminium.
3. Mettez le tian à cuire 1 heure au four. Retirez le papier aluminium, augmentez le four à 180 °C (th. 6). Prolongez la cuisson 25 à 30 minutes. Sortez le tian, dégustez aussitôt.

GRATIN DE POMMES DE TERRE AU PERSIL

Pour **4 personnes** / Préparation **20 min** / Cuisson **40 min**

800 G DE POMMES DE TERRE / **3** GOUSSES D'AIL / **1** BOUQUET DE PERSIL / **50** CL DE LAIT / **30** CL DE CRÈME LIQUIDE ENTIÈRE / **½** C. À C. DE NOIX MUSCADE / SEL ET POIVRE DU MOULIN

1 Préchauffez le four à 220 °C (th. 7-8). Épluchez et hachez les gousses d'ail. Épluchez et lavez les pommes de terre. Lavez et hachez le persil. Coupez les pommes de terre en tranches de 3 à 4 mm d'épaisseur, à l'aide d'une mandoline ou au couteau. Mettez-les dans une casserole avec le lait, la crème, l'ail haché, la noix muscade ; salez et poivrez. Portez doucement à ébullition et laissez mijoter 20 minutes sur feu moyen en remuant régulièrement avec une spatule pour éviter de faire brûler le fond de la casserole.

2 Vérifiez la cuisson des pommes de terre en enfonçant la lame d'un couteau dedans ; elles doivent rester légèrement fermes.

3 Ajoutez le persil haché dans la casserole, mélangez, égouttez les pommes de terre à l'aide d'une écumoire (de façon à garder le lait de cuisson) et mettez-les dans un plat à gratin. Couvrez les pommes de terre avec la crème et le lait de cuisson.

4 Enfournez le plat à gratiner pendant 15 à 20 minutes.

5 Servez aussitôt sorti du four.

GRATIN DE BLETTES AU VIEUX COMTÉ

Pour **4 personnes** / Préparation **20 min** / Cuisson **45 min**

1 BELLE BOTTE DE BLETTES / **10** G DE BEURRE / **160** G DE VIEUX COMTÉ / **10** CL DE LAIT / **30** CL DE CRÈME LIQUIDE ENTIÈRE / SEL ET POIVRE DU MOULIN

1 Préchauffez le four à 180 °C (th. 6). Nettoyez les blettes, retirez la plus grosse partie des feuilles, laissez uniquement la partie la plus près des tiges, puis coupez les tiges en tronçons de 3 cm environ.

2 Faites-les cuire 20 minutes dans une grande casserole d'eau bouillante salée. Une fois cuites, égouttez-les à l'aide d'une passoire.

3 Beurrez un plat à gratin et répartissez les blettes cuites dedans. Râpez le comté dans un bol. Faites bouillir le lait et la crème dans une casserole. Ajoutez la moitié du comté, salez, poivrez et mélangez rapidement hors du feu pour faire fondre le comté. Versez le mélange sur les blettes. Répartissez le reste de comté sur les blettes et enfournez le gratin pendant 20 à 25 minutes.

4 Servez le gratin aussitôt sorti du four.

GRATIN DE POMMES DE TERRE AU PERSIL
GRATIN DE BLETTES AUVIEUX COMTÉ

Gratin de courgettes au parmesan

Pour **4 personnes** / Préparation **30 min** / Cuisson **40 min**

600 G DE COURGETTES
5 CL D'HUILE D'OLIVE
2 ŒUFS
15 CL DE CRÈME LIQUIDE
15 CL DE LAIT
120 G DE PARMESAN RÂPÉ
15 G DE BEURRE (POUR LE PLAT)
SEL, POIVRE DU MOULIN

1 Préchauffez le four à 180 °C (th. 6). Lavez les courgettes et coupez-les en rondelles. Faites-les sauter dans l'huile d'olive 5 minutes dans une poêle sur feu vif.
Salez et poivrez.

2 Dans un récipient, battez les œufs avec la crème et le lait. Salez et poivrez.

3 Beurrez un plat à gratin et disposez-y les courgettes. Versez la préparation à l'œuf, puis ajoutez le parmesan en couvrant bien toute la surface. Enfournez pendant 40 minutes, jusqu'à ce que la surface soit bien gratinée.

POIREAUX GRILLÉS

Pour **4 personnes** / Préparation **10 min** / Cuisson **30 min**

8 PETITS POIREAUX NOUVEAUX / **8** CL D'HUILE D'OLIVE / SEL, POIVRE DU MOULIN

1. Nettoyez les poireaux en retirant bien le vert. Sur chaque poireau, faites 4 entailles de 3 mm d'épaisseur sur toute la longueur.
2. Déposez les poireaux sur un gril en fonte ou dans une poêle, et allumez le feu. Badigeonnez-les d'huile à l'aide d'un pinceau, salez et poivrez. Faites-les cuire 30 à 40 minutes (selon leur diamètre) sur feu doux, en les tournant et en les badigeonnant d'huile régulièrement.
3. Vérifiez la cuisson en enfonçant la pointe d'un couteau (elle doit s'enfoncer facilement). Les poireaux doivent être tendres tout en restant légèrement croquants.
4. Servez chaud ou froid, avec un trait d'huile et de vinaigre de vin ou balsamique.

CHOU ROUGE CONFIT À L'ORANGE

Pour **4 personnes** / Préparation **10 min** / Cuisson **45 min**

600 G DE CHOU ROUGE / **60** G DE BEURRE / **1** C. À S. DE MIEL / **15** CL DE JUS D'ORANGE / SEL, POIVRE DU MOULIN

1. Retirez le cœur du chou et émincez-le finement.
2. Faites-le fondre dans le beurre 10 minutes dans une cocotte sur feu moyen. Ajoutez le miel, le jus d'orange, 10 cl d'eau, du sel et du poivre. Poursuivez la cuisson pendant 30 minutes sur feu moyen en remuant régulièrement.

CHOU ROUGE
CONFIT À L'ORANGE
POIREAUX GRILLÉS

Potirons rôtis aux graines

Pour **4 personnes** / Préparation **10 min** / Cuisson **30 min**

2 MINIPOTIRONS OU MINICOURGES / **2** C. À S. DE GRAINES DE COURGE / **1** C. À S. DE GRAINES DE TOURNESOL / **1** C. À S. DE GRAINES DE SÉSAME DORÉ / **8** CL D'HUILE D'OLIVE / SEL, POIVRE DU MOULIN

1 Préchauffez le four à 200 °C (th. 6-7). Coupez les minipotirons en deux, retirez les pépins avec une cuillère, coupez un peu la base de chaque moitié pour les faire tenir dans le plat et entaillez légèrement la chair de chaque partie avec la pointe d'un couteau.

2 Mélangez les différentes graines dans un bol, puis répartissez-les sur les potirons. Salez, poivrez, arrosez-les d'huile d'olive.

3 Faites rôtir les potirons 30 minutes dans le four.

4 Servez les potirons aussitôt sortis du four.

Topinambours confits

Pour **4 personnes** / Préparation **15 min** / Cuisson **35 min**

500 G DE TOPINAMBOURS / **350** G DE GRAISSE DE FOIE GRAS (GRAISSE RÉCUPÉRÉE APRÈS CUISSON ET PRESSAGE DU FOIE GRAS CUIT ; SINON, FAITES FONDRE DU FOIE GRAS CRU DANS UNE CASSEROLE AU BAIN-MARIE) / SEL, POIVRE DU MOULIN

1 Faites chauffer la graisse dans une casserole sur feu doux pour la faire fondre. Épluchez, lavez et coupez les topinambours en morceaux de taille égale. Essuyez-les dans un torchon propre puis versez-les dans la graisse chaude, salez, poivrez. Faites-les cuire 30 minutes sur feu doux ; la graisse doit à peine frémir.

2 Laissez les topinambours tiédir dans leur graisse de cuisson, égouttez-les puis faites-les rissoler délicatement 3 minutes dans une poêle sur feu vif. Servez aussitôt.

Conseil : on peut remplacer la graisse de foie gras par de la graisse de canard.

Salsifis rôtis au beurre persillé

Pour **4 personnes** / Préparation **20 min** / Cuisson **35 min**

1 KG DE SALSIFIS FRAIS / **1** CITRON / **1** BOUQUET DE PERSIL / **1** GOUSSE D'AIL / **80** G DE BEURRE SALÉ MOU / **2** C. À S. D'HUILE D'OLIVE / SEL, POIVRE DU MOULIN

1 Préchauffez le four à 180 °C (th. 6). Épluchez les salsifis, coupez les extrémités et faites-les tremper dans un récipient d'eau citronnée pour éviter qu'ils noircissent. Lavez et hachez le persil. Épluchez et hachez finement l'ail. Mélangez le beurre mou dans un récipient avec le persil, l'ail, du sel et du poivre.

2 Égouttez les salsifis et versez-les dans un plat à rôtir. Badigeonnez-les d'huile d'olive à l'aide d'un pinceau, salez, poivrez. Enfournez-les pendant 15 minutes.

3 Répartissez le beurre persillé sur les salsifis, puis enfournez de nouveau les salsifis 15 à 20 minutes, en les tournant dans le beurre à mi-cuisson.

SALSIFIS RÔTIS AU BEURRE PERSILLÉ
POTIRONS RÔTIS AUX GRAINES
TOPINAMBOURS CONFITS

OIGNONS RÔTIS DANS LEUR PEAU AU THYM

Pour **4 personnes** / Préparation **10 min** / Cuisson **1 h 15**

4 OIGNONS ROUGES / **500** G DE GROS SEL / **1** BOUQUET DE THYM / **80** G DE BEURRE SALÉ / **25** G DE SUCRE / POIVRE DU MOULIN

1 Préchauffez le four à 190 °C (th. 6-7). Étalez le gros sel dans le fond d'une petite plaque à rôtir.

2 Lavez, essuyez et coupez les oignons en deux dans leur épaisseur, déposez-les sur le lit de gros sel. Éparpillez les brindilles de thym dans le sel et sur les oignons. Répartissez le beurre salé en petits morceaux sur les oignons, parsemez-les de sucre et généreusement de poivre moulu.

3 Mettez les oignons à cuire 1 h 15 dans le four sans y toucher et servez.

CAROTTES RÔTIES AU MIEL ET À L'ORANGE

Pour **4 personnes** / Préparation **15 min** / Cuisson **45 min**

12 CAROTTES DE TAILLE MOYENNE / **30** G DE BEURRE / **1** C. À S. DE MIEL LIQUIDE / **15** CL DE JUS D'ORANGE / **1** C. À C. RASE DE GINGEMBRE EN POUDRE / **1** C. À S. BOMBÉE DE GRAINES DE CUMIN / **5** CL D'HUILE D'OLIVE / SEL ET POIVRE DU MOULIN

1 Épluchez les carottes et lavez-les. Préchauffez le four à 180 °C (th. 6).

2 Dans une petite casserole, faites fondre le beurre sur feu doux. Ajoutez le miel liquide, le jus d'orange, le gingembre en poudre, les graines de cumin, l'huile d'olive, du sel et du poivre, puis faites chauffer 5 minutes sur feu doux.

3 Déposez les carottes dans une plaque à rôtir ou une plaque de four.

4 Versez le contenu de la casserole sur les carottes, roulez-les dedans pour bien les enrober du mélange. Placez la plaque dans le four, faites cuire les carottes 45 minutes en les tournant à mi-cuisson. Servez aussitôt.

CHOU-FLEUR RÔTI ENTIER

Pour **4 à 6 personnes** / Préparation **15 min** / Cuisson **1 h 20**

1 CHOU-FLEUR DE 1,2 KG ENVIRON / **10** CL D'HUILE D'OLIVE / **2** C. À S. DE SIROP D'ÉRABLE / **½** JUS DE CITRON / **1** C. À C. RASE DE CURCUMA / SEL ET POIVRE DU MOULIN

1 Nettoyez le chou-fleur en gardant ses dernières feuilles. Plongez le chou-fleur entier dans une grande casserole d'eau bouillante salée. Faites-le blanchir 5 minutes, égouttez-le et rafraîchissez-le sous l'eau froide.

2 Préchauffez le four à 180 °C (th. 6). Dans une petite casserole, faites chauffer l'huile avec le sirop d'érable, le jus de citron, le curcuma, du sel et du poivre.

3 Déposez le chou-fleur dans un plat à four. Arrosez-le avec le mélange au curcuma. Mettez le chou-fleur à cuire 1 h 15 dans le four en l'arrosant régulièrement avec l'huile de cuisson. Prolongez la cuisson de 10 à 15 minutes selon la taille du chou-fleur. Dressez le chou-fleur sur un plat et servez aussitôt.

LÉGUMES RACINES RÔTIS

Pour **4 personnes** / Préparation **15 min** / Cuisson **45 min**

200 G DE CAROTTES DE DIFFÉRENTES COULEURS / **200** G DE PANAIS / **1** GROS OIGNON ROUGE / **1** C. À S. RASE DE CURRY / **8** CL D'HUILE D'OLIVE / **1** PETIT BOUQUET DE PERSIL / SEL ET POIVRE DU MOULIN

1 Préchauffez le four à 180 °C (th. 6). Coupez les carottes et les panais en deux sans les éplucher, lavez-les. Épluchez et taillez l'oignon en tranches de 5 mm environ.

2 Dans un grand saladier, mélangez avec vos mains les carottes, les panais, l'oignon, le curry, l'huile d'olive, du sel et du poivre pour bien tout enrober d'huile et de curry.

3 Une fois les légumes bien mélangés, répartissez-les sur une plaque de four, mettez-les à cuire 45 minutes en les tournant à mi-cuisson. Lavez et hachez le persil. Sortez la plaque du four, parsemez de persil haché et servez.

Potiron rôti à l'ail et au miel

Pour **4 personnes** / Préparation **15 min** / Cuisson **25 min**

1 PETIT POTIRON D'ENVIRON 800 G / **2** C. À S. DE MIEL LIQUIDE / **10** CL D'HUILE D'OLIVE / **2** PINCÉES DE CANNELLE / **1** TÊTE D'AIL / SEL ET POIVRE DU MOULIN

1. Préchauffez le four à 190 °C (th. 6-7). Coupez le potiron en tranches de 2 à 3 cm.
2. Faites tiédir le miel dans une petite casserole. Mélangez le miel avec l'huile d'olive, la cannelle, du sel et du poivre.
3. Déposez les tranches de potiron sur une plaque de four recouverte d'une feuille de papier sulfurisé et badigeonnez-les avec le mélange au miel. Répartissez les gousses d'ail non épluchées autour des tranches, salez, poivrez, puis placez la plaque dans le four et faites cuire 20 à 25 minutes.
4. Servez aussitôt sorti du four.

Poêlée de champignons aux marrons

Pour **4 personnes** / Préparation **25 min** / Cuisson **15 min**

600 G DE CHAMPIGNONS DE PARIS / **1** GROSSE ÉCHALOTE / **1** PETIT BOUQUET DE PERSIL / **30** G DE BEURRE / **1** C. À S. D'HUILE DE TOURNESOL / **150** G DE MARRONS / SEL ET POIVRE DU MOULIN

1. Lavez les champignons, coupez-les en petits morceaux. Épluchez et hachez finement l'échalote. Lavez et ciselez le persil.
2. Faites fondre le beurre avec l'huile dans une grande poêle sur feu vif. Ajoutez les champignons et faites-les sauter 5 minutes, puis ajoutez l'échalote ciselée. Faites-les cuire encore 5 minutes sur feu vif, salez, poivrez. Ajoutez les marrons grossièrement hachés et le persil, mélangez, laissez cuire 2 minutes et servez.

CONFITURE D'OIGNONS À LA CRÈME DE CASSIS

Pour **un pot de confiture de 300 g environ** / Préparation **15 min** / Cuisson **2 h**

250 G D'OIGNONS BLANCS / **150** G DE SUCRE / **10** CL DE CRÈME DE CASSIS / **40** CL DE VIN ROUGE / SEL ET POIVRE DU MOULIN

1 Épluchez et émincez les oignons. Mettez-les dans une casserole avec tous les ingrédients, salez, poivrez. Mélangez, portez à ébullition et laissez mijoter 2 heures sur feu très doux en remuant de temps en temps. Ajoutez un peu de vin rouge si nécessaire pendant la cuisson si la confiture épaissit trop.

2 Laissez refroidir la confiture, puis versez-la dans un bocal. Vous pouvez conserver la confiture plusieurs semaines au réfrigérateur.

PICKLES

Pour **un grand bocal de pickles** / Préparation **20 min** / Marinade **7 jours**

2 OIGNONS ROUGES / **2** PETITES COURGETTES / **25** CL DE VINAIGRE BLANC / **15** G DE SEL / **30** G DE SUCRE / **8** GRAINS DE POIVRE NOIR

1 Épluchez et émincez grossièrement les oignons. Lavez et coupez les courgettes en rondelles. Intercalez les oignons et les rondelles de courgette dans un bocal avec les grains de poivre.

2 Mettez le reste des ingrédients dans une casserole avec 25 cl d'eau froide, mélangez et, après ébullition, laissez mijoter 5 minutes sur feu moyen.

3 Versez le mélange bouillant sur les légumes. Fermez le bocal avec un couvercle hermétique, retournez-le sur le plan de travail et laissez refroidir.

4 Laissez le bocal 2 jours à l'extérieur puis placez-le au réfrigérateur au moins 5 jours avant de consommer les pickles.

5 Vous pouvez remplacer les courgettes par du chou-fleur ou des radis.

INDEX

INDEX

D

E

F

R

S

T

Éditions du Gerfaut
6-8, rue du Docteur-Maunoury
28000 Chartres
www.editionsdugerfaut.com

Toutes les photographies sont de Pierre-Louis Viel.
Création graphique et mise en pages : Claire Mieyeville, mokmok.agency
Suivi éditorial : Lucie Nédellec, lunedit.com

Dépôt légal : octobre 2023
ISBN : 978-2-35191-309-3

Les éditions du Gerfaut bénéficient du soutien de la Région Centre-Val de Loire, de l'État (DRAC Centre-Val de Loire) et de Ciclic.

PRÉFET DE LA RÉGION CENTRE-VAL DE LOIRE | Direction régionale des affaires culturelles

çiçliç CENTRE VAL DE LOIRE

Centre-Val de Loire www.centre-valdeloire.fr

Imprimé par Rotolito en Roumanie.